The Art and Technique of Digital Color Correction

The Art and Technique of Digital Color Correction

Steve Hullfish

AMSTERDAM • BOSTON • HEIDELBERG • LONDON
NEW YORK • OXFORD • PARIS • SAN DIEGO
SAN FRANCISCO • SINGAPORE • SYDNEY • TOKYO

Focal Press is an imprint of Elsevier

Associate Acquisitions Editor: Dennis McGonagle
Publishing Services Manager: George Morrison
Project Manager: Mónica González de Mendoza
Assistant Editor: Chris Simpson
Marketing Manager: Rebecca Pease
Cover Design: Alan Studholme

Cover art: Tangent Devices CP-200-BK controller photographed by Greg Gills. Boxer image courtesy of Artbeats' Sports 1 HD Volume 1 collection.

Focal Press is an imprint of Elsevier
30 Corporate Drive, Suite 400, Burlington, MA 01803, USA
Linacre House, Jordan Hill, Oxford OX2 8DP, UK

 Recognizing the importance of preserving what has been written, Elsevier prints its books on acid-free paper whenever possible.

Library of Congress Cataloging-in-Publication Data
Hullfish, Steve.
  The art and technique of digital color correction / Steve Hullfish.
      p. cm.
  Includes bibliographical references and index.
  ISBN 978-0-240-80990-8 (pbk. : alk. paper)   1. Color
photography—Digital techniques.   2. Color computer
graphics.   3. Color computer printers.   4. Color display systems.
I. Title.
  TR510.H828 2008
  778.6′6—dc22

                                        2007036364

British Library Cataloguing-in-Publication Data
A catalogue record for this book is available from the British Library.

ISBN: 978-0-240-80990-8

For information on all Focal Press publications
visit our website at www.books.elsevier.com

08 09 10 11 12 13   10 9 8 7 6 5 4 3 2 1

Printed in China

Contents

Acknowledgments   ix
Introduction   xi

PRIMARY COLOR CORRECTION

CHAPTER 1
Tonal Range Primer   1

Monitoring   4
   Video Monitor   4
   Viewing Environment   5
   Surround Environment: Interview with Randy Starnes   7
   Waveform Monitors and Vectorscopes   7
Alternative Displays and Tools for Analysis   11
   First Things First: Black Level   11
   Setting Highlights   21
   Setting Gammas or Midtones   24
   Defining Contrast   25
   Practice Playing Gamma Against Highlights and Shadows   29

CHAPTER 2
Tonal-Correction Tools   31

Main Tools for Tonal Corrections   31
Sliders and Numerical Controls for Tonal Range   32
Don't use Brightness or Contrast Controls   33
Color's Primary In Room   35
Avid Symphony and Color Finesse HSL Controls Tab   38
Histograms or Levels   39

Histograms   39
Forms and Functions of Histograms   43
Curves Tab   44
S Curve Tip   45
Curves Tutorial   47
Isolating Tonal Ranges with Curves   53
Luma Range Display   57
Luma Range Editing   58
Alternative to Luma Range   61

CHAPTER 3

Color Control Primer   63

Balancing an Image   63
Analyzing Color Casts   63
Using Your Eyes   64
Color and the Waveform   65
Color and the Vectorscope   73
Histograms   78
Eyedropper   82
Balancing Color with a Flat-Pass Waveform Monitor   86
Color Contrast   89

CHAPTER 4

Color Control Tools   91

Hue Offset Wheels or Color Balance Controls   91
Hue Offsets with RGB Parade   95
Saturation Controls   101
Histograms   102
Curves   105
RGB Setup, Gamma, and Gain Sliders   112
Channels   123
Printer Lights   126
Filters   126
Conclusion   128

SECONDARY COLOR CORRECTION

CHAPTER 5

Secondary Color Correction Primer   129

The Purpose of Secondary Correction   129
Are You Qualified?   132

Color Vector Isolation   133
  Isolating a Vector in Final Cut Pro   143
  Isolation Practice   146
Spot Color Correction (Vignettes or Power Windows)   148
  Vignette   148
  Geographical Color Fix   152
  User-Defined Shapes   156
  Using Spot Color Correction to Relight   156
  Color Vector with Garbage Matte   157
Color's Secondary Curves   160
Secondaries Are Crucial   162

CHAPTER 6
Secondaries with the Pros   163

Vignettes   164
  Vignetting the Ultralight Flyover Scene   166
  Vignetting the *Kiss Me in the Dark* Bedroom Scene   170
Spot Color Correction   176
  Vignette to Create Day-for-Night Shot   177
Vector and Luma Qualified Secondaries   185
Secondary Corrections Can Focus Attention   191
Using Secondaries to Match   195
Using a Luma Key to Build Contrast   201

PRO COLORISTS

CHAPTER 7
Correcting Shots   205

Three More Grades of the "Banker's Light" Scene   205
Saving a Shot with Bad Color Cast   216
Four Trips Down the "Alley"   221
Three Passes Over the Barn   228
Building Up a Weak Piece of Video   239
Using Many Tools to Fix a Shot   242
Grading with Curves in Primary   247

CHAPTER 8
Telling the Story   255

Color Changes the Story   258
Talk like a Director of Photography   264

The Story Is the Script   266
Emphasize Elements to Further the Story   268
Imposing a Story on the Boxer   276
Conclusion   285

CHAPTER 9

Matching Shots   287

Matching the Lions of the Art Institute   287
Matching Scene to Scene   303
Matching When Lighting Changes in a Scene   306
Conclusion   309

CHAPTER 10

Creating Looks   311

Enough is Enough   312
Preset Looks   312
Festa's PowerGrade Library Revealed   313
Preset Looks in Apple's Color   314
Film Processing Looks   314
Skip Bleach or Bleach Bypass   317
Match the Look   321
Looks for Promos and Opens   324
True Grit   335
Graphic Looks   344
Day-for-Night   350

CHAPTER 11

Miscellaneous Wisdom   361

Starting Off   361
Communicating with Clients   362
Taking It to Extremes   363
The Importance of Color Contrast   363
Maintaining a Look   363
Looking at Real Life for Inspiration   364
Multitasking   364
Smoke   365
Keeping Butts in the Seats   365
The Future of Color Correction   366
Books of Note   367
Conclusion   367

Index   369

Acknowledgments

This book took a huge amount of effort and contributions by people other than myself. Firstly, I must acknowledge the persistence, gentle guidance, and eagle eye of my original editor, Dorothy Cox, and also, the rest of the staff at Focal Press, especially Dennis McGonagle; Mónica González de Mendoza and Paul Temme, who worked to make this a great looking and accurate read. And to my knowledgeable, meticulous, and enthusiastic tech editor, Jeff Greenberg, for keeping me honest and for keeping you, the reader, in mind at all times.

I must thank Bob Sliga, now at Apple Inc., who started me down this road of color-correction knowledge and who helped me with many elements of the book. I also owe a deep debt of gratitude to the rest of the colorists who contributed greatly by allowing me to interview them and watch them in sessions: Greg Creaser, Terry Curren, Janet Falcon, Larry Field, Pete Jannotta, Neal Kassner, Craig Leffel, Robert Lovejoy, Mike Most, Mike Matusek, and Chris Pepperman. It is from their wisdom, experience, and skills that readers of this book will truly learn something valuable. And to all of the employers of the above colorists for allowing me free access to these busy and talented employees. Also, for insightful interviews, I thank Bob Festa and David Mullen, ASC.

To the many manufacturers and their representatives who provided invaluable assistance with their products, including Steve Bayes at Apple, Inc., Bob Donlon at Adobe, Patrick Palmer at IRIDAS, and to Roland Wood (originally founder of Silicon Color, now of Apple Inc.) for enabling many of the sessions with colorists around the country. From Tektronix, I thank Steve Holmes, Leigh Havelick, and others for their support and knowledge in the field of monitoring. I also thank Martin Euredjian for use of his HD monitoring system, eCinema Display; the DR Group in Los Angeles for their support while doing sessions there; Grady Sellers of Eastern Group for his help; and AJA for their gear and support—your stuff is rock solid and your staff's technical know-how is first rate. Also, I thank numerous other resellers, most especially John Ladle of HD Sales, who single-handedly outfitted me to write this book and whose technical support was invaluable from beginning to end. And to noted guru, Gary Adcock, for helping with "HD enlightenment" and for the use of his Panasonic HVX-200. I also thank the folks at DSC Labs for their fantastic camera charts.

There are many great examples of beautiful footage provided within these pages and on the DVD that were donated from several talented individuals and companies. Thanks to ArtBeats and Julie Hill for providing several of their fantastic HD and SD images for use by the readers and the colorists. All of the colorists were impressed by the quality of the color correction of the shots from their stock library. To three good friends and fantastic cameramen who are confident enough in their considerable shooting skills to let me use their footage in the tutorials: Rich Lerner, Randy Riesen, and Charles Vanderpool; trying to find anything that needed "correcting" from the stuff they shoot was a difficult task.

Also, thanks to Barry Gilbert of Seduced and Exploited Films and his director of photography, Robin Miller, for the use of footage from his trailer for *Kiss Me in the Dark*. Thanks for the kind assistance of director Kyle Jackson, producer, Alan Pao and the folks at Tunnel Post for permission to use the *Chasing Ghosts* footage.

Finally, to my family. To my grandmother, Florence, for putting me up and keeping me company during my Philadelphia/New Jersey/New York City sessions. To my parents, Bill and Sue, who have always encouraged my writing, filmmaking, and other creative pursuits, and taught me that you can do anything if you take it one step, one page, or one turn of a bicycle wheel at a time. To my children, Haley and Quinn, who gave up their dad for the good part of a year and to my understanding wife, Jody, who has always been the quarterback of the family and had to take on far more than her share of the parenting as I wrote this book. I love you.

Introduction

The number of applications that allow for color correction of moving images has exploded since I first began doing color correction. This expanding universe of opportunity means that many people have the tools to do great color-correction work without being tied to an expensive telecine or film scanner. As the old saying goes though, "Owning a hammer doesn't make you a carpenter." Although my color-correction experience is more in the context of being a video editor, I wanted this book to provide direct access to the skills and wisdom of real colorists. So I asked about a dozen great colorists from across America to let me sit in with them as they graded a series of real-world images. I also interviewed additional colorists and directors of photography. My part in this book will be to tie information together and provide some context and additional resources, but the book is really formed from the direct experience of some of the top colorists in the business. There are decades of experience and know-how in these pages from colorists who've corrected some of your favorite TV shows, feature films, and commercials.

When I was first introduced to color correction, I knew two things: (1) this has incredible potential to make my projects look better and (2) I have *no* clue what to do with these tools. I was right about both things. Luckily, I found some excellent mentors, including the gracious and talented Bob Sliga, who contributes throughout this book. I also spent a lot of time practicing the craft and, while cowriting my previous book, *Color Correction for Digital Video*, I was able to interview some really great colorists and learn their secrets as well. Eventually, my color-correction skills matured and my skills as a colorist became a way that I made a name for myself as an editor. Many times, after solving tricky editing problems or creating a beautifully assembled story or montage, I would receive no great reaction from my client, but when I broke out the color-correction tools and started actually making the *images themselves* look better, I started hearing "ooohs" and "aaahs" from the back of the room. Eliciting responses like that from paying clients is always a good thing.

Many applications and products now have color-correction capabilities: nonlinear editors, switchers, digital video effects boxes (DVEs), compositors, motion graphics software, as well as stand-alone desktop color-correction systems and color-correction plug-ins. Though some of the tools that are provided may differ from one product to the next, the basic process of color correcting, or *grading*, an image is the same. This book aims to be relatively product-agnostic, meaning that readers should be able to use whatever product or platform with which they are comfortable as they follow along with the lessons and tutorials in this book. Because I interviewed some of the top colorists in the country, I had to use a color-correction product that a wide range of high-end colorists would feel comfortable using and would give them the necessary power and tools to grade the images as they would in their day-to-day work. Because I wanted to be able to save all this work and refer back to it after I monitored the colorists in their sessions, I didn't want them all to use the various systems that they used at work. By and large the colorists featured in this book are used to working on various flavors of **da Vinci**

a

b

Fig. 1 **(a)** da Vinci 2 K panels and **(b)** da Vinci Resolve. Images courtesy of da Vinci Systems.

color correctors, usually the da Vinci 2K. The closest product that I could find with the options that these colorists were used to—and that I could actually afford to use and set up in several different cities around the country—was Apple's Color (formerly Silicon Color's FinalTouch HD). If you, the reader, have access to Apple's Color, you'll have the closest experience to having the colorists sit with you. However, the book does not dwell on specific buttons, sliders, or capabilities of Color, so if you are following along using Final Cut Pro with its three-way color corrector, or an Avid product with its built-in color correction, or another stand-alone desktop color-correction product like IRIDAS's SpeedGrade, a plug-in like Synthetic Aperture's Color Finesse, or Red Giant's Colorista, you shouldn't have any trouble understanding what's happening and what you need to do. Obviously, the more tools that are offered by the color-correction plug-in or product that you are using, the closer you'll be to achieving the same results as the colorists did in this book.

This book is meant to be a companion piece to *Color Correction for Digital Video*, which I cowrote with Jaime Fowler back when FCP and the main body of Avid's product line were first starting to deliver color-correction capabilities. That book was more of a primer on color correction and was primarily concerned with what one can do with the various color-correction tools and how one can monitor corrections using a variety of methods including a video monitor, scopes, and various other references, like sampling RGB (red, green, blue) numbers from an image. How this book will differ from that book is that this is a hands-on guide as you work with the same images that the colorists do. The colorists will explain the hows and whys of each grade. We'll go step by step through numerous types of images to expose you to as many real-world conditions as we can. The footage in this book was sourced from many different formats. You'll see film-originated 2K scans transcoded to high-definition (HD), straight HD from numerous cameras like the CineAlta and Varicam, high-definition video (HDV), standard-definition video from BetaSP, DigiBeta, and mini-DV, and even 8-mm film transferred to BetaSP. Each of these formats has limitations and challenges, but the images themselves provide the real challenge. Some of the images are beautiful to begin with; some are in terrible shape. You'll be able to attack these challenges yourself and see how some of the best colorists in the business dealt with them. Comparing the approach that one skilled colorist takes with the way another one chooses to "make the grade" provides some really interesting insight into the subjective nature of what looks good.

The book is organized with several chapters of introductory information that should prepare you to follow along with the colorists. This includes tutorial information that guides you step by step through some color corrections. The tutorials in the early chapters are designed to give you an understanding of both the tools at your disposal and the standard practices and wisdom of colorists. Then, the later chapters are divided into various technical challenges of color correcting, such as secondaries with the pros, improving weak images, matching images, telling the story with color, and creating "looks." This way, you can refer to specific chapters again, using the book in a nonlinear fashion. But for the most part, the book is designed to be read from beginning to end, with explanations, tips, and concepts that build on each other. Also, with no formal glossary, words that you need to understand will be highlighted on the same page on which they first occur. We'll refer to these highlighted terms in the Index if you miss them in context.

One thing to consider as you grade these images is that even though the DVD has samples of the exact same video files that the colorists were working with, your monitoring may differ significantly from the reference grade monitors and setups that they had access to. As you see the images in the book and on your computer monitor at home, you must realize that the images you're seeing—especially on the printed page—will differ somewhat from the image the colorist saw as he or she graded it. As you grade the tutorial projects, you should definitely make sure you are looking at a well set up video monitor. This will provide you with an experience that is closest to what the colorists saw. You should also be cognizant of the environment in which you are color correcting. The lighting should be balanced as closely as possible to daylight and should not reflect too much on the screen. The lights should be fairly dimmed and the walls and area surrounding the screen should be neutral gray if possible. This will all be discussed at greater length later in the book.

The huge influx of color-correction capabilities have certainly democratized the so-called "black art" of color correction, but the power that these tools provide to manipulate your images is certainly a double-edged sword, and using the tools without the proper knowledge can actually do more harm than good. Using that power for good, instead of evil, is the point of this book! I hope that after absorbing the concepts outlined in this book and learning from the decades of experience of the excellent colorists featured within, you will have more confidence as you begin color correcting your own footage, making the world of film and video a better place! Amen.

CHAPTER 1

Tonal Range Primer

Color correction is generally broken down into two distinct processes: primary and secondary color correction.

Primary color correction is the process of setting the overall tone, contrast, and color balance of an image. Secondary color correction is a further step that refines the image in specific geographical regions or in specific color **vectors** of the image. Don't let the word "vector" scare you. There are a number of definitions for vector that are used when discussing color space. It basically means the specific location or coordinates of a color. A vector can also mean the direction that something is heading from one point in space toward another. So essentially, in the color correction world, vector is just the technical word that defines a specific color.

These two processes will probably *always* be referred to as two *distinct* processes, but the technology itself is starting to change the perception of how and why these two processes are used and when a colorist moves from one process to another.

The first step in any color correction is to assess the tonal range of the picture being corrected. What are the problems with the tonal range and how can you address them? From a purely technical standpoint, it seems like an easy question to answer. As a matter of fact, many color correction plug-ins or color correction systems built in to nonlinear editors have "automatic" buttons that will attempt to spread out the tonal range for you based on purely technical information. These automatic systems assume that the brightest parts of the picture should be as bright as possible while remaining **legal**, and the darkest part of the picture is also set automatically to be as low as possible while remaining legal.

There are two big problems with this. Simply setting the brightest pixel to 100 and the darkest pixel to 0 with all of the intermediate pixels spread evenly between them does not necessarily provide the best spread of the tonal range across the most visually important parts of an image. The other problem is that the image may not need to have either its brightest pixel at 100 or its darkest pixel at 0.

Definition

Vector: A position or coordinate in space or a direction between two coordinates. On a vectorscope, the vector is the specific position of a color in the two-dimensional circle defined by the vectorscope. The "targeted" vectors on the vectorscope are the three primary colors—red, green, and blue—and the secondary colors between them—magenta, cyan, and yellow.

Legal: For video-based images, legal means that the brightness and color saturation of an image does not exceed minimum or maximum levels that have been determined for a specific delivery channel for a video. This usually implies broadcast, but can also pertain to duplication. Each duplicator or broadcaster sets his or her own specific requirements for video levels, but in general, these levels adhere to national and international standards, which state that the darkest portions of the luminance of a picture cannot fall below 0 **IRE** for NTSC digital video (and most other international video of any type) or 7.5 IRE for composite NTSC in the United States. The brightest pixels are not to pass 100IRE when monitoring luminance only, or, when combined with chroma, cannot pass 110 IRE. (There are other ways to measure the signal other than IRE, such as in millivolts.) Also, as our delivery systems become more and more digitally based, **gamut** is also included in legal levels. Not all waveform monitors or vectorscopes can monitor gamut levels. These gamut levels are the legal amounts, or values, of certain colors. It is possible for the luminance of an image to be well under legal levels, but, because of a combination of saturation and luminance, the legal gamut levels can be exceeded (discussed later). In addition to legal levels, there is a second, similar term called **valid levels**.

IRE: One of the units of measurement that can describe a composite analog video signal's amplitude (brightness) where 0 IRE generally represents black and white extends to +100 IRE. 1 IRE is equal to 1/140 of a volt or 7.14 millivolts in NTSC, though in all other systems, it corresponds to 7 millivolts. IRE stands for the Institute of Radio

The first problem is solved with some experience. Great colorists know tricks that can enhance the perception of an image's tonal range. They know that they can sacrifice the detail in a certain tonal range where it may not be noticed so that they can use that tonal range to enhance a more visually important part of the picture. These are tricks that you will learn in this chapter and throughout the rest of the book. Automatic software doesn't know what is visually important, so it treats all areas of an image equally.

Automatic Corrections Are Bad

Let's run an experiment to show that you are already a better colorist than the automatic color correction tools available in most software packages. Even if you aren't tempted to use these automatic features, this little experiment is an important lesson in using your eyes instead of the numbers or doing things technically perfectly.

From the DVD, open the "Popcorn_FD130.mov" file in the Tutorial_footage_and_ files folder (from Artbeats' beautiful "Food 1" collection) in any application that allows you to automatically color correct (see Fig. 1-1a). Most of these tools automatically spread the tonal values and white balance. But since these tools don't know what the image actually looks like, they do everything by the numbers. Sometimes using them can get you in the ballpark very quickly and sometimes it makes an image look worse.

For my example, I brought the "Popcorn" Quicktime file into Avid Xpress Pro and color corrected it using the automatic color correction tools. To be fair to Avid and other applications with these tools, these automatic corrections can sometimes do a pretty good job. If you're in a rush, give each image a shot with them, but be prepared to take matters into your own hands. This need to do things manually is actually a good thing

a

Fig. 1-1 **(a)** Original "Popcorn" image. Courtesy of Artbeats' "Food 1" collection.

for you. If all someone needed to do was push a button, then there'd be nothing special about the skills you're trying to develop.

After running the "Popcorn" image through the automatic color correction (see Fig. 1-1b), it doesn't look nearly as appetizing as the beautifully color-corrected original image.

Most of these tools figure that you want something that looks "white" or neutral with a tonal range that's completely spread out. In the case of the "Popcorn" image, the image *needs* to have a nice, warm golden tone. Also, the original image doesn't really go much beyond 80 IRE in brightness, yet the auto-correction spreads the tonal values over the entire range, which causes the steam rising from the popcorn to take on a harsher feel and the brighter parts of the popcorn come close to clipping out.

This is a good thing to keep in mind as you're manually color correcting images. Not all images *need* to be at 100 IRE and not all color casts are a bad thing. Some images need to be very contrasty and others need to have less contrast. You need to look for the clues in each image to help you find where the image "wants to go." The long shadows of dawn or dusk should indicate warmer tones and lower contrast. The sharp shadows of the noonday sun should indicate higher contrast and maybe a hint of blue, or possibly yellow for heat.

The contrast for "golden hour" and "high noon" *can* be the reverse of what I just said. It depends on where the sun is. If the sun and camera are both pointing in the same direction at the golden hour, things will be very evenly lit, like by a giant soft light. But if the camera is pointing toward the sun or perpendicular to it, it would have higher contrast, since the difference between what was lit by the sun and the shadows would be great. The same goes for high noon. It can have great contrast, throwing deep shadows under the eyes, for example, or it can have lower contrast, because the entire sky is acting as a big bounce light.

Engineers, which defined the unit.

Gamut: The complete range of colors that can be captured, displayed, or broadcast by a device or a system of devices. Most cameras or color-correction devices have a much wider gamut (range of colors) than those that can be used further on in the production stream. For example, the gamut of colors later in the production stream that could require a limited gamut can be those recorded to tape, burned to a DVD, encoded for the Web, broadcast from a TV transmitter, or viewed on a TV set. So there are multiple gamuts that have to be considered. (See definitions for *legal* and *valid levels*.)

Valid Levels: Levels that remain legal when transferred, translated, or transcoded between formats.

b

Fig. 1-1 (*Continued*) **(b)** "Popcorn" image color corrected using automatic correction tools.

Definition

**Tonal Range
(singular):** This is
sometimes also called the
dynamic range, luminance
range, or contrast range,
though these terms can
have slightly different
technical definitions.
The tonal range is the
difference between the
brightest and darkest areas
of an image. The tonal
range of an image, and
how those tones are
spread throughout the
tonal range, defines its
contrast. For some
applications of this phrase,
tonal range indicates the
actual number of *levels* of
tones that a recording
medium can record (256
per channel in the case of
RGB 8 bit, or 1,025 per
channel in the case of RGB
10 bit). For our purposes,
we will refer to tonal
range (singular) as the
range of tones between
brightest and darkest.
Ansel Adams and other
proponents of The Zone
System, break the tonal
range of an image into 11
distinct tonal ranges.

**Tonal Ranges
(plural):** The three
commonly used tonal
ranges that are used to
breakdown the description
(and control) of an image
are shadows, midtones,
and highlights. Sometimes
shadows are referred to
as blacks, pedestal, setup,
lift, or even lowlights.
Midtones are often
referred to as gamma, but
also as grays or mids.
Highlights are sometimes

Fig. 1-2 A classic example of when not to spread the tonal range: a polar bear in a snowstorm. No part of this image should be completely black. Image courtesy of Dan Zatz at www.WildlifeHD.com.

The second problem is that the image may not require an expanded **tonal range**. Most shots should have a pretty wide tonal latitude (range) with rich blacks and sparkling whites. However, there are those images that should not take advantage of the full tonal range (see Fig. 1-2); examples include an igloo in a snowstorm; a dark, moonlit close-up of a Navy SEAL creeping through the underbrush; a foggy, early morning rowboat ride; a long lens shot of a smoggy city at dusk. Each of these may have only a partial tonal range, lacking either deep black or bright highlights. However, these examples are usually the exceptions to the rules, but they do require the colorist to consider the clues in the image itself to determine if anything in the image "deserves" to be completely black or bright white.

Keeping these exceptions in mind, most of the images that we will see will benefit from spreading the tonal range as much as we can.

Monitoring

My first book on color correction, cowritten with Jaime Fowler, *Color Correction for Digital Video*, goes into detail about monitoring. I don't want to thoroughly address those same issues again in this book, but I will touch on them briefly.

Video Monitor

Proper monitoring is crucial. This means that you have a well set up video monitor. There are instructions for doing this in my previous book and on numerous web sites and online PDF files. Although LCD (Liquid Crystal Display) monitoring has been largely shunned by serious colorists, the production of CRT (Cathode Ray Tube) displays for video has halted and the old CRT displays are beginning to die off, leaving many with no choice but to switch to LCDs or some other technology. The main issue with these LCD monitors is how colors and tones shift with a viewer's angle to the screen and how deep a black is able to be displayed.

Many of these LCD video monitors can be set up with look-up tables (LUTs) or by using calibration hardware and software. The cost and accuracy of these calibration units varies widely from several thousand dollars to under one hundred dollars. For my computer monitors, I use a mid-level unit by Gretagmacbeth called the Eye One Display 2. It uses a hardware device and software to create a custom monitor profile that even takes ambient lighting into account. This device would not fulfill the expectations of a serious full-time colorist, but it creates a profile that seems very accurate to me.

Many high-end video monitors also have hardware-based calibration options that can help properly calibrate them. As I mentioned earlier, for video monitors that aren't capable of being set up with a profile or LUT, *Color Correction for Digital Video* offers an in-depth description of how to set up a monitor with color bars. There are also several resources for doing this on the Web and from the monitor manufacturers.

For serious color correction, consulting firms can be hired to set up your suite, making sure that an image is accurate at each stage of the postproduction process, creating a workflow that guarantees the integrity of the image throughout the process.

Viewing Environment

The viewing environment is also of critical importance. The lighting in a color-critical environment is daylight balanced, not tungsten. There is some debate over the exact temperature of daylight, but it's about 6,000–6,500 K. The daylight-balanced light is often only used as *reflected* light as opposed to *direct* light. For example, it is bounced off of a back wall behind the monitor. It is also fairly dim. The eCinema displays we used for most of the color correction sessions come with a separate, external daylight-balanced backlight that actually matches the light used inside a monitor itself. It is designed to be placed behind the monitor, bouncing light onto the wall behind it. The light bouncing off the wall behind the monitor should be one-tenth the intensity of the monitor when the monitor is displaying 100% white.

Any additional lighting in the room can't increase this brightness level. The light sources should be 6,500 K bulbs or be filtered to reach that temperature. No bulbs or light sources should be visible to a colorist's eyes while grading. Some color correction suites have a bulb near the colorist's desk that sends a beam of pure 6,500 K light to a small white

also referred to as whites, gain, luma, or even video. These are not necessarily technically correct terms, but they are terms that were used by the colorists as they were verbally conveying the use of these individual tonal ranges. The terminology in the book will *not* remain the same, because in real life, these terms are often interchanged sometimes even by the same speakers.

card or tile near the colorist to act as a reference for pure white. This light can be turned on or off independently of the other lights in the room.

Walls should be a completely neutral gray, with no tint at all. Paint mixers have a very hard time with this. Bring an 18% gray photo card to your local paint store and see if they can match it. Many color suites aren't painted at all, but covered in gray cloth, which cuts down on reflected light and glare.

Here's a simple test to prove how important the viewing environment is to good color correction. Look at the squares in Figure 1-3 and determine whether the blocks to the right are darker than the blocks to the left. If you're familiar with optical illusions, you can probably guess the correct answer despite what your eyes are really telling you.

The color chips inside the black surround (to the right) appear to be brighter than the ones on the white surround (to the left). The black surround also makes the contrast ratio of the chips appear slightly lower. This is due to a thing called *lateral-brightness adaptation,* which means that a particular retinal receptor in the eye is affected by the brightness of the receptors coming in to its neighboring receptors. This helps us detect edges better. (For more on the color theory involved, check out *Digital Color Management: Encoding Solutions* by Edward Giorgianni and Thomas Madden.)

High-level colorists are very sensitive to their viewing environment. This extends to very small stimuli, such as glowing on/off switches on equipment and the color of the trace of the waveform or vectorscope. Most colorists try to grade using waveform or vectorscopes that have a neutral trace and graticule color, instead of the traditional green.

Fig. 1-3 The environment around your monitor affects how you see what's in it.

This obsession with the surrounding environment used to include the option to turn off the bright-white "Mac menu bar" at the top of the monitor when using Color (then FinalTouch). Color and some other color correction software applications, such as Avid Symphony, go so far as to allow the user to customize the application's **graphical user interface (GUI)** colors to be darker and less saturated.

Surround Environment: Interview with Randy Starnes

Randy Starnes has been the colorist on "Desperate Housewives," "Extreme Makeover: Home Edition," "Dr. Quinn: Medicine Woman," "Touched by an Angel," and others. He tells this story about viewing environment. "To relate how important the surround is, when I first started, I worked in a room that was designed to resemble a living room, since the thought was 'you're going to watch television in an environment similar to this, so let's color grade in this environment.' The monitor was set in a bookcase. It was a warmly lit room with a desk lamp and overhead tungsten lights. A beautiful room, very comfortable, it was like a den, a gentlemen's smoking room. And I think even in those days we smoked in the rooms. The longer you color corrected something, the more red you put into the pictures because your eyes became desensitized. At the start of the day, skin tones look normal, but after six or eight hours, you were correcting skin tones oversaturated, like basketballs, because your perception has changed. The reason you have the neutral background is that you keep the same perception all along. Otherwise, if you bathe the viewing area in blue, you're going to compensate for that. You're going to lose your sensitivity to blue, or red, or warm. And then you become desensitized to that. If you sit in a yellow room, your pictures are going to end up yellow. Or you're going to be constantly fighting what you perceive. So the easiest way to avoid that is to surround the monitor with something that is neutral and daylight. You can also take your monitor to black and white to refresh your perspective. Sometimes I'll use the switcher to put a gray border or a white border around my image to judge what pure white or pure gray should look like. Sometimes that helps the colorist and sometimes that helps the client, whose perception is just as important to the process. If you have an environment that is not neutral, the hardest things to get right are going to be the white scenes."

Waveform Monitors and Vectorscopes

Most of the **waveform monitors** and vectorscopes that are built into the software of desktop applications are barely sufficient for color correction purposes. These scopes have two things going for them: they're free

Definition

Graphical User Interface (GUI): This is basically the screen that you see when working in an application that allows you to interact with the program and execute commands.

Definition

Waveform Monitor: A waveform monitor displays the amplitude level—brightness and darkness — along the vertical axis with the dark parts of an image near the bottom and the brighter parts of the signal near the top. Technically, the horizontal axis of the waveform displays "time," but practically speaking, the horizontal axis of the waveform corresponds to the horizontal placement of picture elements across the image with no regard to the vertical placement of elements in the image.

and they're convenient. Other than that, there's not much to recommend them. There are a number of reasons that they do not stand up to a professional's needs. Depending on the specific application, many of the built-in scopes are not showing you full resolution. Some are designed to only show every other line or every fourth line of your video image! They also don't have the full complement of features that are available on an outboard scope, such as the ability to zoom or position the trace to better evaluate an image. There can also be a problem with lag time between a correction and that correction being sensed by the scope, because the amount of computational horsepower that is required to display the scope is pretty intensive. The main problem with these built-in scopes for broadcast work is that they have no real relation to the signal that comes out of the computer because they're not downstream of the video output. In the initial release of Color, the scopes inside Color didn't match the scopes for the exact same footage inside Final Cut Pro. Largely though, the issue with internal scopes is that they just don't have the resolution needed for color correction.

For a lot of reasons, I recommend having an external waveform monitor and vectorscope. When choosing a scope, find features and tools that you think will be most useful to you. Some brands, like Tektronix, have patented displays, such as the Lightning Display, Arrowhead Display, or Eye Display, that provide you with valuable information that you can't get from other manufacturers. So, shop around for the tools in a scope that make the most sense to you as you color correct.

Also, make sure that the scope is monitoring the type of signal that you are recording to tape. It doesn't make much sense to be monitoring the composite or component video signal if you're laying SDI (Serial Digital Interface) or something else to tape.

I used several Tektronix scopes during the writing of this book including the WFM700 (see Fig. 1-4) and the WVR7100 (see Fig. 1-5). I also own a standard def Videotek VTM300.

Fig. 1-4 Tektronix WFM700. Image courtesy of Tektronix, Inc.

Fig. 1-5 Tektronix WVR7100. Image courtesy of Tektronix, Inc.

Though the colorists who participated in this book could use the internal scopes, I could see that their eyes were really watching the outboard scopes for critical decision making. Many of the colorists used specialized views or amplifications of views that simply were impossible to deliver with the internal scopes. Having a scope that was capable of displaying multiple views at the same time was also important.

All of the colorists used a Tektronix scope for these sessions that enabled them to view four different panes of information on the monitor. They all configured the four-pane view to display an **RGB parade waveform** display and a **vectorscope** (see Fig. 1-6). Some colorists set up an RGB parade waveform showing the entire image and then a second RGB parade that was zoomed in and focused on the 0 IRE line to better see how to balance their blacks. Most also set a fourth monitor pane to see the standard full waveform luminance display. This is similar to what I saw in the suites that the colorists worked in every day. Almost all of them had four dedicated outboard scopes set to different views or displays. This allows them to see information in multiple presentations at a single glance without having to switch between views by pressing buttons on a single scope.

a   b

Fig. 1-6 **(a)** (upper left) This view shows a YRGB parade waveform monitor that has been zoomed in to focus on the shadows only; (upper right) this view shows the full-scale composite standard waveform; (lower right) a standard zoom on a vectorscope; and (lower left) a 5× zoom to the center of the vectorscope. **(b)** This is another set of views using the same video image input (a DSC Labs grayscale chart with a warm white balance) fed to the scope: (upper left) this view shows an RGB parade waveform monitor showing the full-scale composite (not zoomed); (upper right) this view shows the full-scale composite standard waveform (single field only); (lower right) a standard zoom on a vectorscope; and (lower right) an Arrowhead gamut display.

Definition

RGB Parade Mode (Waveform): The RGB parade is simply a display option of a standard waveform monitor. Colorists rely heavily on the RGB parade viewing option on a waveform because it displays the individual levels of the red, green, and blue channels of an image. Each of these channels is displayed in its own **cell** horizontally with red, green, and blue in a "parade" from left to right across the screen. Each of these cells is essentially identical to the regular display of information on a waveform monitor, except that the values only pertain to the amount of that one color in the image. A variation on this display is the YRGB parade display that you will see throughout this book, which has four cells instead of three: the first being luminance (Y), followed by red, green, and blue (see Fig. 1-7).

Vectorscope: The vectorscope displays chrominance and hue. The saturation, or gain, of the chroma, or color, is measured by how far it extends from the center of the scope. Neutral images (black, white, and all levels of gray) register as a dot in the middle of the vectorscope. Hue is indicated by the position of the trace around the perimeter of the circle. Vectorscopes have **graticules** that show each of six different colors (red, green, blue, magenta, cyan, and yellow) in a different, fixed vector (position) around the vectorscope (see Fig. 1-8). Apple's Color includes a three-dimensional (3D) vectorscope that allows you to rotate the vectorscope in 3D space to see luminance displayed as well. Two-dimensional vectorscopes cannot display luminance information.

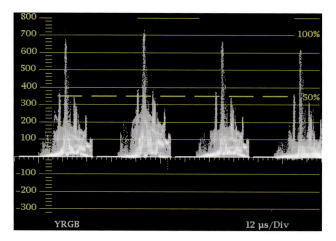

Fig. 1-7 Tektronix WVR7100 YRGB display. This shows a separate cell for overall luminance plus each of the three color channels: red, green, and blue. Also note that this display is presenting the information on a scale of millivolts on the left and percentages on the right. This is a matter of personal preference. Most people find the IRE or percentage scale easier to understand and communicate. The Tektronix display is capable of displaying the graticule for either scale.

Graticule: Graticule is the overlay on the scope that indicates levels and positioning information. The graticule does not change unless the user changes it. The graticule is usually customizable to display various scales and to provide information on how the **trace** signal is being displayed. It is analogous to the legends and lines on a chart or graph. The latitude and longitude lines on a map are the map's graticule. Figure 1-8 is the graticule of a vectorscope.

Trace: The trace is the part of the waveform or vectorscope display that reacts to the incoming video information. The trace is a representation of your video image on the waveform or vectorscope.

Cell: This term is used to describe one of the three (or four) separate images on the RGB parade waveform corresponding to the individual red, green, blue, and, in the case of a YRGB display, luminance signals.

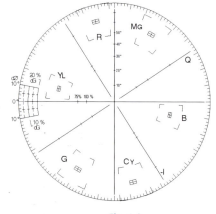

Fig. 1-8

Alternative Displays and Tools for Analysis

There are additional methods for analyzing an image. Most of these are specialized and are only available to specific applications. We'll address these methods throughout the rest of the book where they're applicable. They are also discussed in *Color Correction for Digital Video*.

Some of the analytical tools for video images that are alternatives to the basic waveform and vectorscope include eyedroppering (available in most color correction applications), histograms (available in some color correction applications), and Luma Range view (available in a few color correction applications). Also, some applications, like Final Cut Pro, can superimpose Zebra patterns or warning symbols on video that has levels that are near or in excess of legal limits. Avid products have a similar warning system for illegal and out-of-gamut video levels.

First Things First: Black Level

Nearly every colorist attacks an image by first determining where the blacks should be. Blacks refer to the deepest, darkest shadows and black portions of the image. As has been mentioned earlier, blacks are also sometimes referred to as setup, shadows, pedestal, or lowlights. There is usually some portion of an image that you can pick out that should be corrected to the lowest legal level. If you don't correct at least *some* portion of the image to a black level that is low enough and is basically devoid of detail, the shadows of the image will appear milky and the image will lack "snap" or "pop." The trick is to lower the blacks to the proper point without losing detail that you want to keep.

Some colorists, when working with a monitor that they trust and with which they have a lot of experience, will judge this black level by eye. But while a good colorist knows how to judge these things from a trusted, proven monitor, black levels are generally set by looking at a waveform monitor, preferably set to display in RGB parade mode.

Colorist Mike Most had this to say about black balance and scopes: "The first place I go is black balance. I think it's pretty much the first place pretty much everybody goes. I like to use scopes to do that. Scopes don't lie. I can do it largely by eye, but it depends on what time of day it is, what I've been looking at for the last 20 minutes, and my mood. So for times when you're looking for a pure balance, a scope is kind of your best friend. I know a lot of people who tend to stay away from scopes entirely, and I personally think it's kind of a mistake. I think you get a

Crush: Crush means to lower the black levels to the point where detail is lost in the deep shadow areas. "Crushing" clips the signal on the low end. Sometimes "crushing the blacks" is a desired result, in other words, creating a contrasty look. It is also sometimes a warning that the black levels are too low. For example: "As I lowered the blacks, the picture was looking nice and rich, but I pulled back a little on my correction because I saw that I was crushing the blacks and couldn't see any detail in the shadows."

Low Pass: Low pass is a mode or setting on the waveform monitor that filters out all of the chroma information in the image as it displays the waveform, allowing you to analyze only the luminance values. The opposite of this setting is "flat," which does not filter out the chroma information. On some scopes, especially those internal to many desktop applications, the flat mode is called Y/C, which stands for luma/ chroma. This Y/C mode is often displayed with the luma and chroma information in different colors. On a standard waveform monitor in flat mode, the luminance and chrominance values are indistinguishable by color on the display.

certain sloppiness that you don't need to have by doing that. I don't think you need to be a slave to scopes because a lot of it is just feel. But there are a lot of absolutes, and black balance is an absolute. Either the blacks are balanced or they're not and scopes don't lie. I trust the parade display. The vectorscope is a good guide, but for black balance, the parade display has to be the bible."

Looking at the waveform monitor in RGB parade mode allows you to view the brightness of each of the three color channels: red, green, and blue. Separating the display into these channels allows you to see whether one channel has more detail in the darkest areas of a picture and whether any one color channel has the black levels elevated above the others. This is an important thing to be able to see so that when you are using your color correction tools to lower the black levels, you do not **crush** the detail out of one channel that may be lower than the other two.

Reading the Waveform Monitor Let's take a look at an image and determine the proper black level looking at both a standard waveform image in a **low-pass**, or luminance-only, mode and a waveform image in RGB parade mode. First, we'll identify the picture elements in the video image and find the corresponding areas on the waveform monitor. This will help us judge the affect of our corrections as our eyes move from the waveform monitor to the video image.

Figure 1-9 will give you a good idea on the correlation of the waveform monitor and the video image. Figure 1-9(a) of the boxer is a high-definition still grabbed from Artbeats' "Sports 1" HD collection. Figure 1-9(b) was grabbed from a Tektronix WVR7100; the waveform image is simply an enlarged portion of that same scope. Figure 1-9(c) is an overlay of the boxer and the waveform done in Photoshop.

Take a look at the waveform from left to right and find the matching portions of the picture itself. The large rectangular shape on the waveform is not part of the image itself. This is the black burst. You can ignore that as you **grade**. The first small rises on the left correspond to the very shadowed boxing gloves hanging in the background. Then there is a small ramp leading up to a steeper spike. The small ramp is probably a little atmospheric smoke that is only barely perceptible in the HD image behind and about halfway up the punching bag. The angled spike indicates the left highlight on the punching bag. The ramping of the waveform is because the highlight gradually gets brighter as the light reflects in growing intensity on the curve of the bag then falls away on the right side of the curve. The speckled area above the steep spike appears to be the portion of the yellow rectangle at the top of the bag. I can basically confirm this suspicion by looking at the YRGB parade.

a

Fig. 1-9 (a) High-definition still from Artbeats' "Sports 1" HD collection, SP120. (b) Waveform image grabbed from a Tektronix WVR7100. (c) Artbeats' image from "Sports 1" HD collection overlaid with the waveform display.

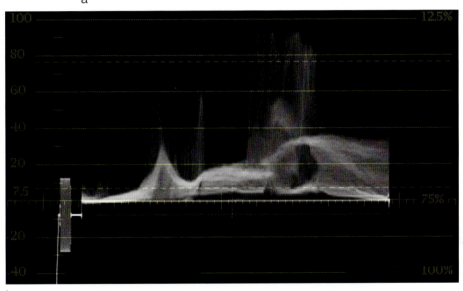

b

c

Grade: A term for the act of color correcting an image. It can be used as both a noun and a verb. For example: "I like the grade you did on this image," or "I'll pull some of the blue out as I grade this." Grade will be a common term used in this book because it's easier to type than "color correct." Also, grade is a preferred term used by many colorists, since it does not have the implication that something needed to be simply "corrected." I think it also tends to imply that it is more art than science. Color correction seems like a very engineering-based term. The term grade seems to have more favor in Europe, but it is widely used throughout the world, including in the United States.

If you look at the same horizontal area on the YRGB display (Fig. 1-10)—the first of the three spikes—you will notice that the spike is taller in the red and green cells and shorter in the blue cell. I explain this in more detail later in the chapter, but the equal combination of red and green in RGB color space makes yellow. Now the yellowish nature of the spike is certainly partly due to the fact that the highlight on the bag is slightly yellowish, but the difference between the amount of red and green compared to blue at that point doesn't correspond to just a small yellowish tint to the highlight. It indicates something that is quite yellow, like the rectangles at the top of the punching bag.

Continuing on across the waveform from left to right, there are four grayish spikes leading up to a thick spear that sits about one-third of the way across the image. These smallish spikes are the highlights in the wrinkles at the top of the punching bag: one along the seam in the middle of the bag and three short, but bright highlights just to the left of the other yellow rectangle. The tall spear in the waveform is the bright highlight at the top of the right side of the bag. Notice that in the tall spear the discrepancy between the heights of the red, green, and blue cells are minimized. This is because the yellow of the rectangle is obscured both by the bright highlight and in shadow. Your brain tells you that this has to be the same color yellow as the rectangle on the other side of the bag, but if you just look at the right-side rectangle, it's very difficult to make out any real yellow tint.

After the spike from the right-side bag highlight, there is a slightly elevated band in the waveform that goes between about 2 or 3 IRE up to about 20 IRE. (On the YRGB parade, it goes from about 15 millivolts to about 150 millivolts if you use the measurement scale to the left, which

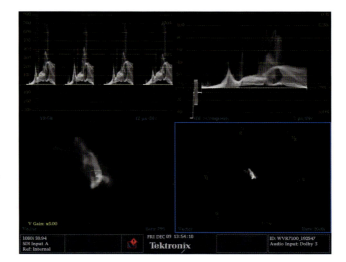

Fig. 1-10 Full display from Tektronix WVR7100 showing a YRGB parade (upper left), a composite (flat) display of the waveform (upper right), a vectorscope set to 5× gain (zoomed in) (bottom left), and a vectorscope set to normal gain (bottom right).

goes from −300 to 800.) This corresponds to the light caught by the atmospheric smoke between the boxer and the bag.

The complex shape to the right of that is the boxer. The highest portions of this shape indicate the reflected highlights from the top of his rear boxing glove, head, neck, shoulders, and left arm tricep. There are also bright portions indicating his white shirt, reflections on his pants, and the brighter flesh of his chest and forearm. The heavy band at the very bottom of the waveform is the shadow of his pants. On the right side of this shape, it falls off precipitously, with only a small ramp around 40–50 IRE. I think that ramp is the highlight from the top of the boxer's back leg.

The rest of the waveform display to the right is the bright haze of smoke. The top of the band is the bright smoke at the top of the picture gradually tapering down to the dark shadow at the bottom of the picture, behind the boxer. Notice that at about 20 IRE on the waveform monitor about two-thirds of the way across there is a circular gap in this smoke band. That's where the boxer is blocking the haze.

Notice that in Figure 1-9c the placement of picture elements in the vertical axis has no bearing on the waveform. In other words, there is no indication on the waveform whether a bright spot is at the top of the picture or at the bottom of the picture.

Looking at the black levels of this picture, they are already set about as low as they can go without crushing the detail out of the darker portions of the picture. This is no surprise really, since this is stock footage from Artbeats that was shot on film and already benefited from a colorist's touch as it was transferred from film to tape.

Setting the Black Level   Now, let's look at an image that needs to have the black level adjusted. The most obvious candidate would be a picture that looks a little washed out (see Fig. 1-11). We're going to analyze the image

Fig. 1-11 This is an interview shot with available light on BetaSP back in 1996. I was the shooter and my brother Brian is the subject. This footage is available on the DVD as the file labeled brian_overexposed.mov.

Definition

Clipping: An electronic limit on the maximum brightness of an image (usually imposed in the camera) to avoid overly bright or hot signals, or simply due to the fact that the imaging or recording medium can't perceive or record any greater brightness. Images recorded with portions where that level was exceeded will have lost picture information, or detail, where the image exceeded the level. Clipping can usually be perceived on a waveform as a "flattening-out" of the top of the trace into a sharp white horizontal line. Clipping is also possible on the low end of the signal, but that is generally referred to as "crushing." It is also possible for clipping to occur in individual color channels. An artifact of clipping is the flattening out of tonal or color detail.

in a number of ways and then look at several tools in various applications to correct the problem.

Please import the file brian_overexposed.mov from the DVD. It is a CCIR601 file size (NTSC video) and color space with interlaced fields, lower field first. You may use the color correction software that is most comfortable to you. I apologize to those of you in PAL or SECAM land. You may have to transcode the tutorial footage from these NTSC Quicktime files to something useable by your equipment.

The very first way that most colorists analyze an image is to view it on a broadcast monitor. This used to mean a CRT display, but increasingly even serious colorists are turning to LCD monitors and projectors as the CRTs are being phased out and the quality of LCDs improves. Future monitor technologies, like SED (Surface-conduction Electron-emitter Display) or OLED (Organic light-emitting diode) technologies, hold great promise, but are not available as of the writing of this book.

For now, you may use the image on the pages of the book itself, but you may also find this image on the DVD as a Quicktime file. The duration of each of the tutorial clips is quite short, in order to get as much data onto the disk as possible.

Import the file into whatever application you choose to use to do the tutorials. This could include Apple's Color, IRIDAS's SpeedGrade, Assimilate's Scratch, Discreet's Lustre, Synthetic Aperture's Color Finesse, any of the Avid products, Apple's Final Cut Pro or Shake, or Adobe's Premiere or After Effects. There are obviously more desktop color correctors, compositors, and nonlinear editing systems with color correction capabilities as well. If you want to, you could even attempt these corrections with Adobe Photoshop.

Looking at this footage, you can see that the image has very little contrast and is quite washed out, with very little "bottom" (see "The Language of Music and Color" boxed text below). There are no darker tones to anchor the midrange and highlights. The subject is poorly separated from the background elements. Looking at the waveform monitor indicates that there is probably some **clipping** of the highlights in the sky area, but there should be plenty of detail available in the rest of the image. The blacks are certainly not crushed because very little of the waveform trace is below 20IRE.

The Language of Music and Color

As someone who has hung out and performed with musicians most of his life and who has had the chance to hear the unique language of colorists as well, I have noticed that the languages of these two groups of artists are remarkably similar.

The example of the word "bottom" is used in both worlds. In music, it refers to having bass tones or low frequencies. To a colorist, it means blacks and deep shadows. Musicians and colorists also refer to images and music as being "warm" or "cool."

"Tone," "color," "midrange," "high end," "low end," and "shading" are often discussed by musicians. These words are obviously important to colorists as well. Adding "sparkle" or "depth" are things desired by both groups. "Spreading the tonal range" and "creating definition" are common goals. Having something that sounds or looks "thin" is bad for either group, while having an image or a sound that is "fat" is usually desirable (and I don't mean "phat"). Other common words include "tension," "contrast," "texture," and "brightness."

To both groups, these are words that cross the artistic divide between the aural arts and the visual arts. What connects them is emotion. Both color and music have a profound affect on our emotions. That is why they are both so important to storytellers and others who use media to influence and affect an audience.

Also, since collaboration and creative communication are important to both groups, it is important to learn to speak and understand a common language with your colleagues. The language used for creative communications is constantly evolving and is also varied by geography and by specific types of film and video professionals, so the exploration of these terms will need to be a personal one.

When you encounter a new word that is tossed at you by another creative professional, you can either ask what it means, if your ego will allow it, or "mirror" the phrase back with the meaning you *think* that the speaker intended. So if someone says, "The bottom seems a little thin," you can say, "So you want me to pull down the shadows to beef it up a little?" If you get an affirmative response, then you know you've translated it correctly.

The standard composite waveform monitor in Figure 1-12 (top right quadrant) shows that there is a small area in the middle of the image that appears to be almost on the 0 IRE line where black should be, but most of the rest of the image doesn't reach all the way down to black (0 IRE).

Looking at the YRGB parade waveform (top left quadrant) shows that nothing is hitting black except a small portion in the middle of the blue cell. This indicates that there really isn't a nice rich black anywhere in the picture and that the black balance has a heavy blue cast to it. We'll deal with the color casts in Chapter 2. For now our goal is to spread the tonal range, focusing first on bringing the black level down to the proper level.

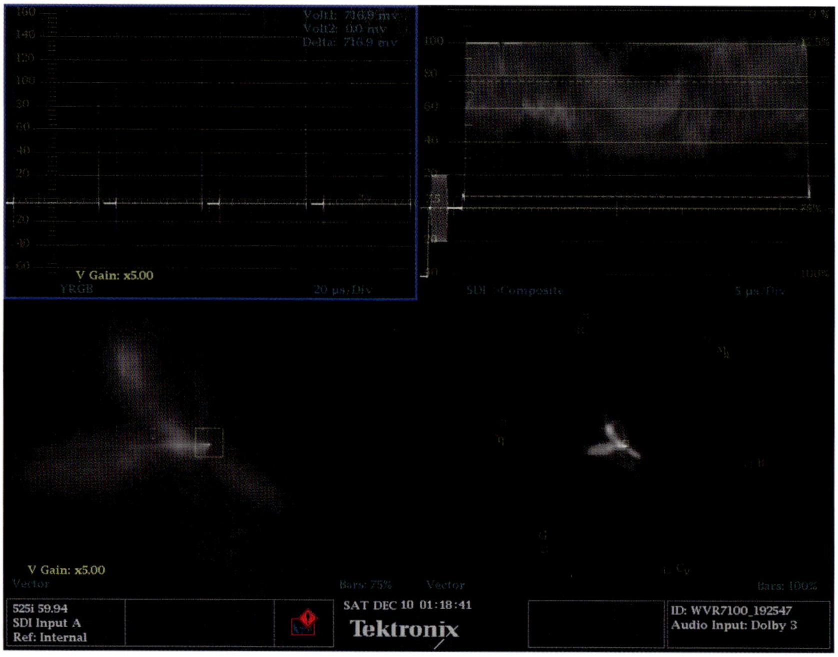

Fig. 1-12 Tektronix display showing a YRGB parade, zoomed in 5× to the bottom of the waveform (upper left), a standard composite waveform with no zoom (upper right), a vectorscope with a 5× zoom (bottom left), and a standard vectorscope display (bottom right).

An experienced colorist would actually tackle this color cast in the blacks at the same time, but we're going to break this task down into its components. Generally speaking, we wouldn't want to pull the overall blacks down on this image very much because we'll end up crushing the blacks in the blue channel while trying to bring down the overall level. That will mean we'll lose some detail there *and* cause some color problems.

So far we've used three methods to look at the black level in this image:

- We viewed the actual image on a broadcast monitor.

- We viewed a composite waveform display.

- We viewed a YRGB waveform display.

We'll learn more ways to analyze the image later in the book. Some of these methods have the widespread support of professional colorists and others are still gaining acceptance as the tools evolve.

Now that we have analyzed the image, it is time to actually *do* something to it. To affect the black levels, we are going to look at a few tools common to many of these applications. I will not show all of the tools from all of the applications, but I'll show you a broad array of tools that are available across the spectrum of applications. Your application may not have all of these tools, but you should be able to find one or two of them that look familiar, even if the specific tool is from a different application.

Often, when I'm teaching color correction, I tell the story of my martial arts training. I never got very far in the art that I studied—Hapkido—but I learned a lot of great lessons. One of the things that we did in Hapkido training was to learn many, many different ways to defend against the same attack. Sometimes there would be a dozen approaches to the same problem. We practiced all of these approaches over and over again, but the more we practiced, the more each of us felt comfortable with just two or three of the methods. That is the way the training was supposed to work. Depending on your physical build, strength, speed, weight, flexibility, and agility, certain methods would almost always work better. All of the methods were taught so that each of us could find what worked best for us. Sometimes the speed, strength, and skill of an opponent would dictate which defense was the best. The same goes for color correction. You'll see lots of tools and techniques. Some you won't be able to use because you don't have those tools at your disposal. Other tools or techniques just won't feel comfortable compared to others. And sometimes, you'll use the same technique 99 percent of the time, but every once in a while, you'll need to try something different on a specific image because of the unique problems it presents. This Hapkido example is an important one to remember as you are exposed to the various ways to both analyze the image and to correct it.

Now, back to setting the blacks on this particular image (see Fig. 1-13). We're going to watch the waveform monitor—and the broadcast

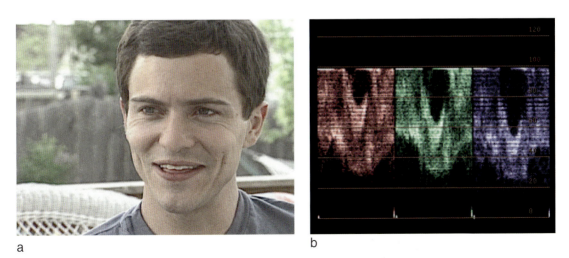

a   b

Fig. 1-13 **(a)** The original source image again. Please remember that the translation between the RGB video color space and the CMYK print color space is not perfect. **(b)** The internal RGB parade waveform display that corresponds to the uncorrected image.

monitor—and find a tool in your application that controls the setup, shadow, or black level. I'll tackle this correction in Apple's Color.

With the clip "brian_overexposed.mov" called up into your application, keep your eye on the RGB or YRGB waveform display. Bring down the master setup level until the trace of the blue channel of the waveform display starts to flatten out at the bottom, then bring it back just a hair. If you don't have an RGB or YRGB display, then bring down the setup (or black or shadow) level until the overall waveform level starts to flatten out at the bottom, then bring it up just a touch.

In Color, there are two ways within the Primary Room display that you can make this adjustment. One would be to drag inside of the black-to-white gradated bar in the Shadows group. I pulled the shadows down to around −0.301 from 0 (see Fig. 1-14). Or, on the right side of the

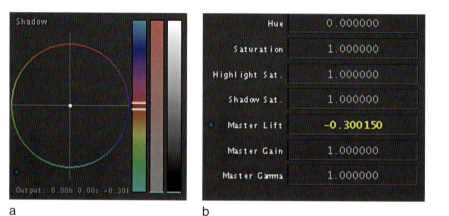

Fig. 1-14 (a) (b, c) This is what the image should look like after the correction to shadows or lift. (d) The internal RGB parade waveform display that corresponds to the first correction to shadows or lift.

a

b

c

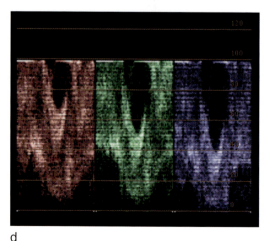

d

screen you could pull the Master Lift down to about the same level. This is done by dragging in the number window and holding down the center button or mouse scroll wheel.

One of my favorite color correction analogies is that making adjustments, especially to blacks and highlights, is like focusing a camera. Point a camera at a subject and look in the viewfinder. The image may, by chance, appear to be in focus. But you don't *really* know if it's in focus or not unless you adjust the focus ring a little bit in each direction, then settle in on the proper focus. Doing color correction is similar. You need to see how far you can push an image *and* when you haven't pushed it far enough.

The black levels can actually come down a little lower in the red and green channels, but we'll get to those kinds of adjustments in another tutorial. I chose to stop when the blue channel reached the bottom because I didn't want to clip or crush the blue shadows. Also I was watching the detail area in the dark portions of the eyes and that's as far as I could go before I started to lose details in the eyes.

Setting Highlights

With the black levels set, turn your attention to the highlights or gain controls. You can see from the waveform that the sky, especially on the right side, is clipped. This is evident from the sharp white line at the top of the right side of the waveform display (see Fig. 1-15). It's never a good thing to see this kind of clipping, but it is very common

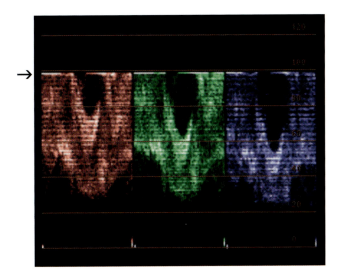

Fig. 1-15 The thin, hard white line at the top of the waveform display (indicated by the arrow) shows where clipping of the highlights has occurred.

in this kind of scenario of an interview shot outside with the sky in the shot. Trying to unclip this is not worth our time at the moment, so all we really want to do is set our gain control to get that clipped part of the sky to be the maximum legal level. We also want to use our focusing analogy to see if we can pull the highlights down to possibly eliminate the clipping. The clipping may be something that is fixable. You don't know until you try to get rid of it. If the shape of the top of the waveform stays flat, then the clipping occurred before it was brought in to the color corrector. This probably happened during shooting.

When the maximum gain is reached, it may have affected your black levels, so adjust them a little bit to get them as close to 0 IRE as possible (assuming your video signal is not set for 7.5 IRE) without "crushing" any detail. Remember, we don't want to see the highlights or the shadows flatten out on the waveform monitor for now. The goal is to spread the tonal range from 0–100 IRE (see Fig. 1-16).

Also, the shapes in the trace representing the brighter portions of your picture that are not already clipped will start to compress. Unless you are going for a specific look, this clipping, flattening, or compressing is a bad thing. It means you are losing detail in those bright portions of the picture. This is similar to the issues we discussed while setting black levels.

When you start to see this flattening in the waveform monitor, try to find the corresponding part of the image in the broadcast monitor and lift, then lower the gain while you watch the actual image. Do you notice

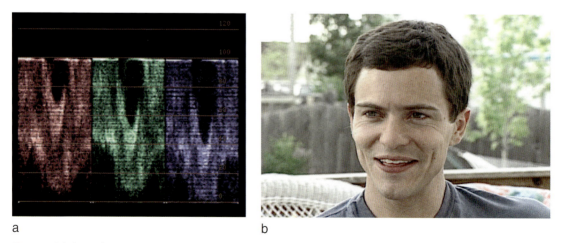

a   b

Fig. 1-16 (a) The resulting RGB parade with a good spread between highlights and shadows. (b) The resulting image with the highlights and shadows spread out.

the point at which the highlights begin to lose detail? Remember that camera focusing analogy here, too.

If you don't have a limiter on your software, then the highlights can be adjusted far above the legal level without the waveform showing clipping (this may depend on your software or your settings in your software to some extent). However, at some point in the broadcast or duplication or distribution chain, these super-bright highlights will get clipped. It's much better for the colorist to determine how and where the clipping occurs than to rely on some "dumb" device downstream to do this, because you'll have no control of the way the signal looks at that point. Plus, if you are doing these corrections with a client supervising the session, they may love the look of what you're doing in the suite, but may be less than pleased when they see what the limiter does to their beautiful corrections.

For an image with highlights that are very high above the rest of the levels in the shot, you may want to set the main brightness using the midtones or gamma so that you have a pleasing level, then use the gain controls to bring just the highlights back down to a legal level. This also can be an instance where you break the rules in regards to clipping. If you have a scene that is perhaps mostly dark except for a couple of very bright **practical lights** that are seen in the shot, or a scene with a very bright window behind a darker subject, you can make the decision to clip or **blow out** that window or practical in order to gain enough tonal range in the area that matters—your subject.

Make one last check to see that your setup change didn't affect your highlights and then we'll find the correct gamma adjustment to make this look as rich and well-lit as possible.

Definition

Practical Lights: Sometimes called *practicals*, these are lights that are part of the scene, such as a table lamp in a scene next to an actor (see Fig. 1-17). Usually the brightness of these practicals is closely controlled by the director of photography by changing the wattage of the bulb or putting it on a dimmer.

Blow Out: A nontechnical term for clipping or letting a bright highlight get so hot that it loses all or most of its detail. An example is: "The only way I can bring the level up enough to see the actor's face is to blow out the window."

Fig. 1-17 The table lamp behind the woman is referred to as a *practical*.

Setting Gammas or Midtones

After setting blacks and highlights, the final tonal correction is to set your midtones. This is where a lot of the mood of the shot is created. With the other two levels basically done by looking for their extreme legal limits, the overall tone of the piece is set using the gamma or midtone.

When I do color correction, I do not have to deal with too many outside opinions. My decision about the look is pretty much the final say. I realize this situation is very different from many colorists.

My personal preference when setting midtones in an image is to create a rich feel with a slightly lowered gamma. If your image seems a little dark, even with the highlights raised to the peak legal level, then raising your gamma can give you a brighter, though usually flatter, feel, sometimes somewhat akin to the look of a sitcom. The reason for this is that often the detail of the image is in the gamma and highlight areas, so the closer those two ranges are to each other, the less contrast there is in this critical portion of the image. Some images with more detail in darker portions of the image would actually look *less* flat by raising the gamma, but in my experience, this is the exception, not the rule.

When setting the gamma, there's really not much to go by except for personal taste. If you're trying to see into the shadows or trying to hide things a little in the shadows, then raising or lowering gamma, respectively, can accomplish much of what you want to do.

Oftentimes I consider the gamma controls to be my postlighting controls. If I feel like the on-set lighting was a little too contrasty or flat, I can often use gamma to get it to look closer to what I want. Lowering the gamma usually increases the contrast in the shadow details of the fleshtones. Raising the gamma tends to flatten out the shadow details. A lot of that depends on the exact levels of the shadows on the fleshtones. On most "normal" footage, though, the shadows on flesh are still in the midtone range, so lowering them tends to increase the contrast between the rest of the lit flesh tones, which are also in the midtones, but are affected by the highlights as well.

To complete the correction on the Brian interview footage, let's set the gamma so that the flesh tones look rich and healthy while making sure that the footage isn't too dark. This is a pretty standard interview clip, so we want something that looks natural and not overly dramatic.

I brought the Master Gamma down about 0.05 in Color from 1.000 to 0.95. I used the focusing technique, looking at the eyes of the subject on the video monitor instead of at my waveform monitor. Actually, this was an instance where the gamma was actually about right where it was.

When I brought it up higher than 1.0, the picture started to look washed out. When I brought it down around 0.90, it started to look too dark and I lost the detail and "sparkle" in his eyes. I ended up at around 0.955. I want to point out that I wasn't being guided by the specific number of the gamma control. I was being guided by looking at the richness of the skin tone, the amount of texture and detail in the hair and eyes, and the overall brightness of the image. I am relating the numbers merely as a matter of reference after the fact. See Figures 1-18(a, b) for the before-and-after correction comparisons.

Remember, that if you are working with color correction software using only a mouse or single trackball to control tonal ranges one at a time, making adjustments to gamma will affect the levels for shadow and highlight that you've already set. Therefore, once you are done with your gamma adjustment, you will need to revisit the corrections you did to highlights and shadows. Then readjust gamma again. Then recheck highlight and shadow levels again after that.

Defining Contrast

Another important concept to understand in developing the tonality of an image is that contrast is not just a global parameter in an image. It is possible to increase the contrast in a specific area of an image by playing either the highlights against the gammas or the shadows against the gammas. This can develop an increased amount of

a   b

Fig. 1-18 **(a)** This is the video image before correction. **(b)** This is the video image after correction. This is not a final correction. This is only the tonal correction in the primary room. The colors, saturation, and secondary color correction have not yet been affected.

contrast in either your shadows, midtones, or highlights. You can use this to draw attention to parts of the image that you want the viewer to focus on.

How does this work? Think of the waveform image of a picture with low contrast. The entire trace on the waveform is squished into a small area. To increase the contrast across the entire image, you simply spread out the trace by making the shadows lower and the highlights higher. Now you can use this same concept to increase the contrast in a specific portion of the image. The goal in that area is to spread out the distance between the bottom of that portion and the top. So if you want to increase contrast in your dark shadows, you lower the shadows and raise the midtones. This is one of those times when having a manual user interface, like the Tangent Devices CP-200, is of great value, because you can play the two ranges against each other at the same time. Now you have a choice of adding contrast to the area between midtones and shadow or midtones and highlights.

In Figure 1-19, notice that the difference in contrast between the tops of the black keys and the sides of the black keys is not that different. If you wanted to increase that contrast so that the sides of the keys were more black and the tops seemed to have more light, you would lower the shadow level, or Master Lift as it is called in Color, while raising the Master Gamma. In addition to seeing a difference in the image, notice that the spread of the trace in the lower portion of the waveform also becomes greater, indicating increased contrast.

a

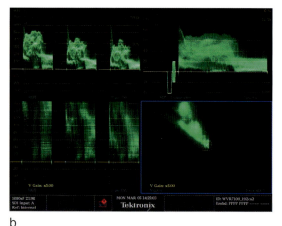

b

Fig. 1-19

I took this to an extreme in this case to make the difference clearly visible. In this instance, I introduced a lot of unwanted noise and a gamut error, but the contrast between the highlights of the black keys and the deeper shadows of the black keys is definitely sharper (compare the front highlight of the black keys in the middle, under the hands), while the hands have become more washed out (see Fig. 1-20).

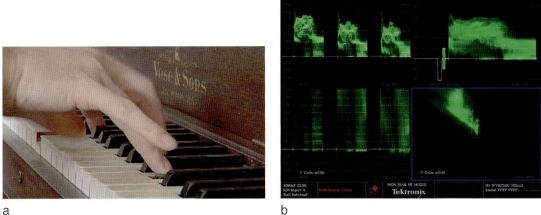

a   b

Fig. 1-20 Contrast increased between blacks and midtones.

Now change the contrasty portion of the picture to the highlights instead of the shadows (see Fig. 1-21).

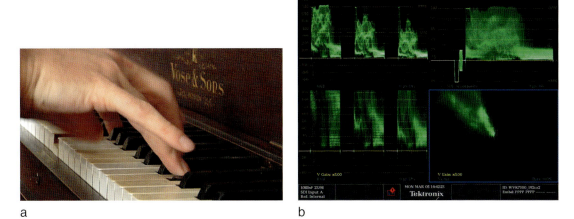

a   b

Fig. 1-21 Contrast increased between the midtones and highlights.

Notice that Fig. 1-20 emphasizes the keys and Fig. 1-21 emphasizes the hands. The name of the piano is also clearer since the contrast has been increased between mid and high. Also, notice the lower portions of the waveform monitor are stretched out when the contrast is in the shadows as opposed to the stretched upper portion when the contrast is in the highlights.

Understanding how to gain contrast in the correct portion of a picture is essential as you develop your skills as a colorist. It isn't enough to simply increase the overall contrast. You need to be able to control contrast within an image, because that helps both in creating distinct looks in your images and in directing the viewer's eye where you want to focus it. Practicing this particular contrast focusing trick will also help you when a client asks you to "pop" something off of a background. To do that, you will need to understand the tonal range of the background and the tonal range of what is supposed to pop off of it and then figure out how to stretch that range. This trick is further supported by eliminating contrast in other areas of the picture, so that the viewer's eye is drawn to the areas of the image that have more information. If you crush the shadows, then there is nothing to look at in that area and the viewer looks elsewhere.

I boosted the contrast even more in an attempt to get the piano name to pop even more off the background (see Fig. 1-22). One thing to be very aware of in doing these extreme contrast moves is that increasing contrast also increases the chroma levels. The hands got

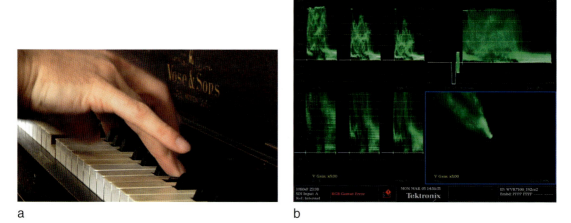

a   b

Fig. 1-22 Contrast increased even more to pop name of piano off of the dark wood.

very heavily colored and unnatural as I pushed the contrast, so I had to also lower the saturation levels across the board. You can control the saturation of shadows, midtones, and highlights separately, so use this ability to create natural-looking color levels and reduce noise in unwanted areas. Some of the most objectionable noise is color noise, so reducing the saturation levels where you see noise can really clean up an image.

Practice Playing Gamma Against Highlights and Shadows

This concept of playing gammas against the highlights and shadows to increase contrast in specific regions of the picture is very important to your ability to quickly and easily manipulate the look of an image. It will help you execute a look that a client has in mind and it will help you match the look of two or more shots in a sequence. Because of the importance of this concept, you should really practice this on your own.

The three images you will need to develop this skill are a ramp like the one on the DVD called "ramp-2-254.psd." Most nonlinear editors (NLEs) have a similar test image built in to them, or you can even make your own. The ramp should start at 0% luminance on one side (usually the left) and then go all the way to 100% luminance on the other side (usually the right). The other image that you will need is the image of the chip chart from the DVD called "grayscale_neutral.mov" And finally, use some of the real video from the DVD or, better yet, from your own projects to see how these gamma versus highlights or shadows corrections affect a natural image.

This practice will be greatly enhanced by using a manual control device with the ability to adjust the highlights, gammas, and shadows all at the same time, like the Tangent Devices CP-200 or CP-100 that the colorists in this book used. The reason for this is that adjusting the gammas will obviously have an effect on the highlights and shadows, so if you can only move one at a time, it will require numerous adjustments back and forth as the various tonal range corrections interact.

Practice with the ramp image by trying to get the dark part of the ramp compressed in a tight dark band on one end while the bright area is spread out more. Then reverse that. If you can copy and paste your color corrections in your application, try applying these corrections to real-life images or to the grayscale chart.

Do the same thing with the grayscale chart. Try to get the chips at the bottom to be all very close together while spreading the distance between each chip in the highs and mid-highs. Then do the opposite.

Try to practice on real-life images from the DVD or your own collection. What if you want to add lots of contrast to the skin tones? What if you wanted to see lots of detail in the shadows? How could you get more detail out of the clouds in the sky? Playing gamma against the other two tonal ranges will deliver these effects. Taking the highlights or shadows *past* the point of clipping and *then* playing with gammas will take these corrections even further, by stretching the contrast over an even greater area.

CHAPTER 2

Tonal-Correction Tools

This chapter describes the tonal-correction tools available in several of the applications and plug-ins for doing color correction, as well as their respective strengths and weaknesses.

Main Tools for Tonal Corrections

Across the range of products, there are lots of tools. Some of them apply to altering tonal range and some are more commonly used to control the color of an image, generically meaning that they'd be used to control hue and saturation, though they'd also have some effect on the tonal range as well.

For tonal corrections, almost every application that has color correction abilities has some slider or numerical controls to adjust brightness, contrast, black level (a.k.a. shadows, pedestal, blacks, or setup), and gamma. Some applications may also include numerous sliders and numerical entry windows for various "tweaks" to the gamma, including knee, shoulder, softness, and width or specific range of each of these gamma adjustments.

In addition to the typical sliders controls (which are sometimes controllable by knobs or dials on an external manual interface like those made by Tangent Devices or JLCooper), some applications also give you tonal control via the manipulation of histograms, which some applications call Levels. Most of these Level controls allow you to adjust the output level, which is a fairly intuitive thing to do, but some also include the ability to adjust the actual *input* levels using a histogram, which will work the reverse of the way you would think.

Another very common way in computer applications to adjust tonal ranges is via Curves. Curves is a popular tonal-correction tool because it offers incredibly precise control and is very intuitive. So you'd figure that it is *the* tool to use for tonal corrections, but there is a caveat: You can *really* mess up your images with this tool. Most applications that have Curves allow you to place as many as 16 distinct points on the curve to control it. All of these points can do some very funky things to your image, includ-

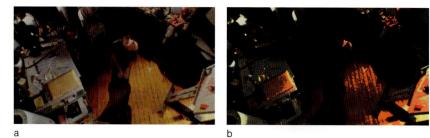

a   b

Fig. 2-1 **(a)** Original image, 16-mm film transfer to high-definition. Courtesy of Vanderpool Films. **(b)** Posterized image.

Posterization: This happens when an image breaks down from having continuous tones to having specific regions of tones where each region has a distinct transition to the next.

Banding: Similar to posterization, banding occurs when a continuous-tone image breaks down into bands of distinct, individual tones. This usually occurs in gradients such as the sky. For example, an image begins as a continuous gradation from light blue to dark blue, then through overcorrection (or a radical change in color space or compression), turns into individually discernable bands of color. Banding is more likely to happen with lower bit-depth images (8-bit instead of 10-bit images).

Chip Chart: A camera setup chart that has several different gray chips that range from white to black. The chart that is used throughout this book is DSC Labs CamAlign GrayScale Test Pattern Chart. It has 11 gray patches, or chips, that have specific reflectance values.

a   b

Fig. 2-2 **(a)** Original image, DV resolution. Courtesy of Randy Reisen. **(b)** Sky exhibiting banding.

ing creating severe **posterization** (see Fig. 2-1) or **banding** (see Fig. 2-2). Curves is a favorite tool of Photoshop and After Effects users and those who move back and forth between Photoshop and video applications. Full-time colorists are much less enamored of this tool, though with exposure to it through Apple's Color, that may change.

Sliders and Numerical Controls for Tonal Range

Let's start the exploration of these tonal-correction tools with simple sliders and numerical input. There are two test patterns that can help you understand the specifics of what these tools can do as you start to explore.

Load the **chip chart** image from the DVD tutorial media folder (grayscale_neutral.mov; see Fig. 2-3) and load a ramp pattern (ramp_0-254.psd). See if your application has one of these ramps. It will have been created for the specific way that your application treats video black. If not, you can use one of the ramps on the DVD.

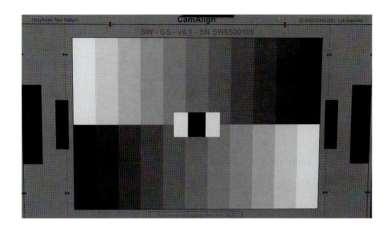

Fig. 2-3 Chip chart image. All charts in this book are courtesy of DSC Labs.

Don't Use Brightness or Contrast Controls

Of all of the controls available in most applications, the Brightness and Contrast controls are the ones that should be avoided. Why? Because they limit the control you have, compared to other sliders.

Watch what happens on a waveform when you use the brightness slider to adjust the image of the ramp or the chip chart. The entire trace of the waveform moves up and down uniformly. Compare this to adjusting the gain. When using gain, there is some movement in the other tonal ranges of the picture, but the largest percentage of adjustment occurs only in the highlights of the picture.

Now grade the chip chart or ramp image using the Contrast control. The Contrast control will compress or expand the entire trace of the waveform equally from each end of the tonal range, by raising the blacks by an equal amount as it lowers the whites, or vice versa. Doing good color correction is all about having control, and Brightness and Contrast rob you of control.

So what do you do if you want to make the picture brighter or more contrasty? Well brightness comes from several things. Bringing the gain up to basically its highest legal level is a key one. Sometimes, because of some very bright highlights, the picture will still seem too dark once you have raised the gain on those highlights to 100 IRE, because the middle tones of the picture, which contain much of the real information, were not raised much. In that case, the real sense of how bright the picture looks is done in the midtones (more on that in a moment). Sometimes, getting a picture bright enough may even involve increasing the gain so much that some of the brightest parts of the image will clip. That is a judgment call that you need to make in deciding what parts of the image

Bit Depth: The number of bits (the smallest data amount, basically on or off binary info) used to describe a color. There's a little confusion about bit-depth numbers. Sometimes what is referred to as 8 bit is the same as 24 bit because they are saying that 8 bits per color channel multiply to 24 bits (8×3); 8 bits of color depth gives you 256 shades of gray, which you then multiply with the three color channels ($256 \times 256 \times 256$) to show how many colors you can describe in that color space (16.7 million colors). 10-bit video has 1,024 shades of gray instead of 256. Obviously 10-bit video is going to be preferable for color correction. The bit-depth computations above generate numbers that are on the theoretical limits. You are really limited in the actual number of levels of tones and colors by your recording and display devices and the color spaces that they represent.

Nonlinear Editor (NLE): A computer based editor that allows source material to be located randomly, and edits to be made non-destructively and non-linearly (out of the chronological order of the edited program) Examples are Avid and Final Cut Pro.

deserve to have the most detail. If the highlights are not important, then you can clip them to the point where detail is lost in order to rescue detail from the high midtones and midtones, because clipping out the highest highlights will also raise the levels of the middle highlights and midtones.

If you are looking for greater contrast, that usually comes from setting nice, rich shadows using the setup control and then getting as much of a range as possible between the darkest portions of the picture and the brightest portions of the picture. The contrast control rarely works for this purpose because, for example, if your blacks are muddy but your highlights are almost at their maximum level, you can only slightly increase contrast before the highlights can't go any higher without clipping. If you want *lots* of contrast, you can ignore all of the warnings about clipping either end of the signal and really stretch out the tonal range. But you will have better results doing an extreme contrast move with a system that does its color correction computations in a higher color space. Color and Color Finesse actually work at a 32-bit floating point, and Avid works at 10-bit. All of them have to convert these color corrections back to the original **bit depth** of the source footage or the highest output bit depth, which is often 8 bit or 10 bit.

Knowing all of that, if you find the need to raise the entire tonal range of the picture *equally* or to compress or expand the contrast (entire tonal range) of your picture *equally* then feel free to use Brightness and Contrast controls. An example of this could be in a **nonlinear editor (NLE)**, if you want to reduce the overall contrast of an image quickly so that a title or text "pops" over the background more, then lowering contrast would be an ideal tool.

Although you may do your color correction with only one of the following products, I hope you'll check out the description of how the corrections are done in each of the products. I can't give descriptions of *all* of the products out there, so I'll show you specific graphical user interface (GUI) tools from a certain representative sample of products. The way your particular product works may not be included in the list, but the basic operating principles probably will be similar to one of the other products mentioned here. Some applications or plug-ins have very proprietary tools, which I'll sometimes mention and show. Other times, the basic tools operate nearly identically across all color correction products. In that case, it's hardly worth describing the same process over and over, so I'll select an application that is representative of them all. Interfaces change from release to release and products come and go, so I'll try to just give an overview here.

As I've mentioned, there are a *lot* of NLEs, stand-alone color correctors, plug-ins, and compositors out there with color correction tools. Covering them all—and knowing them all thoroughly—is impossible, but I will show you some of the main ways that you can affect your tonal corrections.

Let's start with the tools in Apple's Color. Even if you don't use some of these applications, I hope you'll read about them anyway, because certain tips and material may only be covered when I discuss that specific application, even though that information may pertain to more than one application. I also believe that colorists may become more like editors, who need to know multiple applications in order to stay viable and employed. Obviously that doesn't apply to everyone, but many colorists will be able to make a good living by diversifying the products with which they make their living, so knowing the capabilities and limitations of each application will be a valuable career enhancer.

Color's Primary In Room

There are three tools to use for the most intuitive tonal corrections. The first is to use the colored sliders at the top of the screen to the right of each of the three color wheels (see Fig. 2-4). The first rainbow-colored

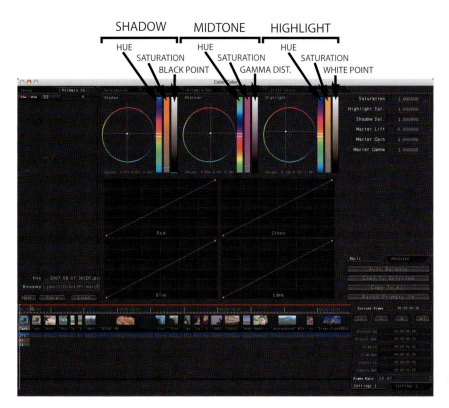

Fig. 2-4 Apple Color's Primary In room.

Hue Offset Wheels:
A circular user interface that looks like a color wheel or vectorscope that allows for the control of both hue and saturation. Hue values are indicated around the perimeter of the circle and saturation is indicated by the respective distance from the center of the circle. With some color correctors with manual user interfaces, these hue offset wheels can be controlled by multiple trackballs. Each wheel controls a different tonal range.

Gamma: Gamma has several definitions, but the primary one that is used by colorists is to describe the midtones or midrange tones of a picture. Gamma can also refer to the curve or steepness of the transition from black to white. These are similar definitions in a way, because by altering the gamma, or midrange, of a picture, the curve or transition from shadow to highlight is also affected. Directors of photography usually refer to gamma as meaning the response curve from black to white instead of meaning the midtones specifically.

vertical bar in each group adjusts hue. The middle bars adjust the chroma or saturation level of the image. The black/white bars to the right of each group adjust the level of the black point, midtone (gamma) distribution, or white point in the shadow, midtone, or highlight tonal ranges, respectively.

Each group, consisting of a circular color wheel (sometimes referred to as **hue offset wheels**) and three vertical bars, controls one of the three tonal ranges. The far left group is for shadows, the middle group is for midtones or **gamma**, and the right group is for highlights.

If you have a JLCooper MCS Spectrum controller, Eclipse-CX, Tangent Devices CP100 or CP200-BK controller, the dials and trackballs on the controller are linked to the various controls on the GUI. On a CP200-BK, for example, each trackball controls the corresponding hue offset wheel on the GUI (see Fig. 2-5). The rings around each trackball control the black point, gamma distribution, and white point (from left to right), and the dials at the top of the device control saturation.

If you are using Color with just a mouse or a trackball, then you can bring the shadows or blacks up or down by dragging the small, horizontal cyan line that is at the bottom of the black/white bar on the left. There is a similar small, horizontal cyan line across the middle of the middle black/white bar. Drag this up or down to control the midtones of your image. To control highlights, drag the cyan line at the top of the right-hand black/white bar up or down.

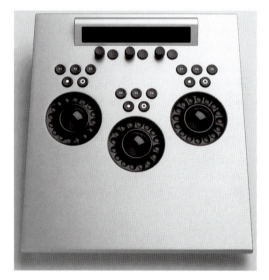

The second tool for tonal corrections is to use the entry windows for Master Lift, Master Gamma, and Master Gain controls along the right side of the screen, near the top. You can type in numbers, but that is hardly intuitive. The best way to control these sliders with a mouse is to use the scroll wheel. Hover the mouse over the numeric lift, gamma, or gain number and then click down on the scroll wheel and drag the mouse left and right to adjust in gross increments, or scroll the wheel itself up and down for fine increments.

The default tab in this location is the Basic tab, but you can also do corrections with the Advanced tab. We'll get into that later in the chapter when discussing color tools, since the Advanced tab is more for making color corrections than tonal corrections. Much of the use of these specific tools was covered in Chapter 1 when we corrected the overexposed interview footage of Brian.

The third tool for tonal corrections is to use the Curves controls, located in the middle of the Primary In room (see Fig. 2-6).

Since we're only discussing tonal corrections in this chapter, tonal corrections would be made using the Luma curve, which is the bottom right control of the four curves. While the previous two methods of controlling tone in Color's Primary In room allow control over three tonal ranges, the Luma curve allows you to alter the black-and-white points by moving the bottom and top corners of the curve. It also allows multiple custom-selected points in between those points that can be adjusted in any direction. For more on the use of Curves, see the "Curves Tab" section later in this chapter.

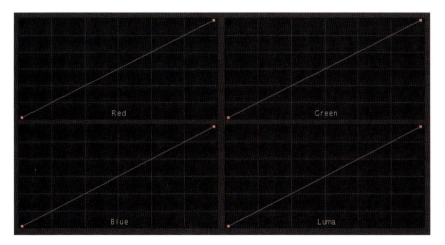

Fig. 2-6 The Curves controls in Primary In room.

Avid Symphony and Color Finesse HSL Controls Tab

For basic adjustments to tonal ranges using sliders or numerical values, Avid Symphony and Color Finesse have several options depending on how much control you want to exercise (see Fig. 2-7). The quick and dirty place to start is the HSL Controls tab of the color correction mode.

There are actually a number of sub-tabs in this area. You can affect the master **hue, saturation, and luminance (HSL)** levels, which include controls for the master highlights, midtones, and shadows, or you can gain more discrete control by adjusting the same controls inside the specific tonal ranges. This means you can control the highlights, midtones, and shadows of the highlights; the highlights, midtones, and shadows of the midtones; and the highlights, midtones, and shadows of the shadows. How are there highlights of shadows? There really are not—instead of simply giving you three tonal ranges, the extra tabs let you restrict your corrections to *nine* discrete tonal ranges: high highs, mid-highs, low highs, high mids, mid-mids, low mids, high shadows, mid-shadows, and low shadows.

If you have Symphony or Color Finesse, you can get a better sense for how all these crazy "shadows of the highlights" and "highlights of the shadows" controls work by putting up the grayscale chip chart in the color correction mode and watching your waveform monitor as you adjust each of the controls.

There are a couple of controls on this tab that you should not use, even though they may seem to be the most obvious ones to start with. The Hue and Saturation controls are not really for doing tonal corrections, so we'll discuss those later. And as I already mentioned at the top of this section, Brightness and Contrast really limit your control over specific tonal ranges, since they affect all areas of the picture equally.

Fig. 2-7 HSL controls in Avid Symphony.

Histograms or Levels

I'm not much of a fan of the Levels controls that are available on many NLEs (for an example, see Fig. 2-8). But if you are comfortable with viewing the levels in histograms, this could be a powerful way for you to have intuitive control over the same basic gain, midrange, and shadow control that was available in the HSL Controls tab.

Histograms

A histogram is a very simple graph. Horizontally across the x axis (redundant, I know, but I'm trying to be clear...) indicates the image's tonal range with black to the left and white to the right. The vertical, or y axis, shows the number of pixels at each tonal value. Most histograms of a well-exposed image will look somewhat like a bell curve, with some pixels at absolute black, some at absolute white, and most in the midrange of the picture. There are some beautiful images that may not look like a bell curve, but if you have a histogram that looks like a bell curve, it should be a pretty well-exposed image.

When analyzing an image with a histogram, the bell curve shape is less important than identifying the danger signs of a histogram, which are sharp peaks or "cliffs" at either end of the histogram. These indicate that clipping is occurring. So you can use this cliff effect to help you judge when your grading is starting to clip.

Look at the following example, which uses the "steve_dark_at_the_park.mov" clip from the "Tutorial_footage_and_files" folder on the DVD.

In the Master tab, at default, the numbers under each histogram are the same (16, 128, and 235). This indicates that black (16 in NTSC levels

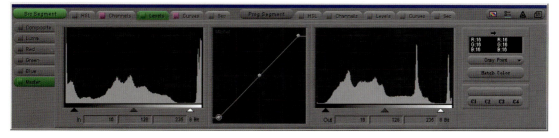

Fig. 2-8 Symphony Levels control allows you to adjust levels while viewing histograms.

for a 7.5 IRE setup) on the source is mapped to black on the output side (see Fig. 2-9).

Now, on the input side, slowly move the black triangle to the right, releasing when the source black side reads 25 (see Fig. 2-10).

Now, the slope on the output side has a nice clean incline, from the black triangle to the peak, but if you slowly move the input slider up from 25 through 30 and 40, you will see that the output side starts to have a significant spike of pixels above the black triangle (see Fig. 2-11).

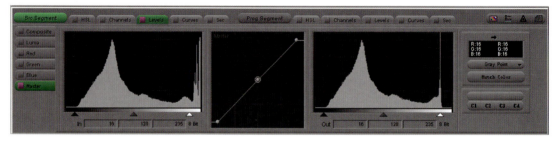

Fig. 2-9

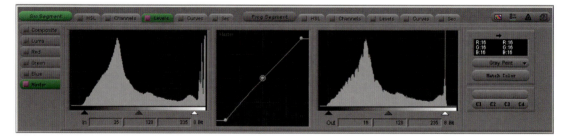

Fig. 2-10

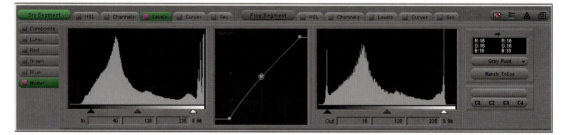

Fig. 2-11

This is because all of the pixels to the left of the black triangle on the input side have "piled up" at pure black on the output side. The more technical description of what's happening is that the levels are being remapped so that all of the pixels in the source footage between 0 and 40 have been now all remapped to 0 and all of the pixels between 40 and 255 have been remapped between 0 and 255. So all of the levels of tonality that are in the slope to the left of the input black triangle have been compressed, or clipped, down to black on the output side. This means you have lost all the detail in the darkest pixels, because where there used to be subtle differences between these very dark pixels, now all of them are at 0. Usually this "crushing" of detail is a bad thing, but it also can be useful to create a punchy, crushed black look. As long as you don't mind losing the detail in the deepest black areas, you're fine. But if you want to preserve that detail, then stop before the big spike gets too big.

Fig. 2-12 is the final position of the Levels, including a midtone correction to lift the face out of the shadows. I wouldn't call this a final correction, but that's as far as we'll take it in Levels. Notice that there is a small spike to the left of the output histogram. I chose to let some of the blacks lose detail, but not a lot. I assume that most of those pixels

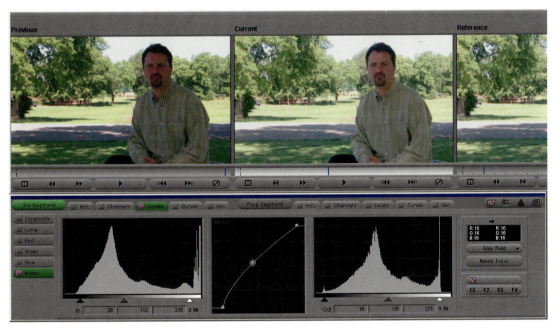

Fig. 2-12

are in the black leg at the bottom of the frame and possibly in my (yes, that's me, or it *was*, back in about 2006) black hair.

Another way to gain an understanding of histograms is to look at the grayscale chart as a histogram. There is a video version of this called "grayscale_neutral.mov" on the DVD (see Fig. 2-13).

If you look at the Luma tab, you can see the five small double spikes to the right of the big middle spike and the five small double spikes to the left of the middle spike. The five left spikes are the five darker chips, and the five right spikes are the five brighter chips. The big middle spike is the middle gray chip *plus* the surrounding gray background. That's why the middle spike is so much bigger. In this case the spike does not indicate clipping, but simply a large area that is supposed to have the same color to it. Remember the vertical axis of the graph doesn't indicate brightness,

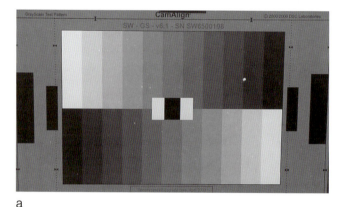

Fig. 2-13 **(a)** Grayscale "chip" chart (DSC Labs). **(b)** Resulting Histogram display of the chip chart in Avid Symphony.

a

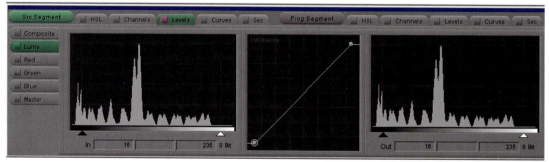

b

but the number of pixels at a given brightness level. So, since there is a greater area of middle gray on the chart, the histogram shows many more pixels at this middle tonal range. Having spikes that do not indicate clipping is very rare in most "natural" video images. Usually there is some kind of gradation or imperfection to the color.

There is also a larger bump to the far left side, indicating the larger patches of black on the sides and in the middle of the chart, and possibly even some of the black text on the chart.

Forms and Functions of Histograms

In some programs, the histogram is not limited to displaying the master histogram. For example, with many applications you can also display histograms of the Composite level (saturation and luminance together), Luma level, and individual levels for each of the red, green, and blue channels.

These individual histograms can be useful for spotting problems with the individual channels. As I mentioned earlier, sharp spikes at either end of the histogram indicate clipping (lots of pixels jammed into the same tight tonal range). You can look at the individual color channels' histograms and see whether a specific color channel is more clipped than another, or if there is an entire tonal range that is weak in a certain color channel. I've actually seen footage from cameras with severe technical problems where there was absolutely *no* information in a particular color channel.

The trick with Symphony's Levels controls is that there are both input and output level controls. These are tied together. The input controls seem counterintuitive because as you move the shadow triangle to the left, the level of blacks goes up, and moving it to the right makes black levels go down. The reason for this is that when you move the black level to the right on the *input* side, you are telling Symphony to map all of the levels to the left of the triangle to black to a lower level. However, if you move the same black triangle on the *output* side to the right, you are telling Symphony that all of the levels of black that are at or to the left of the input black triangle should now be mapped to a higher level.

A way to understand this is to look at the curve in between the two histograms as you move the input then the output black triangles. On the input side, moving the black triangle to the left or right moves the black point on the curve left or right. But moving the black curve on the output side moves the black point on the curve up and down.

Definition

Under Your Fingers:
This is a term musicians use to describe practicing something enough times that the movements become second nature. Basically, it means developing muscle memory, where your body knows what to do without your brain consciously thinking about it.

To best study how this works and get it **under your fingers** is to call up a black-to-white ramp or chip chart and simply slide the faders around, watching the waveform carefully as well as looking at the result on the video monitor.

Curves Tab

Curves in Apple's Color, Avid's Symphony (see Fig. 2-14) and XpressPro (see Fig. 2-15), and Synthetic Aperture's Color Finesse are similar to the Curves controls of several other products, like Adobe's After Effects and Photoshop. They allow pinpoint control over specific tonal ranges. The power of this control is a wonderful thing, but like any kind of power, it can be abused.

Color, Symphony, and Color Finesse give you a Curve for each color channel and a fourth Curve for the master (or Luma). Looking at the default position of Curves makes you wonder: Why are they called Curves? They're straight! That's because at their default position, the Curves are simple graphs that indicate that the input level or source level, which is indicated along the horizontal axis of the graph, is mapped perfectly to the output level, which is indicated along the vertical axis of the graph.

Imagine if you were to draw numbers from 1 to 100 along the horizontal axis and then did the same along the vertical axis. As you trace vertically up from the 50 level on the source side, the diagonal line intersects perfectly with the horizontal 50 level on the output side. Similarly, 0 horizontally matches up with 0 vertically, and 100

Fig. 2-14 Avid Symphony Curves tool.

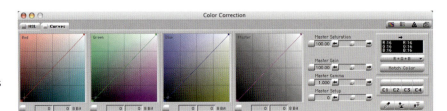

Fig. 2-15 The Avid Xpress Pro Curves Tool adds helpful color coding.

horizontally matches up with 100 vertically, giving you a perfect diagonal graph.

But if you "curve" that graph, by adding or selecting a point along the diagonal line and moving it, you remap the input or source levels to new output levels. For example, to lower the gamma of an image, create a point in the middle of the curve and pull it down a little. Note the numerical values at the bottom of the curve. If you pull down the center of the graph—(128—)to 120, that will mean that the pixels that were originally at a "brightness" value of 128 are now mapped lower, to 120. That also means that all of the other values that were between 128 and 0 are slightly compressed into a smaller tonal range between 120 and 0, and all of the values between 128 and 255 have been lowered but into an *expanded* range between 120 and 255. So each time you place and move a point on the curve, you are not only remapping the tonal values of that point, but also compressing and expanding the tonal ranges on either side of the point on the curve.

A valuable thing to understand about using Curves is that the steeper the angle in a curve, the greater the contrast of the image in that range. Although few professional colorists use, or even have access, to Curves, they utilize the concept of expanding tonal range where it is needed and collapsing it where the eye does not need the information as much. This concept is the basis for a great little tip about how to quickly make images look better using Curves.

S Curve Tip

In the Master curve, place a point by clicking on the diagonal line of the curve about one-quarter to one-third the way up from the bottom of the curve and another about one-quarter or one-third the way down from the top. Now drag the top point slightly upwards and the bottom point slightly downwards. This creates a shallow S curve (see Fig. 2-16).

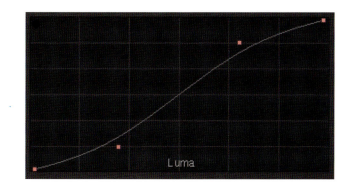

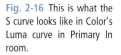

Fig. 2-16 This is what the S curve looks like in Color's Luma curve in Primary In room.

The curve makes the blacks rich and the whites brighter (possibly clipping detail in each of these areas, depending on how much the points are moved) and then spreading the tonal values out over a wider range across the middle of the picture. See Fig. 2-17 for an example.

I think that the fact that most colorists that I talk to dismiss the idea of using Curves for color correction has a lot to do with the fact that Curves are a part of lower cost solutions (like NLEs) and that most of them learned on da Vinci color correction systems that do not have Curves and so were not part of their learning process. The kind of curves we're discussing here is different in practice from the custom Curves available in a da Vinci system, though the basic concept is somewhat similar: to change the curve of the gamma.

Of the colorists who participated in sessions for this book, the biggest proponent of using Curves as the primary place for doing color correction is Avid Symphony Nitris editor Terry Curren of Alpha Dogs in Burbank, CA. While his primary job is as an editor, Terry's corrections stood up very well against those done by the full-time colorists and he made his corrections very quickly and efficiently in Curves. Before Apple bought FinalTouch from Silicon Color, Terry's biggest complaint about the product was that it lacked Curves, which are integral to his approach to color correction. Under Apple's first release of Color, the Curves tool was added.

We will get into using individual color channel curves to fix color cast issues in one of the following chapters, but the Master curve can also

a   b

Fig. 2-17 (a) The video image as it was shot, a fairly washed out, low-con image. **(b)** The video image with the simple S curve applied. The blacks are richer, the highlights pop more, and the contrast in the midtones is improved.

be easily and intuitively used to do either quick or very complex tonal adjustments to a picture.

Curves Tutorial

In the previous chapter we corrected the "brian_overexposed.mov" file. Let's try this same correction again using the Curves in Color Finesse HD.

Launch Color Finesse. Start a new project or open a previous one and import the shot "brian_overexposed.mov."

In the upper left corner, call up the LUMA WFM, or Luminance Waveform. I would prefer that you did all of these corrections looking at an external waveform/vectorscope, such as the Tektronix WM700 used throughout the book, but I will explain these corrections using the built-in scopes in Color Finesse.

Below the built-in scopes, in the lower left corner, are tabs that allow you to select tools with which to do your corrections. Select Curves. The Curves tool presents you with four graphs (see Fig. 2-18). As I mentioned earlier, there are Curves tools in many different applications. If you prefer to follow along in Color's Primary In room or in the Avid Curves tool or one of the other applications, the process will be very similar.

Fig. 2-18 Synthetic Aperture's Color Finesse HD+ user interface showing the Curves tab and the Luma Waveform display.

The leftmost graph, which has a white diagonal line and is called Master, gives you control over the overall signal—the composite of red, green, and blue. The next three graphs to the right give you control over the individual color channels: red, green, and blue, respectively. Each graph has a diagonal colored line indicating the color channel it controls.

How Curves Work

The graphs are interactive. Clicking on a point in the graph and dragging it in a direction alters the relationship between the incoming and outgoing levels. The incoming (source) level is represented along the y axis (up and down) while the outgoing (corrected) signal is represented along the x axis (side to side). So if we want to raise the black level, we click on the point at the bottom left corner and raise it. To lower it, we click on the same point and drag it straight to the right. This remaps the 0 value of the incoming signal, basically stating "all of the values to the left of where I drag this point should be mapped to 0." If you drag the top right corner down, you remap what was 100 on the source down to where you leave the point. If you drag the top right corner point to the left along the top, you are saying "every source value to the right of this point should be mapped to 100." In turn, every value along the line to the next point is also remapped.

The best way to see this visually is to load the "ramp_from_0-254" file. I created this in Photoshop and it has a gentle S shape to it, if you look at it with the waveform monitor. Make some adjustments to it in the Curves tool. Watch the Luminance Waveform monitor (LUMA WFM in Color Finesse) while moving the bottom left point of the graph to the right, straight along the bottom of the graph. Notice that the waveform flattens along the bottom right, corresponding to how far you move the point along the Master graph. Also notice that in the video monitor the amount of the ramp that is completely black has increased. Now move it straight up along the left edge. The black level in the waveform rises and the video monitor becomes washed out since there's no longer anything "mapped" to pure black. In both cases, notice that the most extreme change, visually, is in the blacks or shadows. The gammas move fairly significantly and the highlights don't change much.

Now do the same for the point at the top right corner of the graph, representing the highlights. Move it down along the right edge, watching as the waveform monitor drops along the right edge from 100 and the video monitor becomes less contrasty, because there are no longer any bright whites. Then move the top right-hand point to the left along the top edge. Notice the image in the waveform monitor flattens along the top as all of the values are clipped to 100. Also notice how it changes in your video monitor. The pure-white band to the right of the ramped gradation becomes broader and broader as you move the point to the left.

For now, we will only concern ourselves with the first graph, which controls the master level. We'll start by determining where our black level (shadows) should be. Looking at the LUMA WFM display, you can see that there is almost no part of the image registering below 30 IRE. You can also see that there is significant clipping of the highlights by looking at the tight, flat line along the top of the waveform at 100 IRE. That means that we probably will not be able pull any detail out of the sky.

Let's start with fixing the black levels first. This is usually the first thing that should be fixed, but is doubly important to start with in this instance because that's where the majority of the problem with this image resides.

So, to lower the black level using Curves, you click on the point at the lower left corner and drag it to the right, along the bottom of the graph. If you wanted to raise the black level instead, you'd drag the same point straight up along the left-hand edge of the graph.

TIP

Some applications allow you to "lock" the axis in which you drag the cursor to either horizontal only or vertical only by holding down the shift key.

Under the graph, you can see a numerical value for your adjustment. When you get to about 40 input, 0 output, some of the darker portions of the waveform display start to crush along the bottom. This is where you *start* to lose detail in some of the blacks. From here, the amount that you crush that detail is a personal preference. The image still looks washed out to me and the majority of the darker portion of the image is still around 10 or 12 IRE.

Lower the blacks even more. Somewhere between 58 and 73 on the input of the graph, I think the black is pulled down low enough and the clipping isn't too extreme. As you try to "focus" your adjustment for black somewhere in that range, change from watching the waveform monitor to watching the video monitor. Try to "rack focus" back and forth while looking at some critical areas. In this image, for me, the critical areas are the hair just above his forehead, his eyes, and his skin tone. I don't want the texture of the hair to be lost by pulling the blacks too low. I also don't want to pull down the blacks so low that I lose the sparkle in his eyes. There are a lot of reflections in his eyes that give the image life and if the blacks come down too far, you will lose them. Other colorists who I watched work on this image were less concerned with the eyes and brought the blacks down a lot farther than I did. The other tonal region you need to look at in addition to those two areas is the skin tones in the midtones. You want a nice, rich skin tone that doesn't look too washed out. There are other things you can do to enhance the skin, so instead of trying to get it perfect right now, use the detail areas of the hair and eyes to determine how low to bring your black levels. I settled on a value of 60 for input and 0 for output. That means that in the source footage, everything (on Color Finesse's scale from 1-255) that was below 60 is now remapped down to 0. Then the entire range of the source from 60-255 is now spread from 0-255. See Fig. 2-19.

Fig. 2-19 Note the difference in the image in the split screen between the source image on the left and the effect that the black correction has on the right. Note the bottom of the Master Curve has been moved to the right a significant amout.

Now let's turn our attention to the highlights, which are controlled by the top right point on the graph. Here's where that camera focus analogy comes into play. We can see that the highlights are already clipped, so we don't really need to try to drag the white point to the left along the top. That would just cause the clipping to worsen. But we can try to "focus" the adjustment down a little to see if we can undo some of the clipping. Pulling down the white point a little basically just lowers the overall level and doesn't "unclip" the whites. But the original level was at 110 IRE, so I brought my white level down to 231 to bring the image into "legal" range. (This is just legal for luminance; chroma information could still be illegal.) See Figure 2-20.

To set the midtones of the image (similar to what you did with the gamma adjustment in Color), click on a point about halfway up the diagonal line. Pick a spot at about 160 input, 120 output (looking at the small numbers below the Master Curve). The values of this point actually tell you a little about the mathematics of how the signal is being remapped as you make your corrections. If you hadn't moved the highlights or shadows, all of the points along the diagonal line should match perfectly. The input number and the output number should be identical. But, you remapped the shadow values to have a big difference in value (60 input, 0 output), the highlights had a small drop (255 to 231), and

Fig. 2-20 Highlights have been brought down to legal levels. Note the top of the Master Curve has been brought down slightly.

the middle of the graph kind of split the difference with a 40 value difference. So you can see that by lowering the shadows, we've also already lowered the midtone values somewhat.

You don't need to pay too much attention to the waveform monitor as you adjust the gammas. There's not much that they can tell you. Sometimes, if you adjust the gamma enough, you will create clipping or illegal levels in the shadows if you lower the gamma a lot, or in the highlights if you raise the gamma significantly, but since we're pretty close to the correct level for gamma, all you need to watch is the same detail areas we were monitoring before when we were concerned with setting the shadow (black) level. Watch the eyes and hair for loss of detail and the skin tones for richness as you lift or lower the point in the middle of the line. You can also move the middle point left or right. The move in the blacks richened up a lot of the midtones and the move in the highlights brought down the overall levels as well. Because of this, even though I usually end up pulling down gammas to richen up the image, with this one, I ended up bringing them up a little bit so that the skin tones didn't look too dark. See Figure 2-21.

In Curves you can also make adjustments to very specific tonal ranges. For example, you may be able to soften some of the clipping in the sky areas by adjusting a point near the top of the graph. You won't be able

Fig. 2-21 Notice the slight upward curve in the middle of the Master Curve. This slightly brightens the skin tones and other midtones.

to bring back any detail into the blown-out sky, but you may be able to create some texture in the areas where the clipped sky rolls off or transitions to another element, like the edges of the trees.

Try placing a point on the Master graph less than a quarter of the way from the top. Pull down that point a little while you watch the areas that transition from the clipped sky. See Fig. 2-22. The thing you want to avoid when you use two points on a curve that are fairly close to each other is posterizing. If you adjust the point too radically, it will posterize. As much as you may want to eliminate the clipping in the sky, having posterization is much worse. If you find a good balance before the posterizing occurs, you may be able to create some texture in the areas surrounding the clipped sky. I was only able to bring it down by a very little bit. You can also watch the top of the waveform while doing this and you will see the compressed, clipped area at the top of the waveform start to stretch out. Don't get "target lock" while doing this. You'll be thinking: "Wow! I'm unclipping all of the detail in the sky." But you need to notice on the picture monitor if you are really just introducing noise and banding or polarizing. Be like a doctor: "First, do no harm!".

One of the problems that begins to emerge in this image as the tonal range improves is that a lot of noise and artifacting of the video becomes

Fig. 2-22 Notice the point near the top of the Master Curve that is slightly lowered to ease the look of the clipped highlights.

evident. If you have no means of correcting this noise, you may have to either limit how far you take your correction or determine that the noise is a small price to pay for the improved contrast. Many color correction systems have noise reduction built in to them and you can use that to fix the noisiness that you introduced. The thing with noise reduction is that it must be used with a very gentle hand. Always check the image before and after noise reduction to make sure you haven't applied too much.

Isolating Tonal Ranges with Curves

Another cool thing about working with Curves is that you can isolate specific tonal ranges using points that you don't move so that other corrections on either side don't affect them. Let's try an example.

To best understand exactly what this isolation is doing, open the "grayscale_neutral.mov" file from the DVD and load it into an application with Curves, like Color, Avid, Photoshop, or After Effects. With this example, what we want to see is how we can isolate a specific tonal range so that it is not affected by the corrections that you make in another area. First, let's see what happens when we don't isolate the tonal range.

With the "grayscale_neutral.mov" clip loaded, look at the image on the waveform monitor and on the video monitor. The levels are almost correct. The highlights are a little below 100 IRE, but the black levels are correct and the gammas are just about right. (see Fig. 2-23)

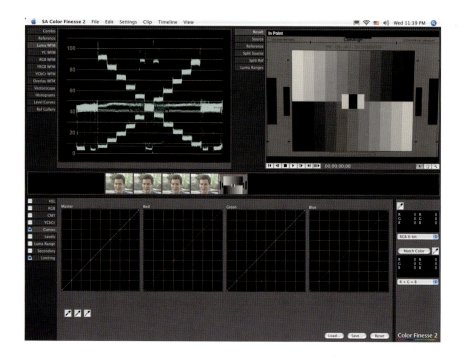

Fig. 2-23 Grayscale_ neutral clip in Synthetic Aperture's Color Finesse Curves tab.

Now, let's adjust the shadow area with a point about 25% up from the bottom of the Master curve. Since the range is from 1–255, that that would equal an input value of about 63. Hover the cursor over the diagonal line in the Master curve while watching the input value just below the Master curve graph. When it gets to around 63, click on the line and drag that point down to around 40 while watching how the trace of the waveform monitor reacts. You'll notice that while the majority of the correction is in the bottom of the waveform monitor (the shadows), the midtones and even the highlights are affected to some extent (see Fig. 2-24).

In some real-world corrections, you may want to affect the deep shadows without changing your midtones or highlights. The key to doing this with Curves is to add points on the curve that you do not move at all. These points will prevent the rest of the curve from moving.

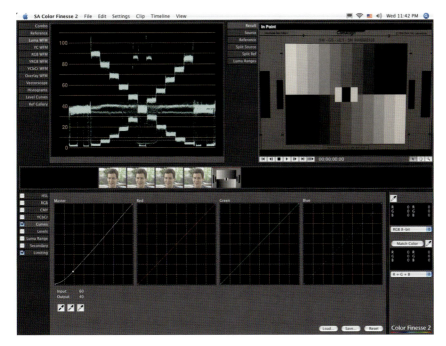

Fig. 2-24 Note the small change near the bottom of the Master Curve.

Reset the Master curve. In Color Finesse, this is done with the reset button in the lower right. In Avid, you can alt-click on the activated tab to reset, or in many applications, simply click on the altered point and hit the delete key on your keyboard. In Color, you can click on the small diamond in the upper left-hand corner of the curve to reset the entire curve, or you just drag the point off the graph to remove it. In Color Finesse, you can also right-click a point on the curve and choose Delete Point from the pulldown menu.

This time, let's place a point on the graph that is just below halfway. I set my point at 120. This point will isolate the midtones and highlights from the corrections we make lower on the curve.

Now, click on the same point (63) that you adjusted before and drag the point up and down as you watch the waveform monitor and video monitor. You'll notice that the changes to the midtones and highlights are much less obvious than before. They still move a little bit depending on what application you use. This is because the point is controlling the curve like a Bezier curve, so the point is not really a hard-and-fast cutoff of the correction. Some applications have much less of a Bezier effect to the curve. Avid should really only require a single point to isolate the correction. If you want to, you can add a second point just above the first "isolation point"—try 130 or 140. This will limit the amount the Bezier curve affects the curve above the higher mark. Now, move the lower (shadow) point again while watching the waveform monitor. Also watch the video monitor and you can see that the shadows are being deepened while the highlights and most of the midtones don't move at all (see Fig. 2-25).

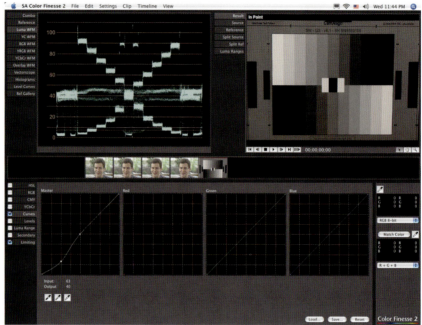

Fig. 2-25 Notice the point in the middle of the Master Curve has not been moved. This protects the areas of the midtones and highlights that are above this point from the affect of the point at the bottom.

If you bring the shadows down far enough, you will see that you start to crush the middle chip that is at 0 IRE. The crushing or clipping is indicated by the waveform trace starting to flatten out. If you want to protect the deepest blacks from clipping, you could also place a point on the curve that is very low. This will protect the detail in the deep blacks while allowing you to pull the rest of your shadows deeper. I placed my point at 16. Then as I brought my shadow point (input 67) down to an output of 51, the darkest black did not clip (see Fig. 2-26).

To practice this some more, continue this same correction without resetting it, and try to get the brightest chip on the right side (the chart was lit a little brighter on the right side) to 100 IRE and the next three chips to land at 80, 70, and 60.

The key to this exercise is to figure out what point on the Master curve corresponds to the luminance value of the chip as it is viewed in the waveform monitor. This is a very valuable skill to have. You should be able to look at a waveform display and figure out approximately what parts of the image on the video monitor correspond to the waveform display.

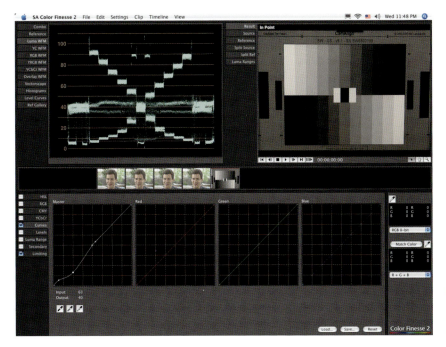

Fig. 2-26 Notice the "protection points" in the middle and at the bottom of the Master Curve.

Luma Range Display

The skill described above (knowing what parts of the image on a wave-form will be affected by a specific tonal correction) isn't only important in using Curves. You also have to be able to do this if you're just using shadows, midtones, and highlights. Color Finesse and Avid Symphony have a nice function, called Luma Ranges, that allows you to develop this skill. In Color Finesse this is one of the main viewing modes at the bottom of the list of tabs in the upper right pane. When you view your source using Luma Ranges, it shows you each of the three tonal ranges as a shade of black and white (see Fig. 2-27). Parts of the image that you would control with the shadows control are black, parts that are considered midtones are displayed in gray, and parts that are considered highlights are white.

Import some of the test images from the DVD, or bring in some movies and images of your own and try to guess what the resulting Luma Range display will look like. This is a fairly simple exercise with a well-lit image, but if it's over- or underexposed, your eye will get fooled into spreading the tonal range. For example, on an underexposed image, you will be surprised how little of the image is considered a highlight.

Fig. 2-27 Color Finesse's Luma Range Tab allows the colorist to customize the definitions of highlights, midtones and shadows. The black, gray and white image in the upper right shows shadows as black, midtones as gray and highlights as white.

In the image of Brian above, I used the Luma Range editing tools so that there would be a good distribution of black, gray, and white in the image. The actual source image shows up as mostly gray and white when no Luma Range editing is done.

Luma Range Editing

With Color Finesse and Avid Symphony, there are ways to alter the *definitions* of the three Luma Ranges: shadows, midtones, and highlights. In other words, *you* can determine what the application considers to be shadow and where it transitions to being a midtone and then where midtones become highlights. For most normal images, you don't need this kind of control. The definitions make sense and give you the kind of control you want. But for certain shots, you may want to alter the definitions of these tonal ranges so that you can gain greater control over specific parts of a picture. I don't have specific technical information from the manufacturers, but I would assume that most applications consider the range from 0 IRE to about 25 IRE to be shadows, from 25 IRE to 75 IRE to be gammas, and from 75 IRE to 100 IRE to be highlights. Obviously these numbers (even if they're right) wouldn't be hard cutoff points. It would work something like this: If you move the shadow control, the darkest 10% would be affected 100% by the control, the next 10% of the darkest part of the image would be affected 90% by the control, and so on, until the brightest parts of the picture aren't affected by the shadow control at all.

Avid Symphony and Color Finesse both have tools to define Luma Ranges. They are essentially the same, though Symphony gives a little bit of added control. At the current time, there is no ability to edit Luma Ranges in the lower-end Avid products or in Apple's Color.

Figure 2-28 is the Luma Range control for Color Finesse. It shows a histogram of the image with three curving lines overlaid and two straight lines that are the controls for the Bezier curves of the shadow and highlight curves. The curving arcs represent the definition of the shadows, midtones, and highlights. The tonal ranges are represented by overlapping curves instead of as strictly defined and delineated areas, because if the definitions of the tonal ranges were defined with a sharp cutoff, corrections to individual tonal ranges would cause sharp, visible transition lines in the picture at the point where one tonal range was defined from another.

In Color Finesse, the curves of Luma Range are interactive. The only way to alter the definition of the midtones is by altering the curve for highlights and/or shadows. In Symphony, each curve can be radically altered by setting numerous points on any of the curves. This is a lot of power, but it can really cause bizarre artifacts in the shot, because the curves can be set to overlap with each other or cutoff with abrupt transitions or even leave entire portions of the picture that are not defined by *any* tonal range at all!

The value of this control is that it is possible to define very specific portions of the picture. One example of where this would be useful would be in a shot with a "hot" window. If the rest of the shot was very well lit and you tried to use your highlight control to bring down the intensity of the window, it may also bring down other highlights in the rest of the room. If you want to limit your correction to the window alone, you could use Luma Ranges to define the highlights of the picture to only include the window values. Then you could use your midtone and shadow controls to control the rest of the image (see Fig. 2-29).

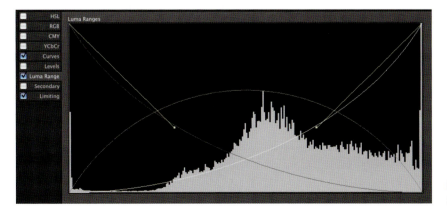

Fig. 2-28 Luma Range control for Color Finesse.

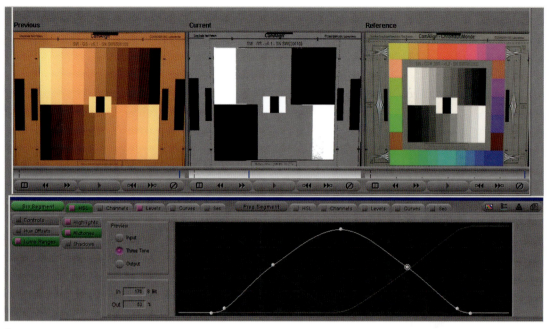

a

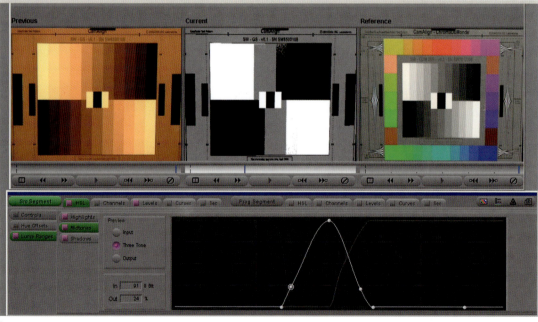

b

Fig. 2-29 (a) The Luma Ranges are basically unedited. Notice what parts of the grayscale image that the Symphony considers shadows, midtones, and highlights in its default mode. (b) The same grayscale image with no color correction, but the Luma Ranges have been edited so that there is much less of the image that is considered by the software to be midtones. This would be useful if you wanted to make an adjustment that affected only a very small range of tones in the absolute middle of the picture.

Alternative to Luma Range

Experienced colorists get a lot of this same ability to isolate a very specific tonal range by creating a matte that **qualifies** a specific tonal range (see Fig. 2-30). Since this type of correction is really defined as a secondary correction, we'll discuss it further in Chapter 3.

Qualify: This term means that an area of the picture is specifically isolated for a correction by any number of methods. You could qualify something for correction using its hue, chroma strength, or tonal value. You could also qualify an area of the image using a "window" or garbage matte; for example: "I qualified the brightest highlights by making a matte of everything over 90 IRE and added a bit of yellow to them."

Fig. 2-30 A key that was created in the Color Secondary Room to qualify the highlights of the "brian_overexposed" shot. The areas defined in white would be the only areas qualified for the correction.

Thinking about the Budget

One consideration before you start to play with the Luma Range editing capabilities is that, like most things, color correction is usually done on a deadline and with a budget.

A sure way to kill a budget is to define the specific Luma Range of every shot, or to add color effects or secondary color correction to every shot. Secondary color corrections and Luma Range definition are fantastic tools that help you accomplish specific tasks, but you need to consider how long you have to grade the entire project and how much time you can devote to each shot. Hopefully, you can make each shot of a longer form project look pretty good in under a minute. I typically had about two days to grade a 600-shot, 48-minute documentary. That works out to about a minute and a half per shot or 20 minutes of color correction work for each finished minute of programming. American dramatic primetime shows are usually in the range of 1,000 shots in a one-hour show and are usually graded in 12–16 hours, averaging a bit better than a shot

Racked: Physically placing the spool or reel of film on the telecine and threading it.

Telecine: This is the machine, or sometimes used as a description of the process, that transfers film to video in real time. The telecine feeds the image to the color-correction hardware. I've heard at least three different pronunciations — TELL-uh-sin-ee, Tell-uh-SEEN, and TELL-uh-sin-uh — and everyone will tell you that the way *they* pronounce it is correct. Most of the interviewees, including Bob Festa, who's probably been at it longer than anyone else, pronounced it "TELL-uh-sin-ee," with the heavy accent on "tell" and a lesser accent on "sin." The other way to transfer film to video (or data, actually) is with a film scanner, which, as of the writing of this book, is not real time, but is getting close.

a minute. Reality shows are closer to 1,200 shots in a one-hour show and only usually budget for a single day including laying it off to tape, which works out to about 170 shots an hour or close to 3 shots a minute. Color correction for digital intermediates can vary greatly, but can average about 20 minutes (about two reels) per day.

Neal Kassner, a colorist for CBS's "48 Hours," estimates that he has about 16 hours to color correct that show's 1,200–1,500 shots per episode. That's 75–90 shots an hour. Other colorists I've spoken to have mentioned averages for a nationally telecast documentary as 6–8 minutes to correct 1 minute of finished program time. On spots, the average is 3–8 hours for a single 30-second spot or a series of spots based on the same material. Some facilities expect certain output from their colorists, such as 100 shots an hour.

Craig Leffel, of Chicago's Optimus, says that it depends if the corrections are from tape or server or if the original camera negative (OCN) has to actually be **racked** on the **telecine**. For film negative, the average is four to six shots an hour if there are only a few shots per reel.

Legendary colorist Bob Festa, of R!OT in Santa Monica, CA, says that for spots he corrects off the telecine, the average is 10 shots an hour. "Unfortunately, today in this world, I'm still racking up film on a day-by-day basis. Today I was working with dailies rolls and we had 30 shots in 3 hours basically. So that's pretty much to my formula of 10 shots per hour." (Most colorists working from telecine have an assistant that threads up the telecine for them.)

Some of these numbers have changed somewhat over the years as colorists are transitioning from a workflow that was originally almost entirely "straight off the tele-cine" to a current workflow where telecine transfers get transferred "flat" to either a digital disk recorder, some kind of a server as a file, or to a tape format like D5, then the colorist basically does a tape-to-tape color correction or color corrects from a file. Back in the day, a rule of thumb for telecine transfers was 1 hour to grade 11 minutes (one 1,000-foot 35-mm reel).

The trick to grading an entire project on budget is to leave enough extra time to work on the shots that really need the additional attention. Until you get more experienced at estimating how long you need to really tweak an entire project, try to get a first pass at all the shots done in half of your budgeted time. Then use the second half of the time to polish the overall corrections and devote extra time to "trouble" shots or those that have high emotional significance or importance to the story. Also, don't forget to leave time for revisions, especially if you don't have absolutely every single decision maker in the session.

CHAPTER 3

Color Control Primer

Many of the concepts that we discussed in the tonal chapters continue to be applicable as we advance the discussion to how we control the hue and saturation of an image. These changes in hue and saturation are rarely done globally, in other words, across the entire image equally, so we'll use elements of the tonal corrections to isolate and qualify our corrections as we continue.

Balancing an Image

One of the most basic chores a colorist must accomplish is to **balance** an image. This means that any *unwanted* **color cast** is eliminated from the image. Along with spreading the tonal range of a picture, which we covered in Chapter 1, balancing an image is the other main aspect of **primary color correction**. Balancing involves removing unwanted color casts from a picture. Notice the word "unwanted" in the last sentence. Very often, color casts are a *good* thing that provide context, mood, and interest to an image, such as the warmth of a scene lit by a sunset. Color casts are rarely of the same strength, or even the same hue, in each of the tonal ranges of a picture.

Just as we started our tonal corrections by working on the blacks or shadows first, we will begin to balance an image starting with the blacks. Before starting the correction, you need to analyze the image to know what you need to do.

Analyzing Color Casts

The three standard tools for analyzing color casts are the RGB parade waveform monitor (or YRGB parade waveform monitor), the vectorscope, and of course the video monitor itself. To best understand what these displays are showing you, we'll check out some standard test images with color casts.

Balance: To remove an unwanted color cast from an image. To ensure that the blacks, whites, and neutral gray tones of the image are free from any unwanted color.

Color Cast: A color that pollutes the pure black, white, and neutral gray tones of an image. Sometimes these color casts are desirable, like in the example of a romantic close-up of a character bathed in the warm, orange tones of a sunset, or the sickly green tinge of color in a scene with a psychotic villain. Oftentimes, we want to eliminate this color cast, but sometimes it furthers the story.

Primary Color Correction: This generally means any correction to an entire image. The other phase of color correction—secondary color correction—is applied only to specific color vectors or geographic areas within the frame. So primary corrections are global in nature and secondary corrections are more specific. Not all images require secondary color correction.

Using Your Eyes

For some images, it will be very easy for even an untrained eye to spot the color cast, but on subtle color casts, it definitely takes some training. You should really spend some time looking at almost any kind of image, but especially film and video images, and try to understand what makes them look the way they do.

Is the image very contrasty? Does it have a color cast? Does just one of the tonal ranges really show the color cast? Where are the blacks, or shadows? Are they crushed? Is there a colored or graded filter on the sky? Watch TV commercials. Other than print advertisements, they have images that have had the most time spent in refining them (see "Thinking about the Budget" box in Chapter 2). Also, if you're checking out images on a video monitor or TV set, make sure it is properly calibrated. Another good visual training tool is to watch an image on your profes-

---

Regional Color Differences

From my interview with Neal Kassner, colorist of CBS's "48 Hours":

One of the things I find helpful to do is to look at life as objectively as you can. What color blue is the sky? Because that can be a very regional thing, I've found. If you're working in the Miami market, I think they want more punchy colors than, for instance, in New York. [CBS] did something where some material that was shot in Manhattan was color corrected by a Los Angeles colorist, and while the colors were technically correct, it didn't have what I felt was a New York feel. So I had the opportunity to go back and regrade it and make it a little more of what I think New York looks like. In a recent episode of "Studio 60 on the Sunset Strip" — it's set in Los Angeles but they had a scene in a corporate board room that took place in New York, which they set up with the standard stock shot of the East River from under the Brooklyn Bridge. But the color difference really struck me. Not that I was so aware of the Los Angeles look, but the New York look was cleaner. It was more contrasty and it was bluer. And that right away, that said to me, "Oh, this is Manhattan." Even the fact that the Brooklyn Bridge was right there in the middle of the shot, that was secondary to the fact that this was just a much cleaner, sharper, crisper looking image than the Los Angeles stuff.

But getting back to what I was originally going to say: What color blue is the sky? Grass isn't really green in television. There's a *lot* of yellow in grass. So if you try to make it look green, it's going to look phony. It's going to look like Astroturf™. You need to look around. You have a white barn in the middle of a field. At noon it's going to be white. Late afternoon, it's still going to be a white barn, but it's not going to look white to your eye. Your brain is going to filter what your eye sees.

sional video monitor, then transfer it to a DVD and watch it on several of the regular TV sets in your home. Look to see how the image changes on each set. It can be a little bit of a depressing exercise to see the way your carefully honed images look "at home." Try to keep your home TV sets set up properly so that you're always watching the broadcast images as close to the way the colorist intended them.

Also, study print advertisements. Though these advertisements often have images that are hard or impossible to replicate on video, you can learn valuable techniques by studying the way print advertisements are retouched (retouchers are the print equivalent of colorists). Since print advertisements don't move, it's much easier to analyze them.

One of the ways to train your eyes to better understand and analyze an image is to confirm what you are seeing with some other method of analyzing the image, like a waveform, vectorscope, eyedropper, or histogram. Let's take that list in order.

Color and the Waveform

We already discussed the basics of the waveform monitor in Chapter 1, but that was just to understand the tonal range of the image as it was displayed. It is also possible to find many critical clues about the color of your image using the waveform monitor.

The standard waveform display is not going to tell you a lot about color, but switching to RGB parade mode or YRGB parade mode is a favorite colorist tool for analyzing color. My guess is that if most colorists were stranded on a desert island with only one scope, they'd choose the RGB parade. The main reason is that the red, green, and blue cells of the RGB parade waveform correspond easily to the red, green, and blue controls available on most color control panels. The RGB parade also gives intuitive visual clues as to which tonal range is exhibiting a specific color cast.

Let's run through a quick tutorial to see how the RGB parade waveform displays color information.

Call up the "grayscale_neutral.mov" and "grayscale_cool.mov" movies from the DVD's tutorial media folder. Hopefully, you've got a nice external waveform monitor to use, but the internal one will certainly work for this tutorial. If you use a YRGB view, remember that the first cell represents luminance and the next three cells are red, green, and blue. I will be doing this tutorial using an RGB view, and I'll do this correction using Apple's Color.

With the "grayscale_cool.mov" movie in the timeline and Color's Primary In room active, you can see that the chip chart does not look the same in each of the color channels. Switch to the "grayscale_neutral" movie. Notice how all three waveforms are identical; this means that in each tonal range, the amounts of red, green, and blue are the same. The chip chart is made up of shades of gray, from black to white. Pure white is the presence of red, green, and blue light in *equal* amounts at "full power." Measured on an RGB waveform set to IRE or percentages, this means that red, green, and blue are each at 100 IRE or 100%. If you were measuring in RGB color space in 8 bits, red, green, and blue would each be at 255. In video color space at 8 bits, they would be at 235. In 10-bit RGB color space, white has red, green, and blue at 1,023. In video space, they would be at 940. Black is the absence of any color, so in RGB color space at 8 bit or 10 bits, it would be 0 for all colors. If the black has setup added to it for NTSC, then black is 16 in 8 bits and 64 in 10 bits.

So, this is a lot of numbers thrown at you. The gist of them all is that pure white, pure black, and pure gray means that the red, green, and blue channels all match no matter what level they're at. Knowing this makes it easy to watch the RGB parade waveform and balance the color by making the top and bottom of the waveform monitor match across all three color channels. You can't really do this with gammas in real-world images usually because the midtones tend to have a specific cast to them for a reason, like skin tones. You don't want to balance a skin tone so that all three color channels are the same, or the skin tone would be gray.

Having learned that black, white, and gray should match across the channels, let's try to use RGB levels to balance the shot. There are other tools that could also do this, but we'll save them for later. In Color, go to Primary In room and use the Advanced tab, which is on the right side of the control screen about halfway down. This calls up a list of numerical selection boxes allowing you to change the **lift**, gamma, and gain for each of the separate color channels. Let's look at the waveform of the correctly balanced chip chart image first (grayscale_neutral, see Fig. 3-1) to see what our goal is.

Fig. 3-1 (a) This image is slightly color corrected to show the ideal. **(b)** This is the way the image should look off the DVD. Though to the naked eye it looks neutral, it is ever-so-slightly warm. Notice that in the "b" image, the red cell is slightly higher than the green and blue cells.

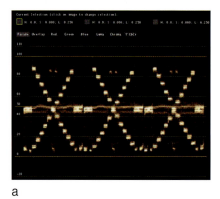

a

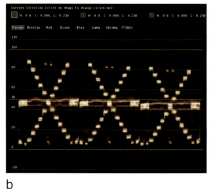

b

Look at the RGB parade waveform monitor and notice the shape that the test chart makes in each color channel. They are all basically the same shape and relative height. The dark black chip in the middle should be all the way at the bottom of the waveform. The white chips should be at the top. Each chip should be at the same level across all channels. The slightly higher red channel compared to the green and blue channels indicate that although the camera was white balanced, there is a *very* slight red cast to this "neutral" chart.

Now, call up the "grayscale_cool" (see Fig. 3-2) shot and notice the height difference between each of the color channels in the RGB parade waveform.

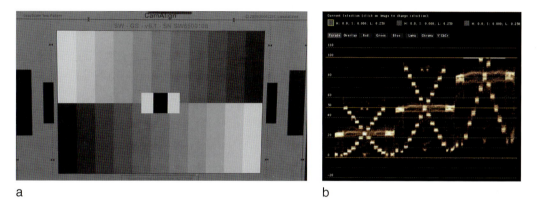

a   b

Fig. 3-2 The red channel is low, the green channel is actually almost correct, and the blue channel is elevated with the highlights very clipped.

To the right of the color wheels in Color's Primary In room is the Basic tab. Under the Basic tab, select the Advanced tab. Use the red, green, and blue lift controls to even out the difference in height between the red, green, and blue cells of the waveform monitor. In Color, center-clicking on the numerical box and dragging it left and right will change the level in large increments. If you have a scroll wheel on your mouse, you can use it to move in finer increments. Pull down each channel so that you "focus" the shadows so that they are near black (0) without being crushed or clipped. Take your correction too far down to see where the clipping occurs, then pull it back up so that the shape of the trace at the bottom of the waveform unflattens.

Remember that the lift controls are for controlling the *bottom* of the waveform—the shadows. Looking at the image on the RGB parade, the shadows of the red are very close to being correct. They could come down a very little bit. The green channel is about three times as high in the blacks than in the red channel and the blue channel is about three times as high as the green. When you are done with your corrections, the red channel should have the least change and the blue channel should have the most.

Note in Figure 3-3 that the blackest chip, in the middle of the blue channel, is still fairly elevated, but if I lower the lift any further in the blues, the chips on the sides start to crush. With the blacks balanced, now you can set the highlight balance. Using the same technique as setting the blacks, use the red, green, and blue gain sliders to properly set the whites all to the same level. The top red levels are 50% of where they should be. The green channel is actually quite close to the correct level, but still needs to come up about 15 IRE, and the blue channels are very clipped. Because of the blue clipping, you will never be able to get the blue highlights all the way up while still getting proper black and gamma levels. Since the blue highlight information is already compromised, we'll concentrate on getting proper levels in the blacks and gammas. When you get the gain for red and green to the proper balance, recheck your black levels; the red channel will be slightly higher than where you left it originally, because of the severe amount of gain needed to get it to the proper level. Green didn't need much alteration in the highlights, so the shadows shouldn't have moved. (Remember, all tonal ranges have some interaction with each other.) Use the blue gain controls to try to get the midtone area (the sixth chip from the top or bottom) to 50%. The midtone on this image is also where the waveform shows a double line all the way across the middle of the waveform display.

Fig. 3-3 The results for my blacks correction look something like this.

Now with the highlights and the shadows balanced, the midtones should fall very close to being right (see Fig. 3-4). You can use the red, green, and blue gamma numerical entries to further tweak the color balance. With gamma, the main swatch of gray that is the background for the chips should be even across all three channels on the RGB parade waveform. As I just pointed out, this gray swatch is indicated on the waveform by the two parallel lines that go all the way across the cell. The most difficult channel to correct will be the blue channel, which was the furthest from correct. Also, due to the clipping, just try to get the gammas and lift correct for the blue. See Figure 3-5.

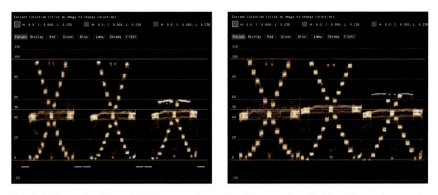

Fig. 3-4 The results for my highlight correction. Because of the clipping in the blue channel, don't attempt to raise the blue highlights to 100. Just raise blue highlights to get the midtones to match red and green.

Fig. 3-5 Note that all of the chips match across the red and green channels from top to bottom and the blue channel matches from the bottom to the midtones.

Now, the "cheat" for fixing the yellow cast in the highlights is to go back to the Basic tab and pull down the Highlight Saturation control to 0. Often in real-world images, this cheat will work. If you pull down the Saturation control to 0, you'll see your waveform for the blue channel will miraculously seem to unclip. However, this will not work in a real-world image, because there will be no saturation at all. That's obviously fine to do with an image that is *supposed* to be black and white in this case.

That's all well and good for a test image, but you would think that with the wide range of colors and hues in a real-world video or film image, that this same concept wouldn't really work. But it does.

Call up the "Art_institute_blue.mov" movie (see Fig. 3-6). This image is definitely incorrectly white balanced. Check out the "Art_institute_proper.mov" shot to see the same scene with the proper white

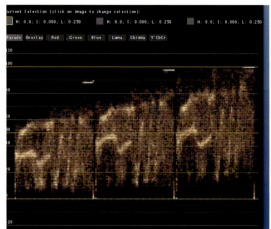

a   b

Fig. 3-6

balance. Notice that the building behind the lion (Chicago's famous Art Institute—a great place to study the use of color and tonality in images, by the way) is not really gray, but a warm, yellowish sandstone. There are lots of different colored elements in the picture with no obvious white, black, or gray reference points, but believe me, they're there.

With the blue cast lion shot called up in Color, let's use those same sliders in the Advanced tab and RGB parade waveform to get a sense for how to balance a real-world image.

Looking at the RGB parade, the color channels almost seem to stair-step, with the red low, the green in the middle, and the blue levels quite elevated. We are going to treat this just like the chip chart and see how close that gets us to the correct color.

The first thing that probably needs work is the lift (blacks) of the blue channel. Bring the level down so that the bottom of the blue cell touches the 0 IRE line. You can focus it up and down a little to make sure you haven't clipped or crushed it.

Now use the green and red lift controls to position that same spot. On the image of the Art Institute itself, the lowest black point in the center probably represents one of the blackish areas inside one of the arched doorways at the top of the stairs or the black area in the arches above them. See Figure 3-7.

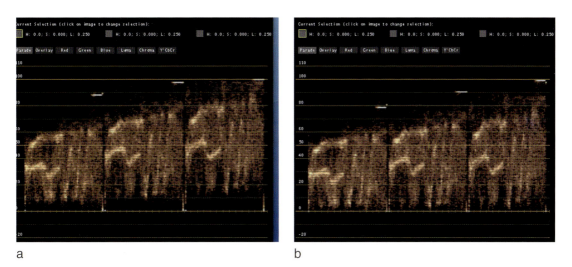

a   b

Fig. 3-7 (a) what the RGB parade looks like on the uncorrected original, and **(b)** What the red, green, and blue lift corrections look like.

Now, we'll make the same kinds of changes to the highlights of each channel. This time I'll start with the red channel gain and bring it up until the part of the image that sits around 60 IRE is up closer to 80, which is where the green channel is. On many images, you'll want to match all of the channels so that the top of them is *basically* at 100 IRE. In the case of this image, there is something clipped on the far right side at 100 IRE in all three channels, but you do *not* want to simply match that in each image. Because that area is heavily clipped, you do not know if the amount of each color channel is clipped *equally*, so you'll need to ignore the clipped area as you color correct. Raise the other levels that are unclipped so that they are close to 80 IRE, but not clipping. There are some bright highlights in the stairs at the bottom of the picture but they probably shouldn't be pure white. You may prefer to balance the highlights at some level higher or lower than I did. To make that determination, you'll need to look at the image in the picture monitor to decide when it starts to get too bright.

Match the red gain levels with the green gain levels. Look at the various shapes in the waveform of the red and green channels and see how closely you can get them to match with the red gain control.

Now use the blue gain control to match the blue highlights back to where the red and green channels are. At this point, the clipped areas of the sky are around 100 IRE for red, 95 IRE for green, and 85 IRE for blue. This is not a good color for the sky. We'll show you how to fix this problem in the secondary section of this book. For now, we're trying to complete the basic, primary color corrections. Just know that oftentimes, a primary color correction is done to get *most* of the image looking good, even if it means that it takes another color correction to fix something that you "broke" in the original. See Fig. 3-8 for where I ended up.

Something else to note is that when we made the gain adjustments to the reds and blues, the shadows, or lift, were also affected. The shadows of the reds got higher and the shadows of the blues went a little lower. So take a moment to get the shadows balanced again.

Comparing the original image with the new balanced image shows a marked improvement in both color balance and contrast. Comparing it to the corrected shot shows that the real image is perhaps a bit warmer. There are exercises in matching shots later in the book. We won't try that right now, but you could pull up the gammas in the red channel a bit to warm up the picture. Also, looking at the lettering in the banners in the arched areas at the top of the picture, you might also see that the lettering on the banners that is supposed to be white is fairly bluish, so you could use the blue gain to pull down the amount of blue in the white of the lettering.

This is a tutorial for a specific purpose—balancing using the RGB parade and individual channel levels—so we are not going to finish the correction right now. This image is not "ready for primetime," but we made significant improvements. If you feel it is too dark, you could use

a

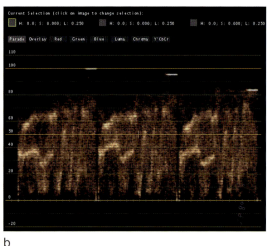

b

Fig. 3-8 Final RGB waveform reading for the correction. The clipped areas of the sky would need to be fixed in secondary color correction.

the Basic tab's Master Gain and Master Gamma to tweak the overall level. You could also bring down the level of the Highlight Saturation control as a quick fix to the yellow tint of the sky.

Making these corrections using the RGB parade and the red, green, and blue gain, gamma, and lift sliders is very intuitive. But this is only one of the ways that you can balance color. The other way is actually the more common way for an experienced colorist to use, but instead of using the RGB waveform, it's much more intuitive to use the vectorscope when using this other tool.

Color and the Vectorscope

Let's look at the blue-balanced chip chart image again (the "grayscale_cool.mov" on the DVD), but this time we'll analyze the signal and fix the image using a vectorscope. When you look at the image on the vectorscope, you see that the some of the trace of the scope is fairly close to the center of the vectorscope, but most of it is decidedly closer to the blue and cyan targets, along the -I line. (See Figure 3-9)

With the vectorscope, pure white, pure black, and pure gray all show up as a tiny point in the absolute center. There is no distinction on the vectorscope of the brightness of an image, so pure black and pure white both look identical to the vectorscope. The further the trace emanates from the center, the higher the amount of chroma or intensity of color.

Each of the three primary additive colors—red, green, and blue—have a target on the vectorscope's graticule (see Fig. 3-10): red is at about

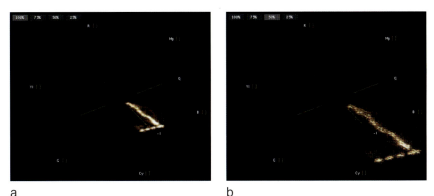

a   b

Fig. 3-9 (a) shows the vectorscope of the cool image at normal power. (b) shows the image zoomed in 200%.

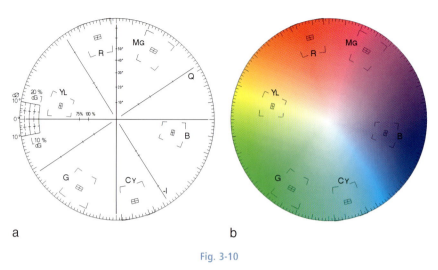

a   b

Fig. 3-10

11 o'clock, blue is at about 4 o'clock, and green is at about 7 o'clock. Then the secondary colors to red, green, and blue are in between them: magenta is between red and blue, cyan is between blue and green, and yellow is between green and red.

Using the color wheels (sometimes called hue offset wheels) for each tonal range while looking at the vectorscope will allow you to "dial in" the color balance for each tonal range. As we have done in the past, let's start with the blacks or shadows.

Your Eyes

It's very important to "reset" your eyes at least every hour. After a long time of staring at a computer or video screen, your eyes become tired and need to get a fresh perspective on the colors that they are seeing on the monitor. The best way to do this is to stop for even a minute or two and look out a window or actually go outside. Refocus your eyes on something far away for a few seconds and remember what real-life images look like in daylight. Some color correction suites provide a small pool of daylight-balanced light on a surface on the color correction desk for this same purpose.

If you can't get up and rest and reset your eyes, another trick that colorists use is to add with a wipe a white or black border to their corrections, so that your eyes get a sense for "absolute" white and black. This is easier done in a typical da Vinci color correction suite that often includes a small video switcher. If you are color correcting in a nonlinear editor, like FCP or Avid, you may want to create and save two effects that add a white border and a black border to your image.

The way to make corrections using these hue offset wheels is to move the cursor that sits in the center of the wheel in the opposite direction of the color cast. So, look at the vectorscope and you'll see that the trace of the vectorscope is in the blue vector. In Color's Primary In room, click on the center of the shadow wheel, which is the one to the left of the interface.

Knowing that the image should be completely free of any color, the entire trace needs to be exactly in the middle of the vectorscope. Since it's off toward the blue vector, we can balance the image by dragging the shadow cursor on the hue offset wheel toward yellow in the opposite direction of the color cast. Slowly focus or aim the trace as closely on the center point of the vectorscope as you can. Not all of the trace will move, because you're only trying to balance the shadows at the moment. And if you are fortunate enough to have a JLCooper or Tangent Devices CP200-BK control panel, you can do these color adjustments using the trackballs instead of dragging a cursor around the user interface (UI).

Once that is done, balance the highlights in the same way. The highlights are also blue, so the move needs to be toward yellow again. It is *possible* that the color cast is not the same *color* in each of the three tonal ranges. It is *highly likely* that the cast is a different *strength* in each of the ranges. Slowly focus the trace in to the center of the image. The key to many of these corrections is subtlety.

The image is almost balanced, so now use the midtone wheel and focus the trace so that the remaining blue cast is balanced out. It's possible that the corrections from the highlights or midtones affected the shadows, so go to each tonal range again and tweak it slightly to better focus the trace in the vectorscope right in the middle of the crosshairs.

Now let's try a real-world image to see how that compares. With real-world images, balancing with the vectorscope is a little trickier because instead of a nice, sharp monochromatic image, every color in the image makes the trace into a big fuzzy ball. Call up the images "Field_museum_proper.mov" and "Field_museum_cool.mov" from the DVD. Compare the images on the vectorscope. See Figure 3-11.

The "proper" image in Figures 3-11(c, d) has some of the trace in the middle and the rest skews off toward yellow and green. This makes sense because the Field Museum is made from the same yellowish stone that the Art Institute has and the green is coming from the pine trees in the foreground. Compare that to the blue image in Figures 3-11(a, b) and the vectorscope is favoring the blue and cyan vectors with almost no yellow or green.

T I P

While trying to balance colors using the vectorscope, it is common to zoom in the scale of the vectorscope to about 5×. In Color, the scale is reversed, so to zoom in, you choose 75%, 50%, or 25% from the small buttons just above the vectorscope. To return to normal scale, choose 100%. See Fig. 3-10.

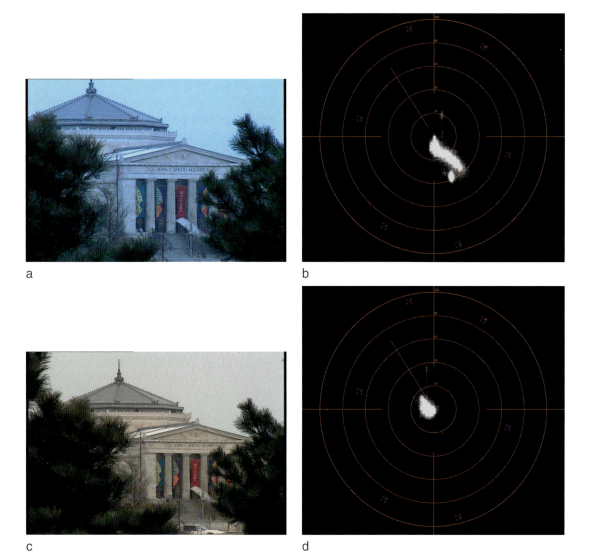

a

b

c

d

Fig. 3-11 (a) The Field Museum with an improper, blue white balance. **(b)** Final Cut Pro vectorscope image of the improper, blue white-balanced image. Notice that the trace aims more toward the cyan/blue vector. **(c)** Chicago's Field Museum of Natural History with the proper white balance. **(d)** Final Cut Pro's internal vectorscope display of the properly white balanced Field Museum shot.

Without looking at the RGB waveform or even the image on the video monitor, let's see what happens if we simply try to dial this image into the middle of the vectorscope using Final Cut Pro's three-way color corrector, which is the same interface that we have been describing as hue offset wheels (see Fig. 3-12). Start with the shadow wheel, then do the highlight wheel, before finishing with the midtone wheel.

What you'll end up with is an image that's a little on the cool side (bluish) and also is fairly washed out. Let's correct the contrast by using the shadow, midtone, and highlight sliders below each of the wheels. Pull down the blacks, pull up the highlights, and move the midtones where they look natural to you. If your correction has become tinged with magenta, this is a very unnatural color, and you should steer clear of it.

Now warm up the image a little by dragging the cursor on the midtone hue offset wheel up toward red, but watch the pine trees to make sure that they don't go red. The trick here is that you want to warm up the midtones of the museum façade, but the brighter pine needles are also in this tonal range, so they will start going too red. There is a lot of the façade that is affected by highlights controls, but moving the highlights too red makes the sky look an odd yellow color. Normally, we'd try to qualify the sky, the façade, or the pine trees with a secondary color correction, but for now, just try to find a nice balance using your primary color correction tools.

With the tonal fixes and the color balancing, Figure 3-13 is now a much more pleasant image.

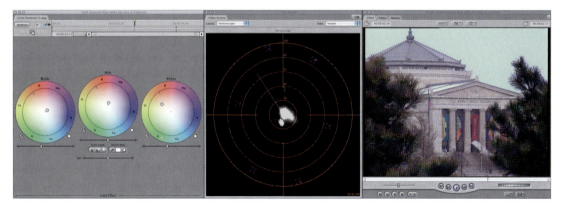

Fig. 3-12 The highlights required the most correction. The small "blob" of trace under the main centered portion of the trace is the sky, which should have some blue in it. Trying to center that part will result in the museum façade becoming quite magenta. Watch the façade of the museum on your video monitor to protect against getting a magenta cast. This image is starting to lean slightly toward magenta here.

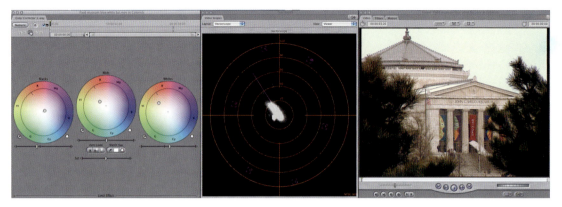

Fig. 3-13 The final corrections are indicated by the position of the small circles inside the color wheels. The vectorscope shows a more centered trace and the image is balanced.

Visual Clues to Color and Contrast

While we usually want to balance the colors so that our blacks and highlights are neutral and the tonal range is nicely spread out, there are certain clues that we need to look for when determining color balance and tone. One of the main clues is the position of the sun in outdoor shots. By looking at the shadows in an image, you can tell whether the sun is high (deep, close shadows) or whether it is low (long shadows). Those long shadows usually indicate a nice, warm "golden hour" feel. The shadows are rich and the colors are reddish-yellow.

Even indoors, you can use shadows and the presence of practical lights in the scene to guide your corrections. Although you don't want an entire scene shot with fluorescent light to look bright green, it's natural to include some of this green cast if your characters are working in an environment typically lit by fluorescents, like a police station. Similarly, with a nice table lamp next to a subject, your audience will be expecting a nice warm light to be coming from it. As long as these colors make sense in the emotional context of the story, use the lighting clues to give you a direction on color and contrast.

Histograms

I am not a major fan of histograms. There is no perfect histogram. About the only thing that histograms are good for is checking clipping and your eyes or the waveform monitor can pretty much give you the same information.

As we mentioned in the Chapter 1, if you used the teachings of Ansel Adams about The Zone System, a perfect histogram would be a beautiful bell curve with small amounts of deep, rich black at one end, a lot of nice midtones in the middle, and a small amount of pure white highlight at the other end. But beautiful images can make a horrendous-looking histogram. Looking at the histogram in Figure 3-14(a), it would seem that the image is terribly underexposed with almost no white or bright portions of the picture. But in reality, the image is a beautifully exposed shot of a woman in a window at night (see Fig. 3-14b). The waveform image of the same picture indicates that while much of the image is dark, the part that is bright, is bright enough (see Fig. 3-14c).

The histogram gives you no clear sense of where the bright or dark pixels are or how bad the clipping in an image is. You can get a general sense of clipping from histograms by looking out for large, sharp "cliffs" in the data. Spikes aren't a bad thing in a histogram as long as they usually have a steady rise in shape. Clipping is seen as a sharp vertical climb or

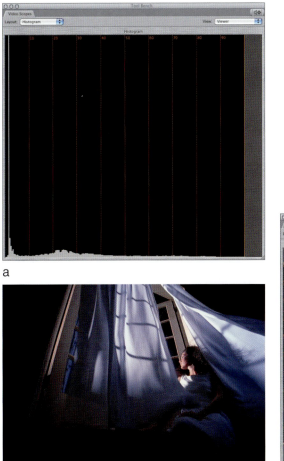
a

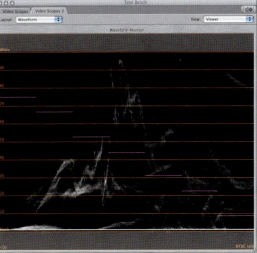

b   c

Fig. 3-14 **(a)** The image looks underexposed. **(b)** Actually, the image has lots of blacks and perfectly exposed whites and few midtones. Image courtesy of Artbeats' LifeStyles Mixed Cuts collection, LM119. **(c)** Final Cut Pro's internal waveform monitor displaying the same clip.

drop at either end of the histogram. The histogram in Figure 3-14 does show a sharp spike in the deepest blacks and the shadows in the waveform also indicate that there is probably clipping in the blacks as well, but the image is very well exposed. You can see that in the waveform, but the histogram gives no sense that the image is well exposed.

The other problem with histograms is that there's not a lot of variety in the way that they can be displayed in most software. You can't zoom in on portions of the waveform to get a better view like you can with waveform monitors and vectorscopes. They are also rarely calibrated with any sort of indication about specific levels or numbers of pixels. Even if they had that kind of information, it still wouldn't help much. Why would you care if there were 6,000 pixels that were a certain shade of middle gray?

In defense of the histogram, many people who do retouching like to use the histogram to set blacks and highlights, because it allows them to see when there's room to either pull down the blacks or pull up the highlights. As soon as they start to see clipping occur (a sharp spike at either end), then they can either stop to retain detail or continue pushing the contrast, knowing that they're clipping their image. For me, and most experienced colorists, you get the same amount of information from a waveform monitor, with the added bonus that you know the specific area (horizontally) that the clipping occurs. This gives you some guidance when you're trying to assimilate what the scope is telling you with what the video monitor is telling you.

For a quick tutorial, try to use the histogram feature in Color to balance the shot of the Field Museum (see Fig. 3-15). I tried doing it

Fig. 3-15 This image shows how to get to Histograms in Apple's Color with right mouse click on the Vectorscope. The image itself is of Color's very cool 3D Color Space vectorscope.

with the Final Cut Pro hue offset wheels with a little success and I got even closer using the blacks, midtones, and whites sliders. In any room in Color, you can switch one of the scopes to a histogram view by right-clicking on the scope that you want to change to a histogram and choosing Histogram from the contextual pulldown menu that appears where your mouse was positioned.

You can view the histograms with all three channels at once using RGB (see Fig. 3-16a), or you can see larger images of each of the color channels individually using the R, G, or B buttons at the top left corner of the histogram. You can also view the luminance of the image using the Luma button.

Use the three lift sliders for each color in the Advanced tab to bring down the shadow end of the histogram so that each of the spikes on the left side of the histogram are even with each other. Notice that the large "mounds" to the left—black—are one above the other (see Fig. 3-16b). Then adjust the three gain controls so that the tall "skyscraper" at the right side of each color channel lines up one above the other (see Fig. 3-16c).

Looking at the histogram itself, there's really no way of telling what to do with your midtones. The shapes in the histograms in the middle of the graph seem to be lining up pretty well. At this point the image seems a little magenta in the midtones. You can use the gamma controls for the individual channels to tweak the image using your eyes on the video monitor to complete the correction. Remember, if you see magenta in the midtones, you either need to lower the red and blue of the midtones or raise the green of the midtones, because red and blue make magenta and green is the opposite of magenta. Which you use depends on whether you want to raise or lower the overall feel of the midtones. If you add green to counteract magenta, you will also be increasing the midtones. If you lower red and blue equally, you will be reducing magenta *and* reducing the overall level at the midtones.

In reality, you simply don't use a single tool to guide you through an entire correction. You have to rely on how the image looks in the video monitor and compare that with the information you're getting from the

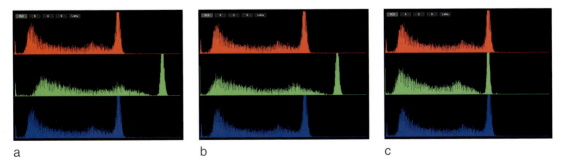

a   b   c

Fig. 3-16 (a) Uncorrected image as analyzed by Color's RGB Histograms. **(b)** shows the Histogram with the black level balance. **(c)** shows the Histogram with the highlights balanced as well. Notice how the basic shapes of each color channel line up.

RGB parade waveform and the vectorscope. You can check out images that have severe problems with histograms to get an idea of what might be wrong with a specific channel, but most colorists would be able to glean this same information from the RGB parade.

Eyedropper

One of the relatively new and very precise methods of analyzing color in most of these software-based color correction applications is to use the eyedropper. Apple's Color and Final Cut Pro, Avid, and Color Finesse, among others, allow you to see the numerical values for sampled pixels. This is valuable information. The eyedropper allows you to sample very precise sections of an image. The big caveat to the eyedropper is that it depends on the specific pixel you sample. Some applications, like Avid, allow you to average the eyedropper sample across a 3×3 grid of pixels around the exact tip of the eyedropper. Other application allow you to choose a 5×5 grid. This averaging is usually a good thing since noise and other odd variations can mean that the exact pixel you chose isn't really representative of the other pixels that appear identical around it. The danger with the larger sampled grids is that they can include pixels of very different colors that are adjacent to the one you chose. For example, if you sample near the edge of a dark line, the sample grid of 5×5 pixels might be reading half of the pixels on the bright edge and half the pixels on the dark edge, giving you a reading that really doesn't correspond to either area.

Aside from those caveats, eyedroppering can give you some very good information about your picture. For this tutorial, we'll use Color Finesse (see following boxed text for use in Color).

Using Eyedroppering in Apple's Color

To use the eyedropper information in Color, choose 3D Color Space as one of your scope quadrants on the right screen and choose RGB mode from the buttons on the top left of the scope. The other choices are HSL, Y'CbCr, and IPT. These choices affect how the eyedropper information is displayed. RGB is the most useful while manipulating the red, green, and blue controls. Color allows you to select three different points on an image to track via the eyedroppers. These points are accessed along the bottom of the 3D Color Space scope. Click on a square to select it and then drag around on the image. It would make sense to use these three points to track a white point, black point, and neutral midtone. As the image plays or as you make adjustments to the image, the numbers to the right of each square update. Many applications provide you with 8- or 10-bit numbers for each color channel, but in Color, they are provided as decimals with 0 being black and 1.0 being white.

Note in Figure 3-17 that on the image to the right, you can see the positions of the three eyedropper points, numbered 1, 2, and 3 (1 is difficult to see in the white veil). The eyedropper swatches in the 3D Color Space scope match the points on the image.

Fig. 3-17 Eyedroppering in Apple's Color allows three distinct eyedroppered positions.

Let's sample some pixels in a few images. From the Tutorial_footage_ and_files folder on the DVD, call up the "ChromaDuMonde_properex-white.mov" and the "ChromaDuMonde_properexwarm.mov" in Color Finesse or some other application that allows you to see the samples from an eyedropper.

One thing to make sure of is that the eyedropper is sampling at a color bit depth that you are familiar with. Basically, this means 8 bit for most people. If you are used to seeing eyedroppered images with whites around 255, then set Color Finesse for RGB 8 bit (see Fig. 3-18). In Color Finesse you set this with a twirl down menu just below the eyedropper on the right side of the UI. In Color, the numbers do not use an 8- or 10-bit scale, but a decimal scale with black at 0.000 and white at 1.000.

Don't worry about viewing a lower bit-depth scale due to quality issues. The numbers are all being crunched by the application at a higher bit depth, but the numbers that are being displayed are purely for reference and do not limit the quality of the correction.

Sample the pure-white chip on the "ChromaDuMonde_properexwhite. mov." In Color Finesse, you click on the eyedropper once, then move over the area you want to sample, and then drag around and release when you've found the area you want. Or you can click once on the eyedropper and then click again on the spot you want to sample without dragging.

As we discuss in other areas of the book, you can tell if there is an absence of color if the red, green, and blue channels are the same. In the case of the eyedropper information, this is a numerical read out. So if the sample reads around 235 in each of the channels, then the white is exposed correctly and it is balanced. If your specific sample does not match across all three channels, you may want to drag the eyedropper around the area. You'll probably see a little movement in the numbers. Try to average them out in your head. Do the numbers flip-flop some-

TIP

One way to get a general idea of the color in an area is to drag the eyedropper throughout the area slowly and watch the samples as they change. Try to get an average of the area in your head. This is good way to avoid being fooled by a strange sample.

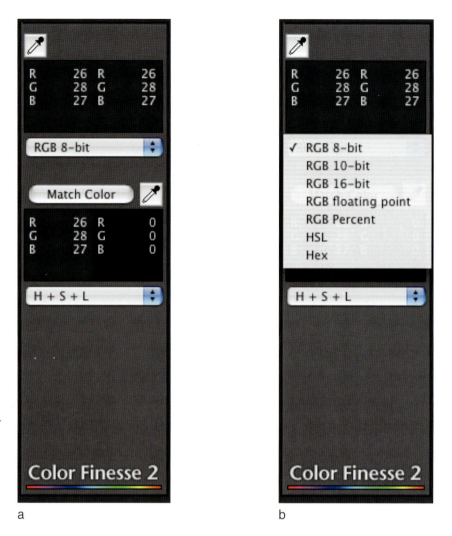

Fig. 3-18 **(a)** Set the bit choice depending on the numerical scale you're used to reading; 8 bit is a scale from 0–255. **(b)** Your other choices are 10 bit, 16 bit, floating point, RGB percentage, HSL, and Hex. RGB percentage would certainly be an easy way to read the numbers from the sampled pixels.

a

b

TIP

To tell if an area has been clipped or crushed, drag the eyedropper around the area. If the number values are "locked in" and don't move at all, then there is no detail in that area.

times? Is one channel consistently higher or lower than the others? You don't want to adjust your levels based on a single pixel.

Check some other areas of the same chart. Drag the eyedropper around the gray background. Check the color of the blackest chip. Check out some of the colored chips. DSC Labs' "ChromaDuMonde" series has a couple of colored chips that represent skin tones. Seeing what the sampled numbers are on these skin-tone chips is valuable information to store away for later.

To see how to use this information for color balancing, call up the "ChromaDuMonde_properexwarm.mov." Now sample the black, white, and gray areas of the chart. You'll see that the numbers are no longer a close numerical match from one color channel to the next. Now the sampled colors are skewed with larger numbers in the red and green channels and lower values for blue.

In most color correction applications, you don't get real-time feedback of your sample as you change it with the color correction application, but Color Finesse *does* update the numbers of your sample as you grade, which is a very cool thing. The numbers to the left are the original sample values and the numbers to the right are the result of your correction. You can also compare the right and left color swatches under the eyedropper values to see where you took the correction.

Sample the black chip in the center of the chart. I got 26 for red, 28 for green, and 15 for blue. I scrubbed around in the area, and while the numbers did change, the blue number was rarely above 16. Even though the red and green numbers occasionally matched, the green number was usually slightly higher than red. This indicates that the blacks are slightly elevated (they should be at 16) and they have a yellowish tint (green and red in nearly even amounts). The blue channel is actually probably just about perfect.

Now, in Color Finesse's RGB tab, you can bring up the red pedestal slider, resampling until you get the sampled number for red down to around 16. Then bring the green pedestal down to 16 as well. I ended up lowering the green and red pedestal to −0.04 and raising the blue pedestal to 0.01.

Now, sample a white chip on the "warm" chart. For me, the sample showed 254 for red, 245 for green, and 186 for blue. This means that the chart is fairly yellow (both red and green are elevated, making yellow) and that red is a little higher than green, so it's a reddish yellow. You can confirm this finding by simply looking at the chip. So to get a legal level, we need to bring down the red quite a bit, bring down the green a touch, and raise the blue levels quite a bit. Let's use our eyes as we do this, or you could check out the RGB parade and then resample the chip. Keep at this until all three color channels read at about 235.

Even after these two corrections, the midtones still look very red. We'll sample the middle gray tone and adjust the gammas to eliminate the cast. I scrubbed around and settled on a gray sample of 136 for red, 118 for green, and 102 for blue. Since there's no absolute value given on the chart for gray, I'm going to match the red and blue gammas to the green gamma.

It also would be possible to attempt this correction using the hue offset wheels. This requires some real knowledge of how the colors combine to make each other. Moving the wheels to match the numbers of the sample is a little like trying to solve the Rubik's cube. Sometimes as you get close to solving one color, one of the other colors drifts away, so it doesn't seem like you can move the hue offset wheels in a direction that solves all three colors. For example, in trying to get highlights of red and green down and blue up, I pulled down toward blue until the number for blue got close to 235, then I had to maintain the distance from the center while I swung the hue offset wheels clockwise and counterclockwise to get the red and green numbers to match. This is actually a good exercise to learn the hue offset wheels. You can also adjust the hue numerically with the arrow keys.

Using very subtle movements in the wheels, try to match numerical values of each channel. Of course, you want to make sure that your sample is of a black, white, or gray image, and that when you are controlling the midtones, the sample is of a midtone area. You shouldn't sample a black chip and try to balance it using the midtone wheel, of course.

Another good exercise is to load up a chip chart like the "ChromaDuMonde_properexwarm.mov" from the exercise above and use the hue offset wheels to balance while looking at an RGB parade. This exercise is considerably simpler with a manual interface like the CP-200-BK or CP-100 by Tangent Devices that allows you to control all three hue offset wheels at once.

Balancing Color with a Flat-Pass Waveform Monitor

Another way to tell that an image has a color cast is with the standard composite waveform monitor set to flat pass (sometimes called YC—which stands for Luma/Chroma—in some software applications).

Of all of the colorists that were interviewed for this book, the only person that utilized this technique regularly was Neal Kassner, the colorist at CBS's "48 Hours," but it's also a technique that I've employed occasionally. Both of us were taught this technique in the days before the widespread acceptance and use of RGB waveform monitors when we were learning to **shade** or **paint** multicamera shoots.

Shading or painting generally involves pointing all of the cameras in a multicamera shoot at a single chip chart, like the grayscale chart or ChromaDuMonde chart by DSC Labs used throughout this book. Then a technician in the truck or control room uses overall pedestal, gamma, and gain controls as well as controls for the individual red, green, and blue color channels to make all the cameras look the same. This was done without an RGB parade waveform monitor and usually in conjunction with a vectorscope.

With the waveform set to flat pass, where you are able to see chroma information in the scope, the shader can match the level of each chip chart on the waveform monitor and balance the color channels by attempting to get the flattest line possible in the shadows, midtones, and highlights.

Let's attempt to dial in a color correction using nothing but a waveform monitor in flat-pass mode. Call up the "grayscale_cool.mov" and "grayscale_neutral.mov" clips (see Fig. 3-19) into Color Finesse or whatever software you're using. If you use Color, you'll need an external waveform monitor, because as of the writing of this book, flat pass is not an option for viewing any of the built-in waveform monitors in Color, though "overlay" is close to what you need. In Color Finesse, the waveform to use is called YC waveform. An external waveform monitor is definitely preferable for this exercise. If you don't have access to a YC waveform or flat-pass composite waveform display, then you can use an overlay-type waveform like the the ones available in Color and Color Finesse. The overlay waveform basically takes the three channels of the RGB parade waveform and lays them over each other. The goal with the overlay waveform is similar to the composite flat-filter waveform: make a thin line. With the overlay, you can see the difference in the three channels and the goal, at least with a pure white, gray, or black portion of the image, is to have them all lay perfectly on top of each other.

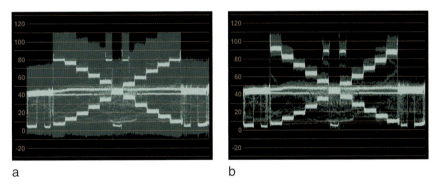

a   b

Fig. 3-19 **(a)** Color Finesse's YC waveform monitor showing the cool chart and **(b)** the same monitor showing the neutral chart.

Looking at the "grayscale_neutral" clip followed by the "grayscale_cool" clip while viewing the YC or flat-pass composite waveform monitor shows you that the neutral clip has much less **excursion** in the trace; in other words, the trace is skinny vertically on the neutral clip and fat on the cool clip.

It took some serious movement in the midtones and the highlights of the hue offset wheels to flatten out the display in the waveform monitor. Figure 3-20 shows the UI of Color Finesse when I got to the end of my correction. Note that Color Finesse has four hue offset wheels and that the first one is an overall, or master, wheel. In order to get enough range out of the midtones, I had to do some of the correction in the master and then counteract that correction in the blacks.

Definition

Excursion: The difference in amplitude between two different levels.

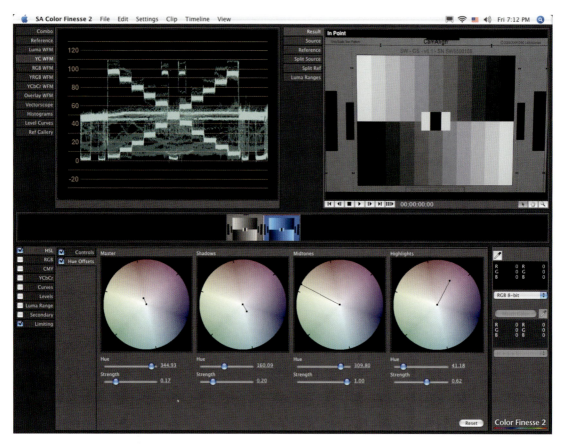

Fig. 3-20 Color Finesse UI at the end of the correction.

Trying to flatten out the color with the composite waveform is something that you would generally only attempt with a pure-white or -black portion of a real-life image. To do this effectively, you need to figure out the part of the image in the waveform that is white or black. This is a similar exercise to what we did with the boxer image in Chapter 1. Once you have identified a section of the waveform that should be black, you can use various tools in the shadows tonal range to flatten out the signal in that area. Then do the same with whites. Once you have balanced the blacks and whites on most images, the midtones will fall into place naturally, or at least be close enough that you can complete the correction using only your eyes and the video monitor.

Kassner provided another helpful tip to refine this flattening technique of eliminating color casts. His tip is just one more reason to use an external scope. While many of the colorists liked to zoom in on their waveforms vertically, in other words, expanding the waveform to closely examine only the top or bottom, Kassner also likes to zoom in *horizontally* to better find and examine the color in a specific horizontal location on the waveform monitor. If your waveform monitor allows you to zoom in horizontally, so that you are not seeing the entire field, give this tip a try and see how much easier it is to isolate what is happening in the magnified area.

Color Contrast

When doing primary color correction, or secondaries for that matter, another thought to keep in mind is that the contrast of colors in an image is just as important as the contrast of tones. If an entire image is warm or cool, the impact of that color temperature can be further strengthened by having some contrasting color to give your eye something to compare.

This concept is applicable to balancing colors in an image. If you are trying to introduce or enhance a color cast, it often creates interest and a heightened sense of the color cast if one of the tonal ranges, usually shadows or highlights, is either perfectly balanced or has a slight color cast in the opposite direction. Oftentimes, this contrast of colors can help your eyes see the color cast better by "anchoring" it with a pure balance. The way that works is that if all of the tonal ranges have the same color cast, your brain starts to color balance the scene automatically, but if your eye has a pure black or white to hold on to, then the color cast elsewhere in the picture can't be filtered away.

In addition to general color casts in an image, color contrast can be enhanced to add interest. The best way to do this kind of isolated color work is in secondaries, however, so we will discuss that in Chapters 5 and 6.

CHAPTER 4

Color Control Tools

In Chapter 3 we discussed two of the most important color-manipulation tools: the hue offset wheels and the individual red, green, and blue gain, gamma, and shadow controls. In this chapter we'll continue to explore those tools but also look at other tools that are available in Color and other applications.

Hue Offset Wheels or Color Balance Controls

The hue offset wheels are analogous to the triple trackballs that most serious colorists use as their main color-manipulation tools. In Final Cut Pro, they're known as the three-way color corrector. Avid has them in their entire line of products, where they're known as *hue offset wheels*, and Color has them, called *Color balance controls*. Many plug-ins have them, Color Finesse has them, and IRIDAS's SpeedGrade has them, though they look a little different.

We did a correction tutorial already using hue offset wheels and a chip chart in Chapter 3, so let's dive right in to a real-world correction using hue offset wheels. I'll be working in Color, but you can use any application that has this same functionality.

With the "piano_cool" clip loaded up in your color correction application, make sure that no previous color correction work is still applied to it. If you have a global reset button, use that before continuing so that all parameters are at the factory defaults and your image is at **base mem**.

I'm going to do this correction with the Tangent Devices CP200-BK control panel attached, but the corrections will work just the same by using your mouse with the graphical user interface (GUI) on the screen.

The hue offset wheels themselves don't have any way to correct for the tone of the picture. On the CP200-BK, I'll use the dials that ring the trackballs to control the levels of the shadows, midtones, and highlights. In Color's Primary In room, you can use the gray bars to the right of the

Definition

Base Mem: da Vinci colorists use this term to describe the state of the image with no color correction applied.

wheels to control these same functions or in the Basic tab to the right, you can use the Master Lift, Gamma, and Gain controls.

I started by bringing down the Master Lift control, using the dial around the left trackball, while simultaneously bringing up the Master Gain control, using the dial around the right trackball, on the CP200-BK panel. This allowed me to adjust the lift (blacks) backdown to where I wanted them with my left hand when they started being affected by the fairly radical gain change I was making with my right hand. I brought the gain up so that the main bright shape in the blue channel reached 100 IRE. This meant that some portions of the image went to about 100 IRE. Basically, there is a small amount of the trace in the blue and green channels to the far left that goes beyond legal. That is probably the representation of the very hot white on the vertical part of the white keys under the hand on the far right. Once I start to balance out the blue highlights, I may be able to bring the gain up even more. (see Fig. 4-1)

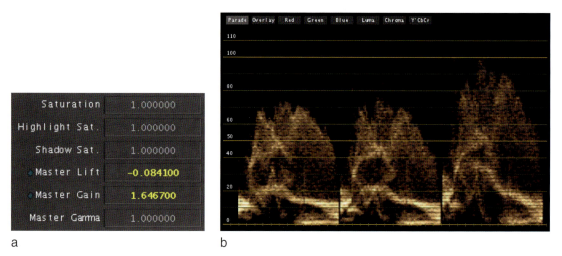

a   b

Fig. 4-1

Then using only the highlight trackball (or highlight hue offset wheel), I pushed toward red and away from blue/cyan to balance the main peak of the shape across the channels in the RGB waveform. You can also look at the vectorscope and try to dial in the black and white piano keys into the center of the scope. Remember that there is supposed to be a lot of warmth in the image due to the skin tones and the brown of the wood in the piano, so having part of the trace of the vectorscope veer off toward red and yellow is fine. There is also the yellow/gold lettering that we don't want to correct away.

Continue to play with the color balance of the highlights. Once the highlights seem balanced and the lift (blacks) is balanced, check out the overall levels. The skin tones seem to be getting washed out, especially the highlight along the pinky side of the hand. I dialed down some of the overall gain so that the red channel was hitting around 90 IRE and the red highlight from the key under the hand was hitting around 100 IRE. That correction crushes the blacks a bit, so a slight raise in the lift is needed.

Use your Master Gamma control to get a nice flesh tone and a rich quality to the wood of the piano. Double check the "focus" on your gain and lift adjustments. Then dial in a nice flesh tone on the hand by using the midtone trackball.

Figure 4-2 is a look at most of the Color Primary In room user interface (UI) and the resulting scopes. You can see where my hue offset wheels ended up, as well as my Master Lift, Gamma, Gain, and Color's built-in scopes (Fig. 4-2a).

a

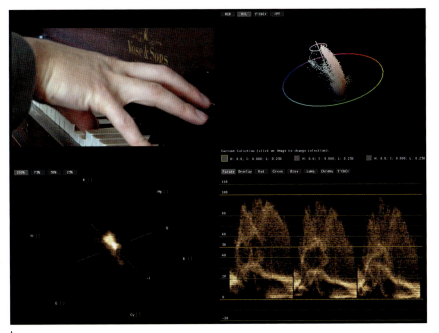

b

Fig. 4-2

When you're using the hue offset wheels and judging images with the RGB parade waveform display and video monitor, you have to be able to figure out what portion of an image is really white or black. In our example, the black piano keys to the right are very obvious and balancing the black portion of the picture so that all three channels are even across the bottom (i.e., balanced) was relatively easy. It's trickier with the skin tone. Obviously, that part of the image needs to have more red than green or blue. Remember that the-I line of the vectorscope is a common reference point for almost all skin tones.

Angle of Attack

Terry Curren from Alpha Dogs in Burbank, CA, has a rule of thumb for balancing images on the RGB parade waveform: "Even though the whites and the blacks end up even, the midtones have this little angle to them with slightly higher reds, mid-greens, and lower blues." Terry demonstrated this by holding up a pen to his RGB parade scope showing about a 15-degree angle from the midtone blue cell to the midtone red cell with the green midtone perfectly in between. The angle of the pen was similar to the red line showing the same angle in the gammas on the RGB waveform display in Figure 4-3. Obviously there are times when the midtones have one of the other channels that is more dominant than in this example, but as we went through correction after correction, this angle on the midtones with reds above greens above blues seemed to be the most common by far.

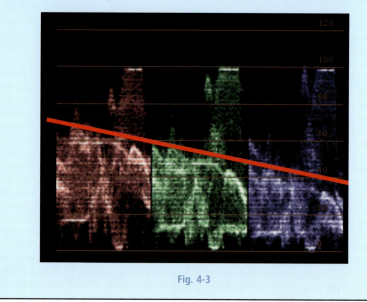

Fig. 4-3

Hue Offsets with RGB Parade

One of the tricky things with the hue offset wheels, or trackballs, is to figure out which way you need to move them when watching the RGB parade waveform. Using hue offsets while monitoring a vectorscope is very easy. It's almost like you're directly manipulating the image on the vectorscope with the wheels. It's the same kind of direct manipulation and response you get with RGB controls or Curves while watching the RGB waveform.

Using the trackballs or hue offsets is one of the most universal, hands-on ways to do color correction and the RGB parade waveform is arguably the most important piece of test equipment for color correction, not counting the video monitor itself. So you really should have a good understanding of how these two pieces of equipment work together.

Load the "grayscale_neutral" clip into your preferred color correction software that has hue offset wheels (or some form of color wheel correction). The goal here is to make the movement of the trackballs or color wheels correspond in your brain to the resulting desired movement for each cell in the RGB parade waveform. This is not something that's going to happen quickly for many people. If you are a musician, think of it like practicing a musical instrument. You need to get the feel of this "under your fingers." It's a question of muscle memory that will develop over some time. The directions should make sense, because they adhere to the color theory that we've already discussed elsewhere. It may appear to be backwards, but if you understand what the color wheels are actually doing, it will make more sense.

Consider pulling the shadow trackball straight toward green (moving toward the 8 o'clock position on the wheel). What do you think should happen to the RGB parade waveform? If you consider that pulling the wheel toward green is adding green and that you are doing this in the shadow wheel, then you should guess correctly that the green cell will rise at the bottom and the red and blue cells will come down, because the opposite of green is magenta, which is comprised equally of red and blue.

From that position, swing the point on the color wheel from 8 o'clock toward 9 o'clock: green stays essential the same, red (which is in that basic direction) moves up, and blue (which is in the opposite direction) moves down. Swinging from 8 o'clock toward 6 o'clock raises the blue channel while keeping green fairly even and lowering red.

After you've tried those moves, reset the shadow wheel to the default. Practice trying to move specific combinations of cells with specific moves of the wheels or trackballs, specifically:

TIP

To follow along with this series of moves visually, see the figures on the pages (97–101).

- Moving toward green raises green while lowering red and blue.

- Moving toward yellow raises red and green while lowering blue.

- Moving toward red raises red while lowering blue and green.

- Moving toward magenta raises red and blue while lowering green.

- Moving toward blue raises blue while lowering red and yellow.

- Moving toward cyan raises blue and green while lowering red.

Another important trick to learn: If you want to maintain the position of one cell while moving the other two, imagine a line drawn from the color that you want to remain stationary across to the color opposite it. For our example, we'll try to keep the green channel stationary while having the red and blue channels move up and down on either side of it. Draw the imaginary line from green to magenta. To move red and blue while maintaining the green cell's position, simply move the trackball or wheel perpendicular to the imaginary line. For us, this perpendicular line is from about 10 o'clock (raising red and lowering blue) to 4 o'clock (raising blue and lowering red). This corresponds almost perfectly to the I line on the vectorscope.

Thinking about what you are doing from a color theory perspective, this makes sense. You are not moving toward or away from yellow at all. You are maintaining the cursor's distance from green while moving it toward yellow-red or blue-cyan.

Trying to maintain the position of the red channel while moving green and blue in different directions means a move that corresponds to the Q line of the vectorscope; this is approximately from 2 o'clock (lowering green) to 8 o'clock (lowering blue). (Let's make a shorthand for these clock positions by dropping the "o'clock." For the next couple of paragraphs, numerical entries will refer to clock positions around the color wheel or vectorscope. Technically it would be best to use degrees, but clock positions are easier, I think.)

Trying to maintain the position of the blue channel while moving green and red in different directions means a move from 1 (lowering green) to 7 (lowering red).

If you are not following along with the tutorial in an application right now, you may need some visual support. Here are some examples. I will drag the midtone hue offset wheel to extreme values around the circumference of the color wheel and show the corresponding RGB parade waveform. Remember that the starting point for all of the midtones is about 50 IRE and not quite perfectly balanced, but close. Note the direction of the hue offset change (exact degrees are indicated by a number under the hue offset wheel) compared to the movement of the midtones in the RGB parade.

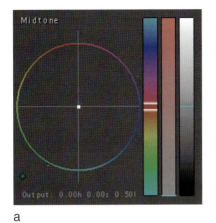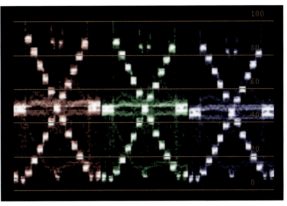

a   b

Fig. 4-4 This is the starting point for all of the corrections.

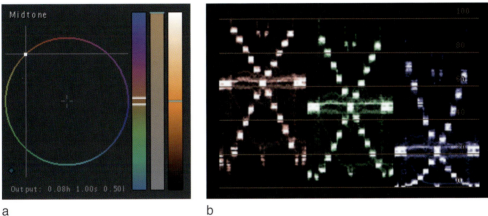

a   b

Fig. 4-5 This correction raised red, lowered blue, and green stayed the same.

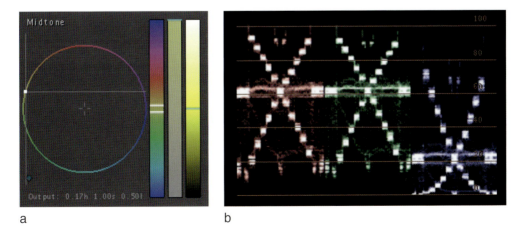

a   b

Fig. 4-6 This correction raised green and red equally and lowered blue.

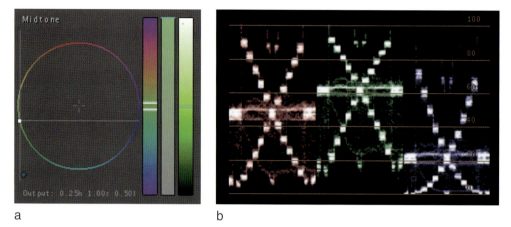

a b

Fig. 4-7 This correction raised green, lowered blue, and red stayed the same.

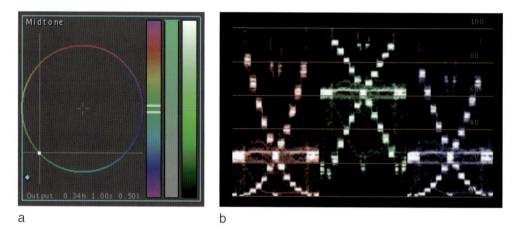

a b

Fig. 4-8 This correction raised green and lowered red and blue equally.

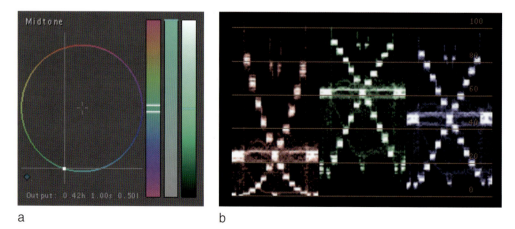

a b

Fig. 4-9 This correction raised green, lowered red, and blue stayed the same.

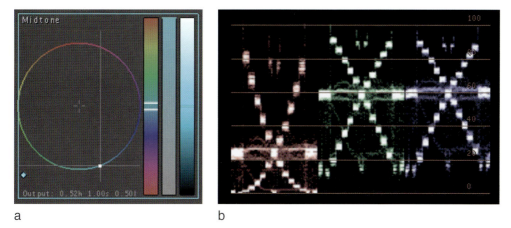

a

b

Fig. 4-10 This correction lowered red and raised green and blue equally.

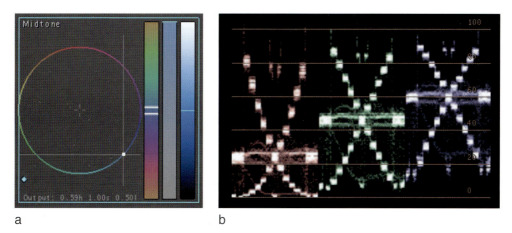

a

b

Fig. 4-11 This correction lowered red, raised blue, and green stayed the same.

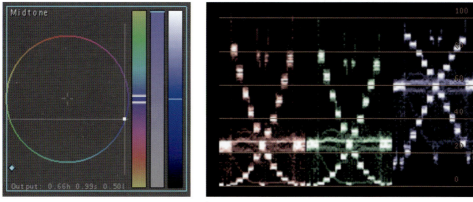

a

b

Fig. 4-12 This correction raised blue and lowered green and red equally.

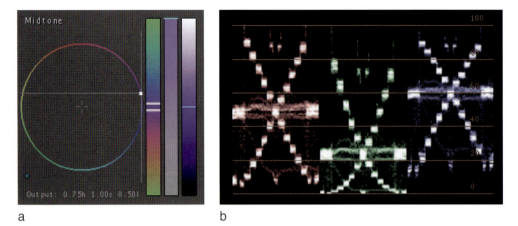

Fig. 4-13 This correction lowered green, raised blue, and red stayed the same.

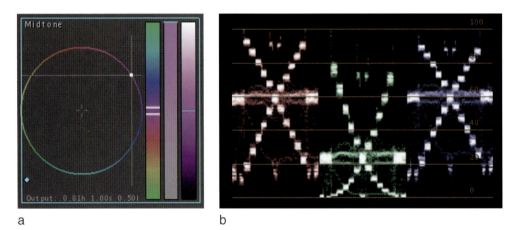

Fig. 4-14 This correction lowered green and raised red and blue equally.

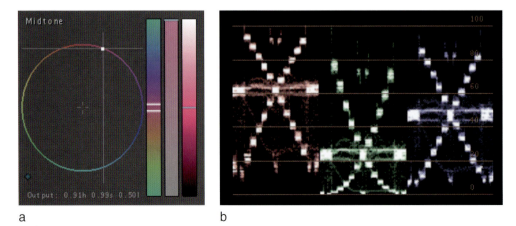

Fig. 4-15 This correction raised red, lowered green, and blue stayed the same.

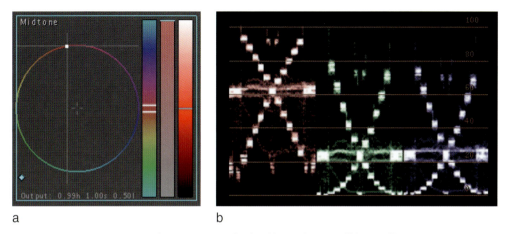

a   b

Fig. 4-16 This correction raised red and lowered green and blue equally.

Saturation Controls

Before we discuss some of the other tools for making color corrections that are available in some of the color correction applications and plug-ins, we have to discuss saturation controls. Any good color correction application should have the ability to control saturation in the highlights, shadows, and across an entire image as well.

It's kind of fitting that I've left the discussion of saturation so late in the part about primary color correction because as I watched the expert colorists, most of them didn't do changes to saturation until fairly late in the process. As with so many things in color correction, this is not a hard-and-fast rule, but it does make a lot of sense because of the way that many of the other primary color corrections can alter saturation. Changes in black level, brightness, contrast, and color balancing can all affect saturation. So until these things are all set, the real saturation of the image remains "fluid."

Once the tonal range and color balance of the level is set, there are several reasons for adjusting the saturation controls. Obviously, we need to have "legal" colors and if raising the gain has also raised the saturation of certain colors, then we need to use saturation to bring those levels in to the correct range. Also, corrections such as raising the blacks or stretching gamma can increase saturation and cause color noise in various portions of the picture, and using the high or low saturation controls can help diminish the appearance of noise in these areas.

One of the other important reasons for adjusting saturation is in matching shots. Oftentimes, if you are trying to match shots that were white balanced differently, adjusting saturation in certain tonal ranges after balancing the colors will help tweak the match in a way that simply balancing the colors cannot do.

The other important reason for adjusting saturation is in creating a look. So many of the great looks that the colorists developed for the later chapters of this book relied on the creative use of saturation. Usually this meant lowering the saturation, but sometimes it meant taking saturation to the extreme upper limits.

Saturation adjustments are also important when you're trying to take an image in a very different color direction than it was intended to have. The reason for this is that if you are trying to introduce a totally new color scheme to an image, then the old colors must be nulled out so that they don't "pollute" the colors you're trying to add. For example, if you are trying to create an icy-blue skin tone on a person with a normal skin tone, the reds and yellows of that skin tone will blend in with the correction you're trying to make. If you first lower the saturation in the areas of that skin tone or across the entire image, you will find that your icy-blue look will be much easier to achieve and much more satisfactory in the end.

One of the important reasons to adjust saturation is simply to make it look good. Saturation levels are very subjective, like gamma levels. When you're doing primary color correction, you sometimes "break" something that needs to be fixed elsewhere. That is often the case with saturation. If you had to add warmth to the midtones of an image in order to get a nice healthy skin tone, it's possible that other areas of your midtones will need to have saturation reduced. Possibly the addition of warmth in the midtones means that some cool element in the midtones becomes desaturated, so you may be able to bring the saturation up in that case, though the only real way to fight this would probably be a secondary color correction which we will discuss in Chapter 5.

Histograms

Trying to do color balancing with histograms would definitely not be my choice, but it's certainly possible if your application has the tools. Avid Symphony has a tool called Levels that allows you to correct using histograms. Color Finesse's histogram tool is also called Levels.

The basic concept for using histograms to fix color casts is similar to using Curves. You are remapping the incoming levels to different outgoing levels. In Curves, the relationship is on a grid where the horizontal and vertical axes define the relationship between incoming and outgoing signals. In Symphony's Levels, you basically have two horizontal axes and you attempt to match the position that the histogram levels sit with their ideal location.

In our tonal range correction that we did with the histogram (see Chapter 2), the goal was to spread out the tonal range across the histogram as much as possible. With color correction you attempt to do the same thing in three different color-channel histograms. This gets very difficult with severely mis-white-balanced images.

Call up the "ChromaDuMonde_cool" clip into an application that allows histograms to be manipulated and look at each color channel. The green channel appears pretty good, but the red and blue channels don't have much that's recognizable to match to the green channel (see Fig. 4-17).

The way I approached this correction was to try to match the blacks, whites, and grays using an eyedropper tool, constantly adjusting the levels and resampling. The things to adjust are the small triangles under the histogram. The default positions for the outgoing black and white histogram triangles correspond to the correct legal levels of black and white. That's why I did most of my corrections on the input (left) side. The basic concept is to match the points on the histogram on the left side so that the histogram on the right looks like you want it to look. Fig. 4-18 shows the results of my correction.

The whites, dark grays, and blacks are correct, but there is a blue cast to the upper grays. This is probably because the blue channel is clipped in the high end (due to the cool white balance) so all of the colors between the clipped blues and the midtones are more blue than they should be. The only way to fix this would be to try to lose the blue cast in the upper midtones by making the whites too warm, then using a secondary color correction to either pull all of the saturation out of the clipped area, or try to balance just the highest whites.

One of the ways we can check to see what the clipping in the blue channel looks like is to look at another color correction tool in Avid Symphony called Channels, which is similar to After Effects' ability to display the individual color channels using the controls at the bottom of the Composition window (Fig. 4-19).

a

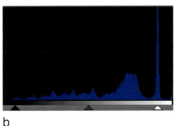
b

c

Fig. 4-17

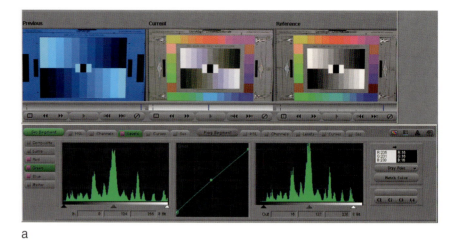

a

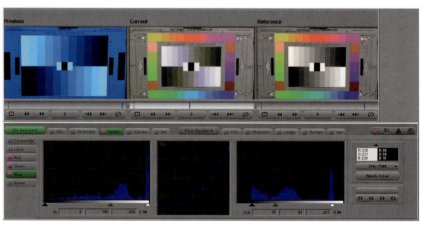

b

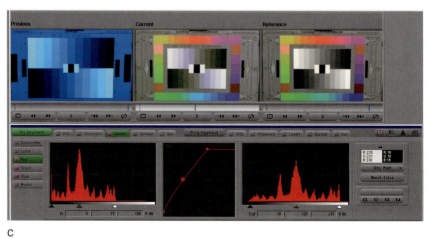

Fig. 4-18   c

Fig. 4-19 After Effects can show you what the individual color channels look like using the red, green, and blue buttons at the bottom of the Composition window. (The white button next to them shows the alpha channel.)

Curves

Curves seems to be the Rodney Dangerfield of color correction. It just doesn't get any respect. I'm not entirely sure why this is. I've spoken to many colorists. Some are confused between the Curves that I'm talking about and the implementation of Power Curves on a da Vinci.

a

b

Fig. 4-20 (a) da Vinci 2 K panels and (b) da Vinci Resolve. Images courtesy of da Vinci Systems.

The most common Curves tool is probably the one available in Adobe Photoshop (See Fig. 4-21a). This tool is also available in Color (see Fig. 4-21b), After Effects, Color Finesse, and all Avid products (see Fig. 4-21c).

We discussed Curves in Chapter 2, but only in the context of making adjustments to the tonal range of a picture. Curves can also be used to adjust color in a very quick and intuitive way.

To show you the power of Curves, let's run through a quick tutorial. Call up the "flowerbench" file in an application that has Curves, like Color, After Effects, Color Finesse, or Avid. As we showed in Chapter 2, Curves can make tonal corrections easily in the Master curve. I'll be doing this tutorial in Avid Xpress Pro because I like the nice color coding of the Curves in that application.

When dealing with Curves, the RGB or YRGB parade waveform is the most intuitive way to monitor your image while you are making corrections. Take a look at the RGB parade waveform with the "flowerbench" image up (see Fig. 4-22). All of the black levels are elevated but the red

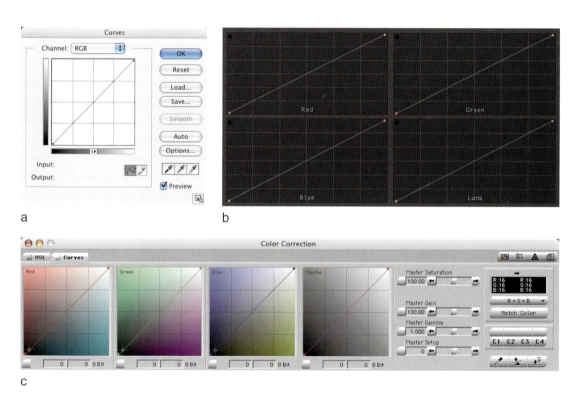

a   b

c

Fig. 4-21 (a) Curves in Photoshop (b) Curves in Apple's Color Primary In Room, (c) Curves in Avid, which is definitely the sexiest Curves interface.

is the closest to being down at 0 IRE where it probably should be, followed closely by blue, and the greens are highest of all. The red highlights appear to be clipped and they are as high as they can go. The green and blue highlights are low. Let's take care of these things first, then see what else the image needs.

Drag the bottom of the red curve to the right to pull down the shadows in the red channel. Watch the red cell of the RGB parade waveform until the lowest part of the shape gets to the bottom. Your image will not look any better but the tonal range of the red channel is much improved. My correction pulled the 0 black level in red over to 24. That means that everything that was between 24 and 0 on the original image has now been pulled down to 0 on output. See Figure 4-23.

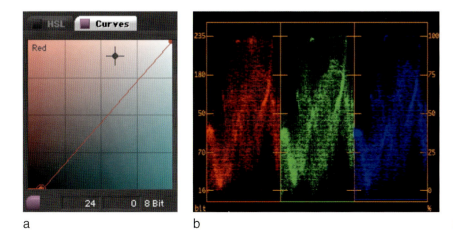

a   b

Fig. 4-22 (a) The original "flowerbench" file and (b) with the RGB parade waveform.

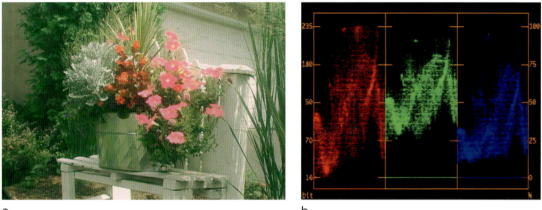

a   b   Fig. 4-23

Now, drag the same points to the right on the green and blue curves. I took the black point of the green curve to 65 and the blue curve to 24. The image starts to look better and the three cells of the RGB parade waveform are much more even. See Figure 4-24.

Grab the upper right corner of the red curve and pull it down just a little to see if you can get rid of some of the clipping in the highlights. You don't want to bring it down too low. There are lots of bright whites in this image and you need some part of all three RGB channels at the very top. I ended up bringing the top of the red curve down to 252. Greens are pretty low. To bring a highlight level up in Curves, you need to drag it to the left along the top because you can't drag it any higher. Drag it to the left while watching the highest spot in the middle of the green RGB parade cell. Line the high spot on the green channel with the high spot on the red channel. This point corresponds to the bright white leg of the bench at the middle, bottom of the image. My correction put the top of the green curve to 230. Do the same thing with the blue channel; my correction put the top of the blue curve to 240. See Figure 4-25.

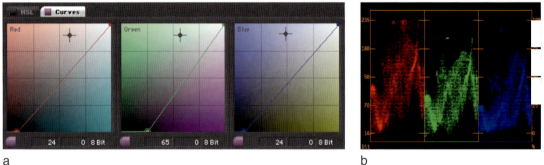

a   b

Fig. 4-24

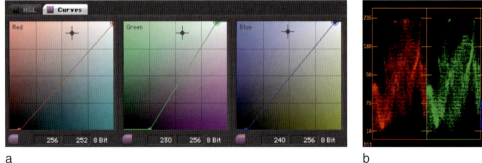

a   b

Fig. 4-25

The image is looking even better at this point but still seems a little yellow. If you look at the RGB parade waveform, this yellow tint is evident by the fact that the red and green channels appear stronger (and red and green make yellow; plus a weak blue channel means that the opposite color from blue, which is yellow, is stronger).

Looking at some of the shapes in the waveform monitor, we can try to see if the corresponding parts of the image are white or black and figure out what we need to do to get them to be balanced white or black. Notice that the far left sides of the red and green channels on the RGB parade are higher than the blue channel. On the red and green channels, that portion of the trace comes up to about 40 IRE. On the blue channel it's at about 25 IRE. To pull this part of the waveform up, click on the blue curve about 25% of the way up the diagonal line and drag it straight up. We'll watch the blue channel of the RGB parade but we'll also watch the video image. That part of the waveform is on the left side, so we need to be looking at the left side of the video image as well. We're also pulling up part of the image that is fairly dark, so we want to keep our eyes on the shadows on the left side of the video image.

I was able to get the blue channel to match the red and green channels, but when I did, I noticed that the shadows in the pine tree in the background to the left became very blue (see Fig. 4-26). So I'm going to undo that correction.

What I know about the real-world scene is that the extreme left side of the image is actually the siding of my house. That siding is painted a warm tan color (reddish yellow). The bluish tinge to the shadows gave us the clue that we didn't want that part of the waveform to match.

Let's try something else. Looking at the RGB parade waveform, we can see that even though we have the brightest part of the blue channel up as high as it can go, the rest of the blue highlights aren't as strong as the highlights in the red and green channels. Knowing that the bench has a lot of white in it and the garage door in the background is also

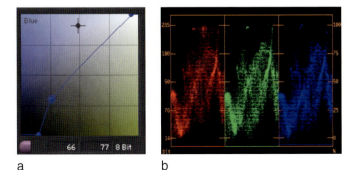

a   b   Fig. 4-26

probably white tells us that we need to bring up the highlights of the blue channel.

Grab a point on the blue curve about 75% of the way up the diagonal line and drag it upwards. We're trying to get the area on all three channels to look about the same at 75 IRE. Before doing this correction, notice that there's a peak in both the red and green channels at about 75 IRE; bring that same area of the trace in the blue channel up to match them. My adjustment was to bring the point at 185 on the blue curve up to 207. When I did that, I also brought the highest highlights on the blue channel up too far, so I made an adjustment at the top point of the blue curve back down to 246.

You could look at the RGB parade and decide that the highlights in the red channel are too strong but I think that the extra "weight" at the top of the red channel trace on the waveform is probably due to the red and pink flowers that are in a corresponding position to the strongest parts of the red channel of the waveform monitor. If you want to, you could play with the red channel to get it back into line with the blue and green channels, but you'll see that the white highlights in the picture quickly turn cyan, which is the opposite of red.

The image looks significantly better at this point, but there's a lot of green in the tin flower can on the bench and I don't think the green foliage pops very well. Let's see if we can pull out some of the green in the midtone areas.

Start with a point in the green curve that's about halfway up and pull it down a little. Using the tip in the sidebar, you know that you're moving the midtones of green down, so you need to be looking at the midtones of your video image to guard against having the image go too magenta, which is the opposite of green. As soon as you see the midtones turn magenta, you have to back off the correction. For me, the magenta cast started almost immediately when I pulled the gammas down, so I returned it to its original place (undo—CMD or CNTL-Z—should work on most applications, or simply select the point and delete it).

I still feel that there's a bit of a green cast to the middle shadows, so this time let's place a point that's much lower on the green curve and pull it down subtly. I brought the point around 106 down to 57. This may not seem like a very subtle move, but remember that the black level of green was already pulled down quite a bit, which pulls down all of the other points on the Curve as well.

Looking at our original image compared to our correction shows a significant improvement (see Fig. 4-27). These are changes that would not be quite as easy to make using the traditional hue offset wheels, because the changes to the midtones of the blue and green channels wouldn't work as well as the specific changes we made to the high midtones of the blue channel and the low midtones of the green channel.

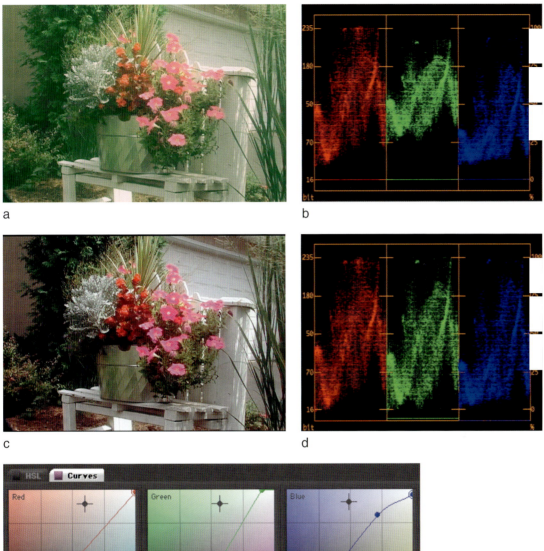

Fig. 4-27

TIP

Some applications, like Avid, allow you to eye-dropper a point on an image and see exactly where on the Curve that point lies. This is a great instructional tool to develop your ability to know where these points would fall without letting the software do it for you. A good photographer knows how to use a light meter, but most also pride themselves on being able to set exposure by eye if they have to. Developing a good sense of the luminance levels of various parts of an image will make you much faster as a colorist, because your corrections will be more intuitive.

Use extra points on the Curve to protect portions of the Curve that you *don't* want to affect. For example, if a correction to the midtones of the red curve is working great for the midtones but is adding too much red to the high-lights, place a point on the red curve between the top of the curve and the area that you are moving in order to protect the red highlights from being affected by the red midtone point. When you do this, you want to be careful not to place the points too close to each other or it will cause banding or posteriza-tion. You can use the previous tip about eyedroppering the image to determine where the pro-tection point should go.

The important thing to remember when choosing a point is to determine a specific portion of the picture you're trying to change, like the tin watering can in the example above, and to try to guess where that tonal range lies on the Curve. Don't be afraid to make mistakes. Pick a point and move it a bit. If it's not affecting the tonal range you want, then delete it and pick another point. Use the information you gathered from the first point to determine where the second point should go. Did the first point affect a tonal range that was slightly above or below the range you really wanted? That will guide you in picking the correct spot.

RGB Setup, Gamma, and Gain Sliders

A tool that works similarly to Curves are the red, green, and blue numerical or slider controls for setup, gamma, and gain. Virtually all color correction software includes sliders like these. They are available in the Advanced tab of Color's Primary In room and they are available in Color Finesse as well as many Avid and Final Cut Pro color correction plug-ins, such as 3-Prong's ColorFiX AVX plug-in or Magic Bullet's Colorista plug-in for Final Cut Pro. Figures 4-28 through 4-33 are a range of options from various products and plug-ins that allow you to color balance your images using RGB sliders or numerical values in each tonal range.

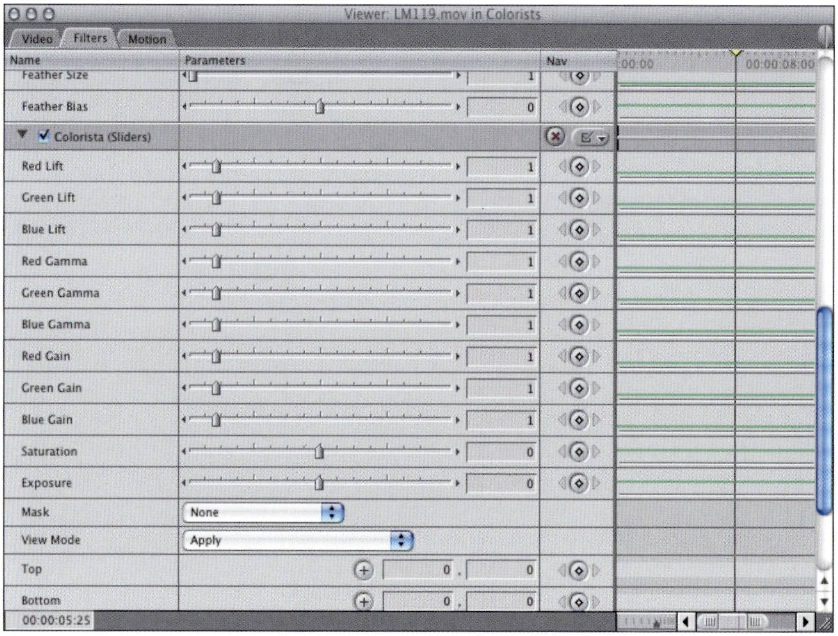

Fig. 4-28 RGB sliders for the Final Cut Pro Colorista plug-in.

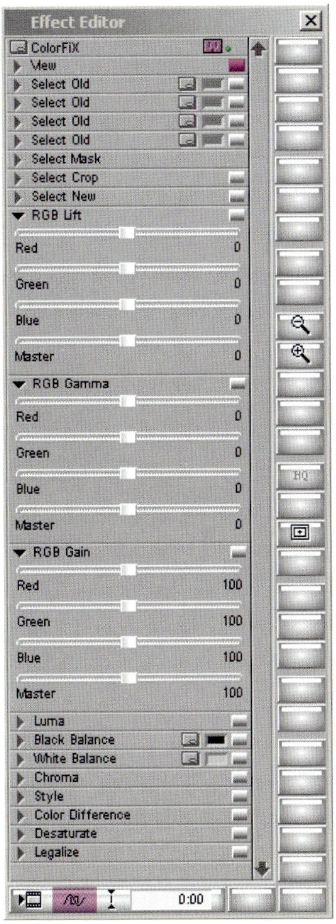

Fig. 4-29 RGB sliders for 3-Prong's ColorFiX plug-in for Avid.

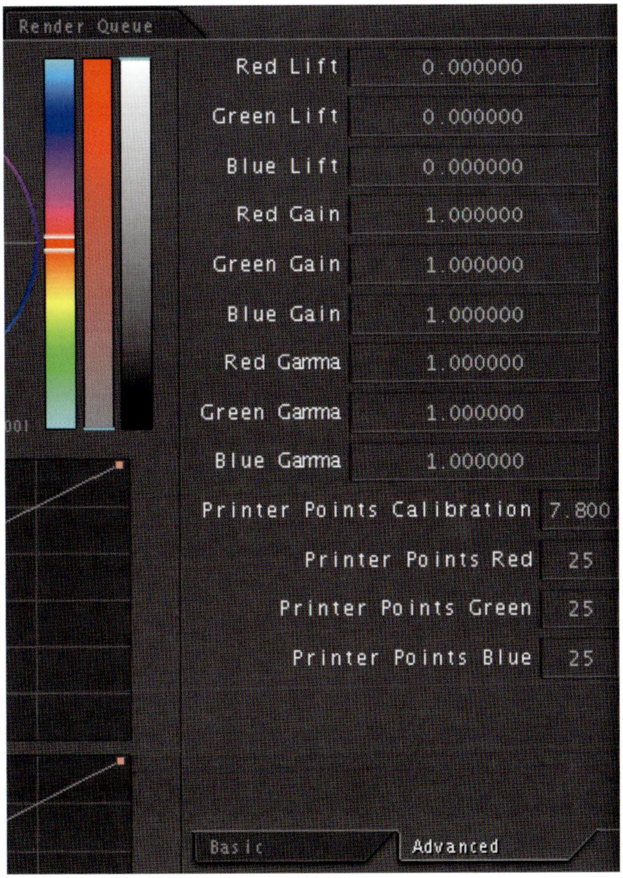

Fig. 4-31 Color's RGB sliders are in the Advanced tab of the Primary In Room.

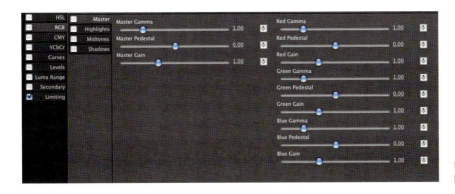

Fig. 4-30 Color Finesse's RGB sliders.

Fig. 4-32 After Effect's built-in RGB color balance UI found in Effects > Adjust > Color Balance.

Fig. 4-33 IRIDAS's SpeedGradeDI primary color correction controls.

Although we're going to do this correction in Color, any of the above applications or others with a similar RGB-level UI, will work similarly. For this tutorial, we'll use the "ChromaDuMonde_warm" clip from the DVD.

Looking at the "ChromaDuMonde chart" is a little more complicated on the vectorscope and RGB parade but it is still very similar to the grayscale chart (see Fig. 4-34). To familiarize yourself with how the chart should look on the scopes, import the "ChromaDuMonde_properex_white" clip from the DVD. (see Figure 4-2b) Notice the way that the colors from the color chips evenly surround the center of the vectorscope and how they aim toward the six color vector targets. Also, the various skin-tone chips

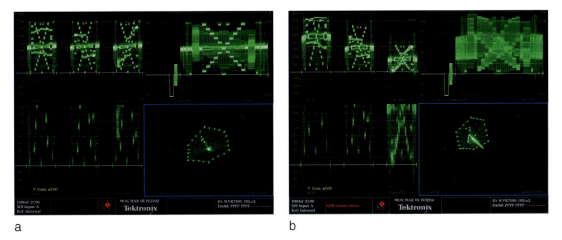

a   b

Fig. 4-34 (A) Tektronix WVR7100 display of the "ChromaDuMonde chart" with a neutral balance. (B) The same chart with a warm white balance.

should form a line that follows the-I line of the vectorscope. The-I line runs diagonally across the vectorscope from about the 5 o'clock position to about 10 o'clock. Many people refer to this as the *skin-tone line* on the vectorscope. Technically though, this line along with the Q line, which is on a 90-degree angle from the I line, are actually the in-phase and quadrature phase lines for the color-difference signals in NTSC. What does that mean? Nothing to a colorist, so we might as well call the top half of the I line the skin-tone line, since for us, that's what it's good for.

Back to our tutorial. Ignoring the color chips, the goal here will be similar to the tutorial we did with Curves. We want to use the red, green, and blue channel sliders or numerical entry boxes in each of the tonal ranges to color balance the gray chips. We'll use the red, green, and blue lift data boxes to control the bottom of the trace as it appears in the RGB parade display. This is similar to the tutorial at the beginning of Chapter 3.

In Figure 4-34b, notice in the top left RGB parade display the difference in levels between the channels, with the red channel (the first cell) having higher levels in all three tonal ranges and the blue channel (the third cell) having the lowest levels of the three. The green channel is relatively close to being correct. If you look at the RGB parade display at the lower left, you are looking at a 5× vertical gain. You can see that the black levels of the red and green channels are elevated somewhat. Looking at the composite waveform display in the upper right corner, you can tell that there is some kind of color cast because of the excursion in the trace for each chip. If the chart was neutral, the lines for each chip in this waveform display would be tight and bright, similar to the black chip at the bottom center. The vectorscope shows the red color cast, because the color chips are all pushed up toward the red vector instead of being evenly disbursed around the center of the scope.

For this tutorial, our main focus will be the standard RGB parade waveform display because it will match up very nicely with the specific red, green, and blue sliders or numerical entry controls.

The controls in the Advanced tab of Color's Primary In room are actually laid out in the order you should use them: lift first, gain next, and gamma last. Watching the RGB parade waveform, bring down the red, green, and blue lifts until the center black chip rests on the 0 IRE line. Remember the focusing analogy and only bring the level low enough to get a good clean black without clipping the signal or creating an illegal black level. The center black chip in the blue channel reads much higher than the darkest chip to the left. In the red and green channels, the lowest chip is the center chip. We may have to determine which chip we try to put at 0 for the blue channel. For now, we'll put the center chip for the blue channel at 0. Remember, once the relative positions of various parts of the lower part of the trace start to change, you need to stop, since that is showing clipping. See Figure 4-35.

Next are the gain controls. Bring them up so that the brightest part of the white chip is at 100 IRE. Note that the chart is not quite evenly lit, so the left side of the chart is slightly brighter than the right side of the chart. Seeing this slight difference in luminance between the right and left sides of the chart is very difficult to do visually but is quite obvious with your scopes. Also, you may notice that as you start to bring up the green channel gain, you can't really get to the top (100 IRE) before the green channel starts to compress and a strange interaction starts happening with the red channel gain, which almost seems to start unclipping. Once this happens, stop raising your green gain and bring down your red gain quite a bit (I brought mine down to about 80 IRE) until you can get the green channel to 100 IRE without compressing. Then bring your blue channel up to match green. See Figure 4-36.

Fig. 4-35 Here are my numbers for the lift correction from Color.

Red Lift	−0.037700
Green Lift	−0.037700
Blue Lift	−0.033350

As you make changes to the gain, and especially to the gamma, you may notice that your lift (black) has changed. This is because the gain corrections were so drastic that they affected the lift. This is common. If you were grading these sequences with a manual UI like the Tangent Devices CP-200 that allowed you to tweak the red gain and red lift at the same time, you could do this much faster. By using a single mouse, you'll need to go back and forth between the gain and lift controls until you've both of them in equilibrium. Figure 4-37 shows the numbers for gain and lift. Check the minor difference between these and the numbers in Figure 4-36a.

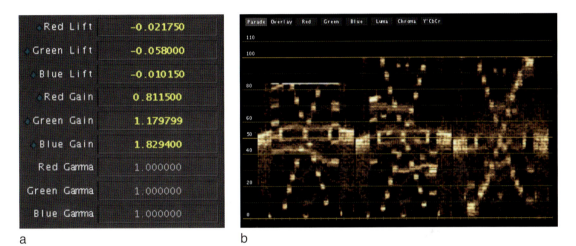

Red Lift	-0.021750
Green Lift	-0.058000
Blue Lift	-0.010150
Red Gain	0.811500
Green Gain	1.179799
Blue Gain	1.829400
Red Gamma	1.000000
Green Gamma	1.000000
Blue Gamma	1.000000

a

b

Fig. 4-36 (a) The numbers for the gain corrections. (b) the resulting waveform.

Red Lift	-0.023200
Green Lift	-0.063800
Blue Lift	-0.007250
Red Gain	0.783950
Green Gain	1.191399
Blue Gain	1.820699
Red Gamma	1.000000
Green Gamma	1.000000
Blue Gamma	1.000000

Fig. 4-37 The difference in the numbers for lift between figure 4-36a and 4-37 indicate revisions to the lift numbers because of the changes the resulted from the gain corrections.

Now it's time to make sure that the midtones are also balanced. With the highlights and shadows balanced already, the midtones should be pretty close. Notice though that the similar shapes that sit just under the 60 IRE line in the RGB parade are not quite at the same level in all three channels even though the white chips and black chips are even. I'm going to match the red and blue midtone shapes to the green midtone. The midtone corrections will have a fairly strong affect on both the highlights and shadows, so I'll have to do some back-and-forth corrections between the three tonal ranges until I have the shadows, midtones, and highlights all even across the three color channels. Figure 4-38 shows my final results with the numbers and RGB waveform.

With the amount of clipping in the red channel, this correction is problematic but you can see from the vectorscope and the 3D color space that most of what is supposed to be neutral is actually fairly neutral. There is still a slight red cast in some of the chips due to the clipping of the red channel. In a real-world image, you could determine whether this slight warming was appropriate or not and what you were willing to sacrifice in other colors or tonal ranges to try to get these into "spec."

Let's apply this to grading a real-world image with these same tools. Call up "piano_cool.mov" from the DVD into your chosen color correction application or plug in (see Fig. 4-39). I'll do this one in Color Finesse.

Fig. 4-39(b) is the starting RGB parade waveform display for the "piano_cool" image. It shows that the black levels are slightly elevated across all three channels. Looking at the right side of the shadows, the

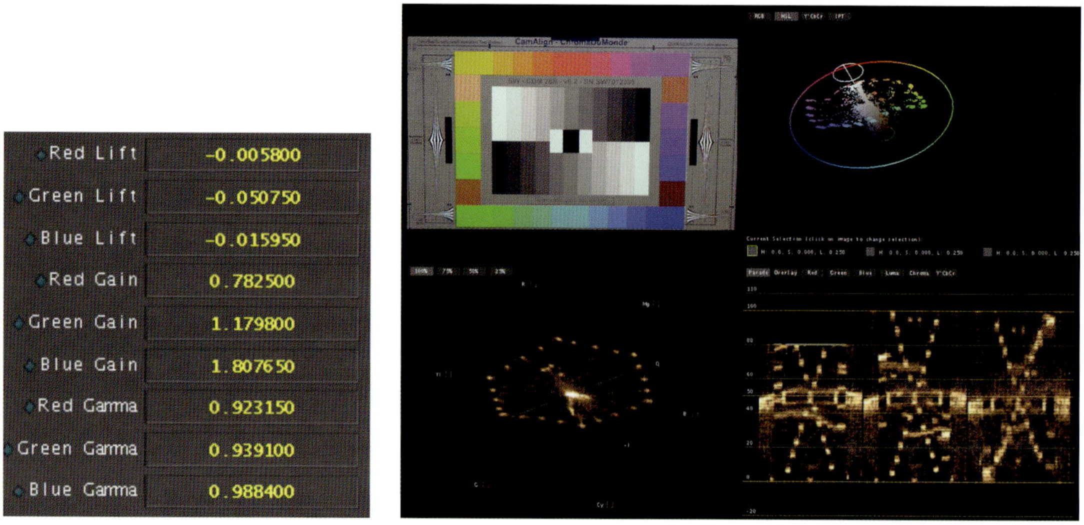

Red Lift	-0.005800
Green Lift	-0.050750
Blue Lift	-0.015950
Red Gain	0.782500
Green Gain	1.179800
Blue Gain	1.807650
Red Gamma	0.923150
Green Gamma	0.939100
Blue Gamma	0.988400

a   b

Fig. 4-38

blue channel starts at about the same level as the other channels at its lowest point but the portion of the trace from about 0 IRE to about 20 IRE shows that the deep shadows above black are elevated above the other two tracks. Also, looking at the highlights, the red channel is the lowest and the blue channel is the highest. Midtones are a bit hard to judge at the moment. Let's set our black or pedestal level first across all three channels (see Fig. 4-40). We have the nice black piano keys on the right to use as a very clean black, so that should be relatively easy.

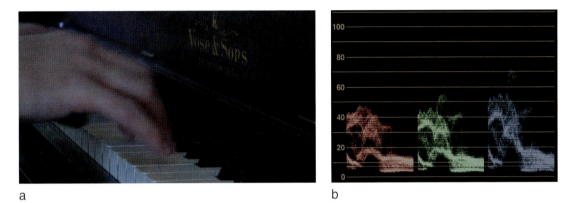

a   b

Fig. 4-39 **(a)** The "piano_cool" image, **(b)** the starting RGB parade waveform display.

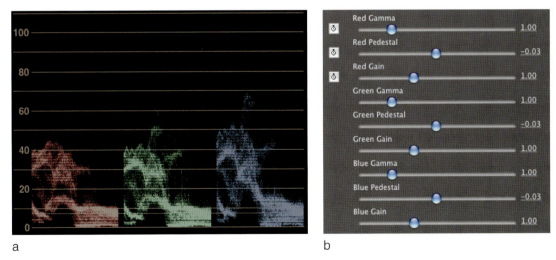

a   b

Fig. 4-40 **(a)** The RGB parade waveform and **(b)** the numbers at the end of the pedestal correction.

Now we'll move to the highlight or gain correction (see Fig. 4-41). Once again, we have nice white keys to use as we set our highlights. The blue channel is closest to being correct and the red channel needs the most help. Let's set all of these so that the highlights on the white keys in the middle of the frame are at 100 IRE. That might be too bright but we'll start with that goal to spread out the tonal range as much as possible, then we can look at the video monitor and determine if 100 IRE is too bright for this image.

From Figure 4-41, where I left the gain controls, there is some green above 100 IRE but the main shapes across the 100 IRE line match across all three channels. Notice though that the blacks in the red channel are slightly elevated now because the gain change was so radical. We'll need to fix that (see Fig. 4-42), then decide what we want to do with the gammas.

Now that I'm satisfied that the gains and pedestals match across the three color channels, we need to decide what to do with the gammas. First, let's look at the RGB parade display in Fig. 4-42 and figure out what we're looking at. We only have a couple of elements to figure out. There are the hands, the brown piano wood, and the black and white keys. What is what in the waveform? Well, the area between 0 IRE and 20 IRE to the right of each cell is the black keys and probably some of the dark wood to the right of the image. The area in the middle of each cell between 90 IRE and 100 IRE is the highlight on the white keys in the middle of the screen. The area to the left and extending past the middle of each channel between about 80 IRE and 30 IRE is the hands. In the red channel, this shape goes up to about

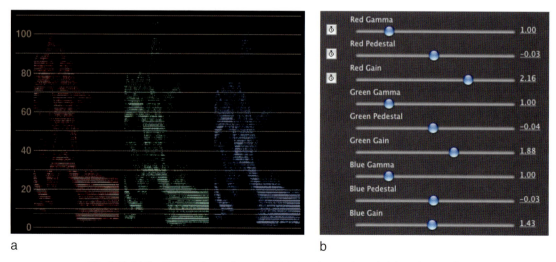

a   b

Fig. 4-41 (a) The RGB parade waveform and (b) the numbers at the end of the gain correction.

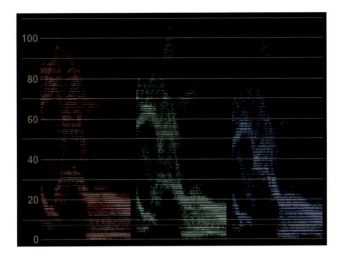

Fig. 4-42 This RGB Parade shows the revision to the black levels after the gain correction elevated them after the first black level correction.

90 IRE, probably due to the highlight on the pinky-finger side of the hand.

You may think that we need to even out the discrepancy in the levels in the 80 IRE to 30 IRE zone, which is definitely defined as gamma, but consider the color of flesh. It's pretty red and fairly yellow without much blue. Considering that, the RGB parade may be sitting just about right.

But we wouldn't be doing our job, and I would be contradicting my own advice, if we didn't try to focus our correction and see what we can do with the skin tones and any other colors in the gammas. However, trying to focus color in gammas is not something you can generally do with scopes. This is where you have to turn your eyes to the actual image and find where the image is most pleasing or correct visually.

I started by making an adjustment to the blue gammas and the skin tone and the tops of the piano keys quickly started getting too yellow as I dropped the blue gammas. Raising the blue gammas added too much coolness to the flesh tones in the hands.

Changing the green gammas downward pulled some green noise out of the wood and skin tones, though going just slightly too far quickly started making the image go very magenta. Lowering the green gamma also added a nice richness to the dark wood of the piano. Raising the greens instantly started looking sickly.

Bringing down the red tones certainly doesn't help the skin tones. Raising them creates a nice warm glow to the dark piano wood, but moving it too much adds an unnatural oversaturated look to the hands first and then to the wood.

Figure 4-43 shows where we started and where we ended up after all corrections.

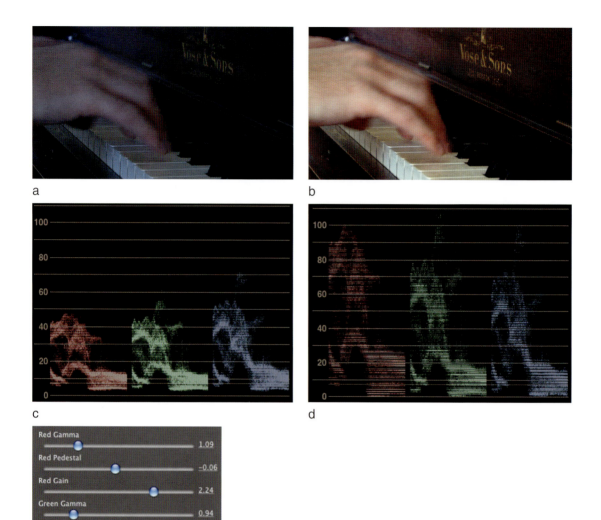

a

b

c

d

e

Fig. 4-43 **(a)** The source image, **(b)** the final corrected image, **(c)** the source RGB parade waveform before correction, **(d)** the RGB parade waveform after correction, and **(e)** Color Finesse RGB sliders in their corrected positions.

Channels

Avid Symphony and After Effects allow you to see the individual channels as black-and-white images and Symphony allows you to blend the channels together in combinations that include not only red, green, and blue, but also Luma, Cr, Cb, and an offset percentage.

The black-and-white views are handy visual tools, but don't give you too much more information than the RGB waveform. Figure 4-44 shows the individual channels for red, green, and blue.

Green looks pretty much like you would expect for a black-and-white representation of the "ChromaDuMonde" chip chart, except that the dark grays are a little stretched out and the upper grays are a little compressed. The red channel looks like nothing is really clipped or badly crushed but all of it is pretty dark compared to the green channel. The blue channel really shows the clipping in the upper whites, just as I suspected it would, but notice that the chips from the blacks up to the midtones match pretty well between the green channel and the blue channel. Nearly all of the upper gray chips are almost the same luminance value in the blue channel; this explains why our previous correction looks like it does. Compare what the three channels are showing you visually against the Tektronix RGB parade waveform image in Figure 4-45.

In the RGB parade waveform, you can see how compressed the chips above the midtone are in the blue channel. This is actually giving you more information, but it's just not so visually simple to digest. The waveform is showing you that even though the green channel image looked pretty good, it actually has quite a bit of clipping going on in the upper grays.

Fixing these issues with channels is a different matter than *seeing* them, though. With channels, the way to fix the problems is to combine channels with each other. This is basically way too unintuitive for most color corrections, but it can save you—if you have access to a channels-like interface—with some really nasty corrections.

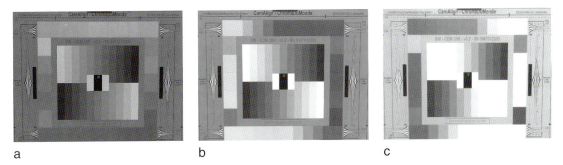

a   b   c

Fig. 4-44 The individual black-and-white channels for **(a)** red, **(b)**, green, and **(c)** blue.

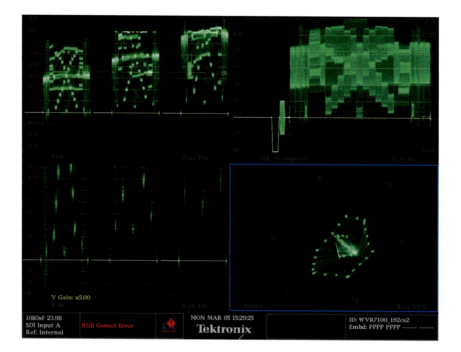

Fig. 4-45 Tektronix RGB parade waveform image.

There are two main situations where I find myself turning to channels. The first is when a color channel is completely or almost completely missing. Sometimes this happens on multicamera shoots where a single color channel gets shorted out going to the isolation (iso) deck. The camera seems fine going into the switcher, but not the iso deck. When this happens I can try to "fake" the missing color channel using channels.

I also use channels with very noisy video. Nine times out of ten, the noise primarily resides in a single channel. By reducing the strength of the noisy channel and mixing it with the cleaner channels, I can take out the noise.

You should know that channels are only going to get you so far in saving things. In almost every color correction that I start in channels, I have to use other tools to fix what I broke in the image.

I'm not going to get into a detailed explanation of this tool because very few applications have it. What I did here (see Figure 4-46) was to look at what was wrong with a given channel and try to correct it by reducing the percentage of the problem channel and mixing it with a percentage of a channel that had attributes that would address the missing elements of the bad channel. Sometimes this causes some whacked-out color shifts.

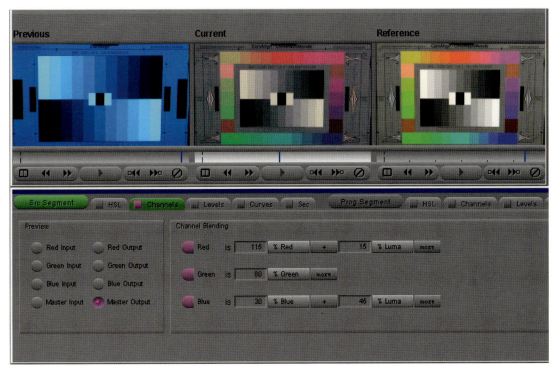

Fig. 4-46 Avid Symphony's Channel Tab in the color correction mode.

The goal here is to try to make the picture look more normal than what you started with. For me, channels is really only a last-ditch stop for fixing bad technical problems. If you have access to channels in your application and want more information on how to use it properly, I would suggest checking out one of the many Photoshop color correction books, such as *Photoshop Color Correction* by Michael Kieran. There is an entire chapter on blending channels in that book. Photoshop offers a much greater capability to blend many different channels using options beyond those available in Avid Symphony.

After Effects also has a similar color correction tool called Channel Mixer, which can be found at Effects > Adjust > Channel Mixer. The Channel Mixer defaults to having the red channel be 100% red, the green channel be 100% green, and the blue channel be 100% blue. You can also combine each color channel with one of the other two color channels by percentage or you can choose the Constant ("Const") option, which specifies the amount of the input channel to be added to the output. Color can't do this type of correction but there is a channel mixer plug-in for Final Cut Pro that does this.

Printer Lights

There is another option on several color correction systems including Color and IRIDAS's SpeedGrade DI. You can choose to alter the color the way the film industry has done it for decades: with printer lights. This is *not* going to give you a lot of control.

Basically this process turns your highly specialized, finely tuned digital color correction workhorse into an analog processor that harkens back to the dawn of color film: changing the color correction of scenes with a paper tape reader controlling the relative light levels of the red, green, and blue printer lights that create the film print from the negative. This additive color timing of a film print uses printer points or printer lights calibrated with intervals from 1 up to 50 for each channel. See Fig. 4-47. Typically, a printer is set up to the default exposure of 25 red, 25 green, and 25 blue, which is right where Color's default levels are set. To raise any given channel, you lower its numerical value. If you want to raise the overall brightness of a scene, you lower all three color channels evenly. There is no ability to change relative levels for each tonal range. Of course in SpeedGrade and Color you can combine the use of printer lights with any other tools in the system.

Filters

In addition to the various tools that give you primary color correction control, there are numerous effects plug-ins for color correction, editing, and compositing software that allow you to place filters on your image to make global corrections such as **duotone**, **sepia tone**, **bleach bypass**,

Fig. 4-47 This is the actual control device for color correcting major motion pictures. I took this at Deluxe Labs in Hollywood, CA, while timing a trailer print. Note that, in addition to adding and subtracting red, green or blue, there are also buttons to increase or decrease the overall density (+D and −D, on the little black box in the middle of the picture).

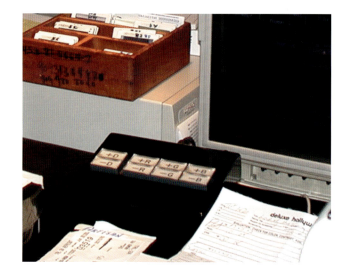

Fig. 4-48 This is the original image to compare filter effects in following figures. Image courtesy of Charles Vanderpool.

Fig. 4-49 Duotone filter applied.

Fig. 4-50 Sepia filter applied.

Fig. 4-51 Bleach bypass filter applied.

a   b

Fig. 4-52 An image with **(a)** no graded filter, and **(b)** with a graded filter. Image courtesy of Artbeats.

"film look," and **gradated filter** looks ("grad"). There are really too many of these to mention and the filter choices are constantly expanding and evolving, but the ability to use them creatively to affect color in your images certainly exists, and I felt I should at least mention the possibility of its use. Use Figure 4-48 as a starting point for all the shown filter corrections in Figures 4-49, 4-50, and 4-51.

Conclusion

The previous four chapters have discussed how to analyze your images as well as the basics of spreading the tonal range of those images and properly balancing the colors.

Many methods and tools were discussed. I hope you'll explore all of the ways you can color correct before getting locked in to a favorite method. One of the things that you will see as you explore deeper into the book is that every colorist develops a different methodology and approach to their corrections and they are all valid and deliver excellent results.

With a solid understanding of primary color correction, we're ready to explore secondary color correction in the next two chapters.

CHAPTER 5

Secondary Color Correction Primer

While primary color correction affects the entire **raster**, secondary color correction limits its affect on specific geographic regions or color vectors. Secondary color correction can also affect specific tonal regions, but these regions are more specific than the shadows, midtones, and highlights that are used to qualify corrections in primary color correction. Figures 5-1 through 5-5 show a few of the interfaces for secondary color correction.

As color correction tools have become more nonlinear, the distinctions between what is primary and what is secondary are beginning to blur. For the purposes of defining workflow, this distinction will probably never totally evaporate, but the boundaries between these two terms are more vague than they have been in the past. As a matter of fact, the boundaries of where secondary color correction ends are also beginning to fall as more color correction applications are offering the ability to add effects and filters to create exciting new looks. I briefly touched on this at the end of Chapter 4 in the "Filters" section, but it could be easily argued that this new effects capability belongs in a discussion of secondary, rather than primary, correction. Where to include effects work depends on whether you feel that primary color correction is a workflow term. If primary and secondary simply define logical steps in a workflow, then effects work is decidedly in the secondary category. On the other hand, if you regard the definition of primary color correction as "global" corrections to the image and secondary corrections as being "qualified" or "targeted" corrections to a portion of an image, then effects is probably a primary correction since many of these filters and effects are applied to an entire image.

The Purpose of Secondary Correction

Virtually every color correction application or nonlinear editor (NLE) with color correction capabilities has a part of their product demo where

> **Definition**
>
> **Raster:** This is computer terminology that has crossed over to video to represent an image created from horizontal lines of individual pixels. The raster refers to the entire video image.

Fig. 5-1 Color's Secondary room. Image courtesy of Artbeats.

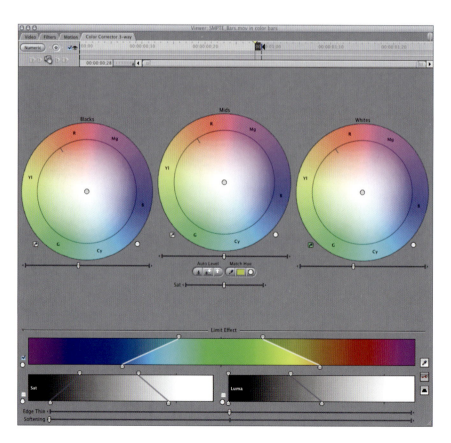

Fig. 5-2 Final Cut Pro's Secondary Effect, called Limit Effect, accessed from a "twirl down" triangle at the bottom of the three-way color corrector.

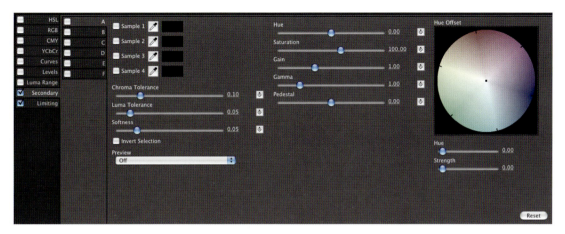

Fig. 5-3 Color Finesse's Secondary tab.

Fig. 5-4 Avid Symphony's secondary color correction tab.

Fig. 5-5 IRIDAS's SpeedGradeDI secondary correction mode.

they turn a car, a shirt, or a product package a different color using **secondaries**.

When I first started color correcting, I rarely used secondaries because I didn't find myself correcting car commercials where they filmed a car with the wrong color. I soon learned that serious colorists rarely use secondary color correction for such obvious chores. Instead, secondaries are used subtly for much more natural corrections. Some of the main

D e f i n i t i o n

Secondaries: Shorthand for secondary color corrections. The plural is often used because most applications allow you to have multiple secondary color corrections on a single image.

D e f i n i t i o n

Vignette: One of the noncolorist meanings for this word is for a photograph or other image that has edges that shade off gradually. To a colorist, vignette is both a noun and a verb. The noun describes a shape placed in a picture to allow a different correction inside and out. Usually this correction is used to create the effect of fading out (darkening usually) the edges of the image. As a verb, it is simply the action of making the vignette or the affect the vignette has on the image, as in "I vignetted it, so the center of the image pops a little better." Additionally, Color uses the word to describe *any* use of a shape to create or modify a secondary.

targets for secondary color corrections are skin tones, sky, water, and grass.

Often, primary color correction has to be done with an eye on the "big picture" and an understanding that the goal is to make *most* of an image look good, but that certain things, like skin tones, may need additional work with secondaries. If you notice, the items I just mentioned—skin tones, sky, water, and grass—are all things that people have a natural understanding and preconceived notion about what colors these things should be. And oftentimes, getting a primary color correction to look good across most of an image will take these specific items out of the color range that most people are expecting. Sometimes, if you want to warm up an entire image, the skin tones will go much too orange. Or by pulling the unwanted blue cast out of an outdoor scene, the grass will turn yellowish. Or by bringing up the levels of the foreground elements of the picture, the sky will become overexposed. All of these things call for a secondary color correction that isolates, or qualifies, the problem area and fixes *just* that portion while leaving the rest of the primary correction alone.

Secondaries are also often used to make the subject of the shot "pop" or to focus the viewer's attention on something important. This is often done with a **vignette**, which slightly darkens the edges of an image and "points" the viewer's eyes to the main focus of the shot. It can also be done by qualifying an important part of the image and increasing the saturation or contrast in that portion of the image to draw the viewer's attention to it.

Are You Qualified?

For me, the biggest issue of secondary color correction is qualification. I'm not talking about whether the colorist is skilled enough to do the work, rather, I'm talking about what portion of an image you are trying to "qualify" as the section in which you make alterations.

In case you missed the earlier glossary item for this word in Chapter 2, "to qualify" or "qualification" means that an area of a picture is specifically isolated for a correction by any number of methods. You could qualify something for correction using its hue, chroma strength, tonal value, or a combination of all three. You could also qualify an area of an image using a window or garbage matte. This is an important concept to grasp. So much of this chapter will be devoted to methods and techniques for qualifying parts of an image. Once a portion of an image is well qualified, altering it is largely based on the skill sets presented in the previous four chapters.

Creating effective qualifications when doing secondary color corrections requires a good understanding of your tools and of your ability to
analyze an image and understand what can be selected and how. Since
this book is not really about developing specialized skill sets with specific
tools, I'll leave that exploration up to you. As for developing an ability
for understanding what can be isolated in a shot, that is a matter of some
experience and, for even the best colorist, a good deal of experimentation.
Of course, the more experienced you are at making these qualifications,
the less experimentation you need. Getting that knowledge and practical
experience is what the rest of this chapter is about.

Qualifications in secondaries are done in three basic ways:

1. Isolating a specific color vector or luminance range, or a
   combination of the two.

2. Using a shape to define a portion of an image.

3. Using a combination of 1 and 2 above.

For all three of these methods, the basic concept is to create a matte or
mask that limits the correction to a specific portion of the image.

There are also three basic steps to doing a secondary color
correction:

1. Determine what you are trying to accomplish.

2. Figure out how you can qualify the correct portion of an image
   without qualifying unwanted areas.

3. Make a correction inside or outside of that qualified area.

Let's take a look at the three methods of qualification and walk
through each of the three steps with each method.

Color Vector Isolation

One of the main secondary color correction qualification methods is to
isolate a specific color vector and alter it in some way. This is a very good
way to do secondaries compared to vignettes or "spot" color correction
because you don't have to worry about camera movement or things
crossing the foreground. The color corrections that you apply to a specific color vector isolation or qualification stay with those pixels as long
as those pixels stay relatively the same color. Passing shadows or other
active lighting effects or semitransparent foreground effects like smoke or

fog will have an effect on color vector isolations though, since they will change the color of the image behind it.

Each color correction application has a slightly different set of controls to accomplish isolating specific color vectors, but most of them work similarly to Color. You can try to isolate the vector in the old-school way by guessing at the correct hue, saturation, and luminance (HSL) values and moving the HSL sliders until you have a clean matte, but nearly everyone will start their qualification of the selected color by sampling it with the eyedropper first.

Nearly all color correction applications have the ability to sample a portion of an image with an eyedropper. Symphony uses a "syringe" for sampling large areas. Each application has slight differences in how the eyedropper works. Some, like Color, allow you to add and subtract from your qualifications using the eyedropper and certain modifier keys. Some applications only allow you to click on a color with the eyedropper, while others allow you to drag over large areas to qualify multiple shades of a color. Some of these eyedroppers only sample the precise pixel that is at the tip of the eyedropper, while others allow you to set a user preference of sampling and averaging a 3×3 grid of pixels around the tip of the eyedropper or even a 5×5 sample. Consult the user's manual for your application on how the eyedropper works (and stay up to date on your application's current way of doing things, since applications evolve and gain new abilities or ways of doing things all the time). Learn the options for the eyedropper tool when creating qualifications.

Let's try doing a color vector qualification in the old-school way so that if you're in an application that doesn't have an eyedropper, you can get something accomplished. Also, learning to do it the hard way helps understand exactly what's going on and makes doing it the easy way even easier.

As we pointed out earlier, the first step of making a secondary correction is to determine what you are trying to accomplish. For this tutorial, our goal is to make the lion be the star of the "Art_institute_proper" clip. The second step is to figure out how to make a qualification that will enable you to accomplish that goal. Looking at the "art_institute_lion_proper" image from the DVD, the lion is fairly green-blue and there doesn't appear to be too much else in the image that is the same hue or saturation as the lion. Much of the rest of the image contains similar luminance levels, so the obvious place to start is to create a key using the hue information.

Load the "art_institute_lion_proper" clip into your color correction application. I'll be using Color for this secondary tutorial. In Color, you go to the Secondary room (which is like a tab) and enable one of the secondaries (there are eight) (see Fig. 5-6).

Fig. 5-6

Before making the qualification, there are a few things you should know: To view the matte that you create with your qualification, make sure the Previews tab under the shadow hue offset wheel is active. In the Previews tab, the left window shows you the clip and allows you to see and manipulate any vignettes or garbage mattes you've created. The right window shows you the matte of any isolations you've made by color vector selections or luminance selections. To the right of that window, there are three small icons, called the Matte Preview Mode buttons. The top one has red, green, and blue rectangles. This is for viewing the image normally in RGB, which is essentially the same image that is in the Scopes window. The middle one has gray and green rectangles and is called the Desaturated Preview. It is a view of your qualified areas in full color and your unqualified areas in black and white (monochrome). The bottom icon has black and white rectangles. This is the Matte Only button and displays the isolation as a black-and-white matte image, with qualified portions in white and unqualified in black.

Click on the icon to see the black-and-white matte on the second monitor. The display is white, indicating that the entire image is selected. Start by selecting only the hue slider and drag the small white left-hand line above the hue bar toward the right. This will narrow the hue selection and pull in the small white line on the right-hand side an equal amount. Then drag the white line inside the hue bar so that it is over the bluish green area of the hue bar. Now use the white lines on top of the hue bar to adjust the width of the hue selection. Moving either white line will move them both. If you want to move just one side of the hue selection, hold down the shift key while you drag. The smaller white lines above the hue bar control the falloff of the selection and will be crucial to creating a nice matte. If you can't see the falloff controls, then use the eyedropper and click on the lion. This will add two little gray triangles with gray handles above the HSL bars. You can adjust the falloff in the same way as the hue selection. See Figure 5-7.

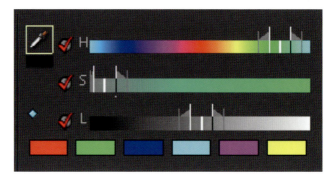

Fig. 5-7 HSL Color Selector in Color's Secondary Room with the qualification for the lion using the eyedropper.

Disable the luminance and saturation controls if you used the eyedropper. Just adjust hue until you get the best selection possible. Use that focusing analogy. Try to get the greatest amount of the lion selected with the least selection of other picture elements. Some of the things to look for in this particular image when selecting with hue are the sky and the banners in the arches of the museum. Even the grayish shadows on the inside of the lower arches have some green in them. They can become qualified depending on the angle and spread of the hue, but you should be able to do a good job of isolating just the lion. Figure 5-8 shows my isolation version.

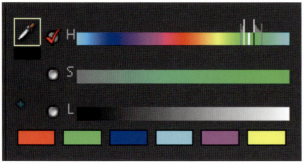

a

b

Fig. 5-8

The correction shown in Fig. 5-8 is not perfect. We want to see if we can isolate the lion more and get less of anything that is not the lion. Also, we need to soften this matte or the correction will look very nasty. In Color, choosing a Key Blur of about 1.0 or 2.0 is a good starting point (see Fig. 5-9). Key Blur is located just below the HSL selectors.

Fig. 5-9 In this image, a keyblur of 2.0 has been added to the matte from 5-8b.

We could further qualify just the lion using a garbage matte created in the vignette section, but for now, see if adjusting the saturation or luminance controls will clean up this qualification any further. After a bit of experimenting, I found that the hue control by itself worked to get the best key.

Before we try to improve the qualification any more, let's see if we can accomplish what we want to do to the lion with the qualification we already have. This is part of the time management of color correction. You could try to really "dial in" a perfect matte for the lion, but it is possible that the fairly rough qualification that we have now will suffice, so why waste any more time on it? Later on, you may discover that in order to really take the secondary correction where you want it to go, you need a better qualification so that your adjustment does not "pollute" other areas of the image.

Our goal with this correction was to make the lion "pop" from the background and be more prominent. I started by taking the midtone hue offset wheel all the way down to cyan on the outside edge of the wheel, then I decided that I didn't want to have the lion's hue swing to a new direction, I just wanted to increase the saturation and contrast of the color that already existed. So I reset my hue offset wheel and just increased the saturation and lowered the gamma, lift, and even the gain a bit. Figure 5-10 shows the numbers.

Key Blur	2.000000
Hue	0.000000
Saturation	2.023650
Highlight Sat.	0.000000
Shadow Sat.	1.787850
Master Lift	−0.069600
Master Gain	0.881100
Master Gamma	0.618650

Fig. 5-10

Figure 5-11 shows the before (a) and after (b). This isn't a final correction, just a secondary on the lion. I also included a diagonal split image to see the difference (Fig. 5-11c).

Before moving on to the spot color corrections, or vignettes as they're known in Color, let's take a look at color vector isolations in Avid Symphony. I realize that Symphony is not a widely popular application for color correction, but even if you don't have Symphony, don't skip ahead, because Symphony has an interesting graphical user interface (GUI) that allows you to better understand and visualize what you are doing as you isolate these color vectors. See Figure 5-12.

Notice the two vectorscope-like images in the bottom center of Figure 5-12. The one to the left shows the vector you've selected. The one to the right shows the way you have moved that selected vector.

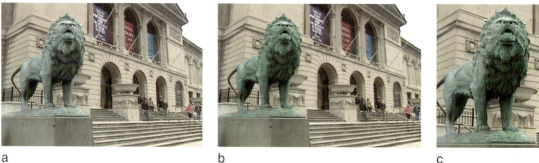

a   b   c

Fig. 5-11 Seeing the subtlety of the correction may be difficult in the color space of the printed image.

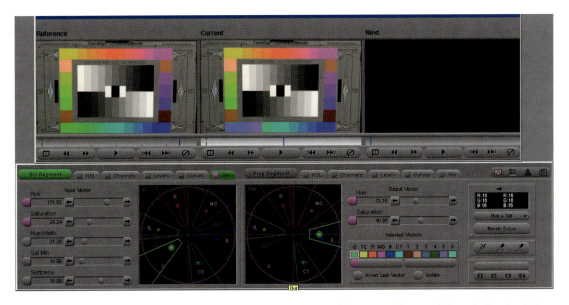

Fig. 5-12 Avid Symphony's secondary UI. Note that the green "wedge" in the left "vectorscope" is moved above the blue "wedge" on the right "vectorscope." This moved all the green chips on the chart to blue.

Actually, the entire bottom of the user interface (UI) is split in two to divide the functionalities of the two sides. To the left, all of the sliders under the words "Input Vector" are controls to *define* the vector that you want to qualify or isolate. To the right, under the words "Output Vector," all of the controls *affect* that selected vector. So, the left controls *define* the vector that you want to isolate and the right controls *affect* that vector. Not all applications break it down into this nice, obvious division of tasks, but they all work the same way. You need to figure out in your application what are the *defining* tools and what are the *affecting* or controlling tools. Once you understand that, everything will make sense.

Note: At the bottom of the right side of this UI is a section that is called "Selected Vectors." This section actually belongs on the left side logically, because it allows you to *define* a vector by clicking on one of the colored squares, but Avid's UI designers probably didn't have room for it on the proper side and there was space to the right. These "Selected Vectors" was how I actually selected the green vector for this image. You can see that the green color square is highlighted in white.

To understand what defining and moving the vector does, look at the reference image of the ChromaDuMonde chart at the top left. This is the source image. Notice the green color chips at the bottom left of the ChromaDuMonde chart. These are the colors that fall within the area defined by the green vector that has been selected for correction (see Fig. 5-12).

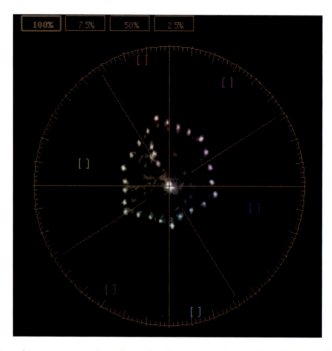

Fig. 5-13 Looking at the vectorscope, you can see the location of the green color chips on the vectorscope. The three selected color chips fall within the area on the vectorscope defined by the green vector area on the Symphony UI.

Notice these same color chips in the center image in the UI. The green color chips are now bluish purple because the green vector was swung toward the blue-purple vector in the output vector.

Notice the numbers on the input and output sides. On the input side, the numbers define a specific degree of hue and amount of saturation that have been selected. On the output side, you see the new angle to which the hue has been swung and the fact that the saturation has been increased. This saturation increase is also displayed visually by the vectorscope image, which has the green vector pulled out slightly further on the output side than the input side. Just like a vectorscope, the distance from the center of the vectorscope shows the amount or power of the saturation.

To get a better understanding of this, it is possible in the Symphony UI to isolate the vector you are trying to define and to display all of the unselected vectors as gray. To make it more clear what we are selecting, we'll switch to the "isolate" mode. (Many other applications have a similar mode.)

In Figure 5-14, we spread the input vector, which could also be known as our "isolation" or "defined" or "qualified" vector, and rotated the hue a bit so that we isolated only the bottom row of green color chips. Notice the numbers for hue are slightly different than in our first example. I needed to rotate the hue slightly so that only the color chips in the bottom row were isolated. Also notice the hue width number is much larger, which allowed us to select all nine of the bottom color chips instead of just the three that were selected in the first example. You can see this visually on the left vectorscope-like image in the UI, which has expanded to cover

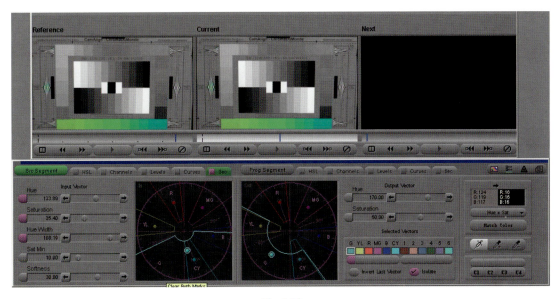

Fig. 5-14

a larger portion of the vectorscope. (The small dot with the circle around it in the middle of the chosen vector is the control point for moving the vector.) You can see in the Current window at the top center of the UI that all of the color chips at the bottom have been chosen.

If we rotate the hue one direction or another, we would deselect some of the chips along the bottom and start to select chips going up one side or the other of the ChromaDuMonde chart. In Figure 5-15, the vector was swung toward blue. Notice that we haven't changed or affected the colors in this example. We are simply defining a slightly different set of colors by rotating and spreading the hue.

Symphony also has a set of vectors called custom vectors that are the vector selections you create when you use the syringe or eyedropper to pick colors off of the source clip. Instead of looking like arcs joined by straight lines, custom vectors are round or oval shaped. I created a custom vector by clicking on the top left skin-tone color chip on the ChromaDuMonde chart. (see Fig. 5-16) (The color chips ringing the ChromaDuMonde chart are meant to mimic the colors around the vectorscope, except for the four chips just above or below the corners. These four chips are "skin tone" color chips, representing various racial skin tones, or just people with really good tans.)

I picked a skin tone because skin tones are common things to target for secondary color corrections. Notice the very tight selection area on the source vectorscope image (Figure 5-16). This has selected only the top left color chip, while leaving the other three skin-tone chips unselected. This is one of the goals of isolating a vector for secondary color correction.

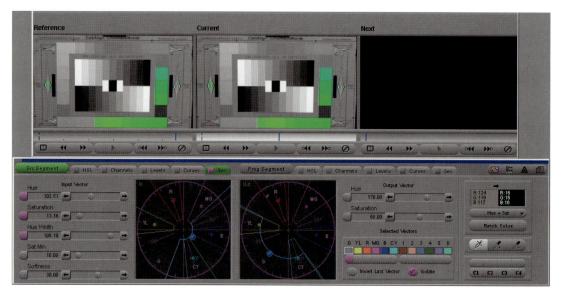

Fig. 5-15

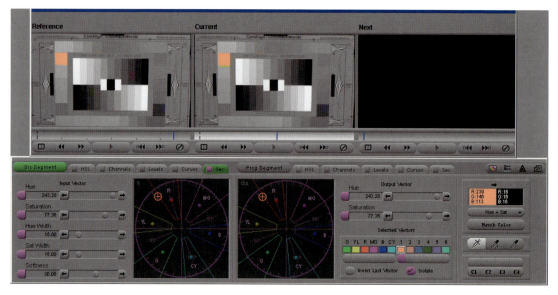

Fig. 5-16 A single skin tone chip on the ChromaDuMonde chart selected.

To select the other skin-tone chips, you could see if swinging the hue or increasing the hue width would select them, but as I've mentioned before, almost all skin tones line up right along the -I line of the vectorscope, regardless of race. So, to select the other skin tones, the other choice is to increase the saturation width (see Fig. 5-17). Notice how the

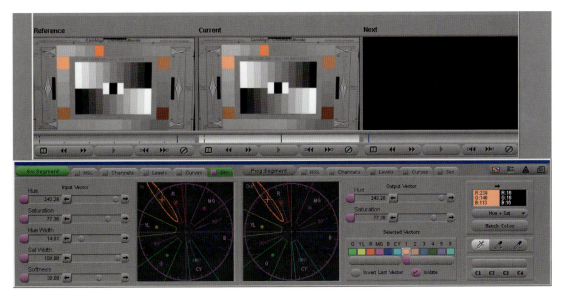

Fig. 5-17 All four skin tone chips plus the red chip on the ChromaDuMonde chart selected.

custom vector in this image selects more levels of saturation extending from the middle of the vectorscope outwards. This effectively selects the other skin-tone chips as well as one of the regular color chips that is also very similar to skin tone.

I'd be remiss if I didn't also show how to pull off a color vector isolation in the ever-popular and ubiquitous Final Cut Pro (FCP), so here it is.

Isolating a Vector in Final Cut Pro

In FCP, import the "ultralight_field" clip from the DVD. Add a color-corrector three-way to your clip and drag that tab over to the side so you can see the color-corrector three-way UI and the clip at the same time. At the bottom is a small "twirl down" triangle to the left of a line with the words "Limit Effect" in the middle. Click on the small triangle to reveal the Limit Effect UI (see Fig. 5-18).

Click on the small eyedropper to the right of the long HSL color bar. We're going to try to isolate the green grass. In a later exercise in this chapter, we'll isolate the grass with a spot correction or vignette. The best way to do this is with this color vector isolation because the camera tilts up, and for the spot correction to work, it needs to be tracked or animated to match the move. With this color vector isolation the correction will go wherever the grass matches the color of the selected vector, so even if the ultralight lands on the grass, the color correction will still work. With a spot color correction, the ultralight would change colors if

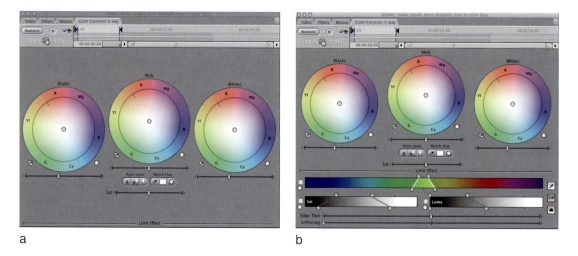

Fig. 5-18 FCP color-corrector three-way effect **(a)** with Limit Effect twirl down at the bottom **(b)**.

it violated the area defined by the spot color correction (or vignette in Color's terminology).

Once you have the Select Color eyedropper active, click or drag on the grassy area. This will define an HSL range on the controls of the Limit Effect UI. Then click on the small icon of a key under the Select Color eyedropper. This is the View Final Matte/Source button. It will change the viewer from a display of the image to the matte that is being created by your selections in the Limit Effect UI.

The goal here is to select all of the grassy color without selecting any of the sky or ultralight. Looking at this image, this should be a pretty easy task, since the sky is such a different hue from the grass. Both the sky and the grass have a range of luminance values and saturation levels. Trying to isolate the grass with luma or saturation alone is probably not going to work, but using hue alone might work. Turn off the check boxes next to the Luma and Saturation control bars, then start to spread out the width of the Hue controls by clicking on the little gray control handles and spreading the hue range out. You can control where the hue range is centered by clicking on the bar itself. When the cursor becomes a hand, you can drag the bar one direction or the other. You want to get as clean a line on the horizon as possible in this case. If you don't get enough blue in the selection, the horizon gets raggedy on the left side. If you get too much blue, you start to select the ultralight. Keep spreading the range until you get as much grass selected without selecting the ultralight. It also helps to soften the matte a little. If you soften it too much, you will get a strange glow of your correction where you don't want it. The Softening control is at the bottom of the Limit Effect portion of the color-corrector three-way UI. With the green grass selected, you can swing the midtones toward green to create a nice, spring-like feeling. See Figure 5-19.

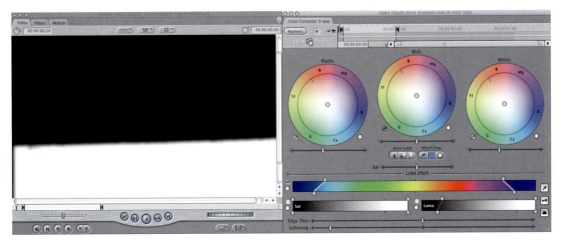

Fig. 5-19 I ended up with a very wide selection; basically every hue except blue and purple.

If you want to continue the correction and work on the sky, add another color-corrector three-way effect and make the exact same correction that you made for the grass, repeating the above steps exactly. Once you have properly qualified the grass, click on the small icon that looks like a keystone under the Select Color eyedropper and View Final Matte/Source button (the one that looks like a key). This keystone icon is the Invert Selection button and allows you to color correct the opposite side of the selection. I pumped up the gain and brought down the midtones of the sky and then boosted the blue using the midtone hue offset wheel and balanced some of the blue out of the clouds by edging the highlight hue offset wheel toward yellow (see Fig. 5-20).

Fig. 5-20 Compare the matte shape in Figure 5-19 to the actual image in Figure 5-20.

Isolation Practice

To practice the ability to isolate a single color in an image, use the "ChromaDuMonde_properexwhite" clip from the DVD and work with your secondary color vector selection tools to isolate individual color chips or specifically choose sets of two or three or more chips from the others. Using the ChromaDuMonde chart is good for getting the basics of hue selection "under your fingers" but you'll need something more natural for making other selections based on various levels of saturation. The ChromaDuMonde color chips are all basically the same saturation except for the skin-tone chips.

Plus, one of the other skills that you need to practice is in determining the right falloff or softness levels that allow you to grab, for example, all of the skin tones on a face that is half in shadow, or all of the tones of a shirt that has numerous levels of chroma and luminance because of folds, shadows, and highlights.

Choose some other clips from the DVD and see if you can isolate various portions of the image. Want a challenge? Try these:

- Isolate the skin tones in "piano_correct." The highlights of the skin are similar to the aged yellow of the tops of the white piano keys. As I've stated before, skin tones are one of the big things that colorists like to tweak as a secondary.

- In any of the ultralight clips, try to isolate the entire wing of the ultralight while keeping other colors out of the selection. This would be a common correction for a number of reasons. If the video is for the ultralight manufacturer, they may require the color to be a very specific shade to properly represent the product they're delivering. For other purposes, the producer may just want to "pop" the ultralight out of the image, calling attention to it through color contrast.

- In the "Jackie_interview" clip, try to isolate her skin tones without selecting the same tones in the wall to the left or in the door behind her. (This can't be done without the addition of a garbage mask of some sort, but practicing with this real-world image is a great experience.) What would you do if a director of photography asked for a specific correction to the skin, but didn't want to see that correction in the rest of the image?

- In the "Railroad_LM112" Artbeats' clip, isolate the suitcase. In an image like this, it would be common to ask for more emphasis to be placed on an important prop so that the audience would think of how it relates to the storyline or so that they remember its presence in the scene at some later point.

- In the "8mm_loading_gear" clip, attempt to isolate the yellow jacket or orange life jackets. With the jacket, I found it helpful to turn off saturation (in other words, *not* to limit by saturation) because the jacket's saturation levels go from white to yellow. Yellow is one of the colors that people often wish to tweak specifically. Oftentimes, a shade of yellow with more red in it is desired, yet that red cast is *not* desired in the rest of the image.

- In the "Football_SP123H1" Artbeats' clip, try to isolate the football and hand from the grass. To attempt the impossible, try to isolate the ball from the hand. This isolation figures prominently in some of the upcoming corrections by our panel of colorists later in the book.

- Figure 5-21 ("DeltaE_8bit_gamma2.2.tif" on the DVD) is another good image, created by noted color scientist Bruce Lindbloom, to use for many experiments, because there is shading in the image and various levels of saturation in many different hues.

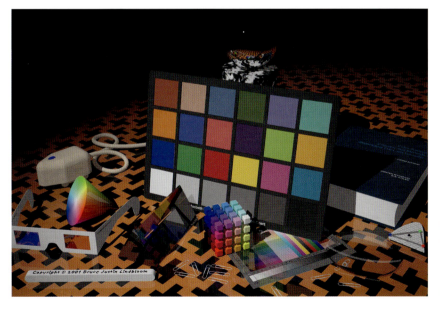

Fig. 5-21 The "DeltaE_8bit_gamma2.2.tif" image from the DVD. Image courtesy of Bruce Lindbloom (www.brucelindbloom.com).

Spot Color Correction (Vignettes or Power Windows)

Another form of secondary color correction is called *spot color correction*, or *vignettes* in Color, and *Power Windows* in da Vinci. The basic concept is to draw a shape on the screen and color correct inside or outside of that shape. In the early days of Power Windows, you could only use geometric shapes—variations on circles and squares. Now, most of the file-based color correctors like Color and others allow you to draw custom shapes using Bezier curves or B-Spline Curves. Many of these vignettes, windows, or spot correction shapes can also be tracked to the movement of the shot, which is important in many shots.

Shot movement, whether it's camera movement or movement within the frame of a locked-down shot, will be a big factor in whether or not you choose to use a spot color correction. In the example we just did of the lion at the Art Institute, the camera is locked down, the lion doesn't move, and no one crosses in front of the lion or even gets near it, so that shot is a great candidate for a spot correction or to use a garbage matte to further isolate the color vector correction. We'll discuss this in the next tutorial.

There are a couple of reasons to use a spot color correction. One of the ways is to use it very globally to darken the corners of an image and focus attention on the subject in the middle—called "vignetting." This is usually done with a very soft oval shape placed right in the middle of the image. With this use, you don't really have to worry too much about shot movement because the spot correction is supposed to look more like an in-camera effect anyway. Another reason for a spot correction is to pick a portion of the frame and affect it in much the same way as the color vector secondary would be used: to pick an area to enhance or fix a problem with the primary correction. The third way to use spot correction is almost as a postlighting tool. You can add this kind of selection to almost spotlight certain regions of the frame. If you are familiar with making prints in a darkroom, this can be similar to dodging and burning. Let's do a tutorial for each of these reasons.

Vignette

Vignette is Color's term for spot correction. One of the meanings of the English word "vignette" means a photograph whose edges fade off gradually. The following tutorial is not about Color's meaning, but the creation of a vignetted image.

The vignette is often used to focus the audience's attention in the middle of the screen. It can also create the point-of-view feeling that you are watching the image through someone else's eyes (as opposed to being a third-person participant). Vignetting is also a common trick to salvage large flat areas of a shot, like a boring sky or a huge, blank wall that was lit flatly. The vignette add interest and texture to images.

Faking Spot Corrections

If you don't have a color correction application that allows for spot color correction, you can usually fake it with the tools in most NLE systems. Copy a clip from your timeline and edit it on a track directly above the clip from which you copied it. Correct one of the clips for the optimum look of the inside of the correction and correct the other clip for the look that you want on the outside of the correction. Use a soft-edged wipe to transition between the two of them. You may need to actually create a matte and place it on another track. Each NLE deals with mattes differently, so consult your user manual about the channel on which to place the matte and the channels for the "darkened" and "proper" versions of your color corrections.

On an Avid, for example, the recipe would be to put the correct clip on the bottom track (V1), the darkened clip on the second clip above it (V2), and a matte clip with black around the edges and a soft, white center on the top track (V3). Then add a matte key effect to the top track. See Figure 5-22, and the matte for this effect, "mattekeyvignette.psd" on the DVD.

In Final Cut Pro, the effect would be accomplished slightly differently. Place the dark clip on the bottom (V1), the correctly graded clip on the top track (V3), and the matte clip goes in between. Then right-click or Control-click on the top clip and select Composite Mode from the pulldown menu, then Travelling Matte—Luma. In FCP, you could also generate your gradient for the second track right inside of FCP using the Generator button on the Viewer and choosing Render, then creating a radial shape and placing the start point somewhere near the middle or wherever you want it. See Figure 5-23.

Call up the "Kissme.mov" clip from the DVD into Color or some other application that allows you to make spot color corrections. In Color, go to a secondary and enable it and enable the vignette. Then draw an oval that goes from edge to edge and almost from top to bottom (see Fig. 5-24a). You can soften this circle by either center-dragging (center-dragging on many mice is the scroll wheel) in the circle or by changing the softness in the vignette control area (see Fig. 5-24b).

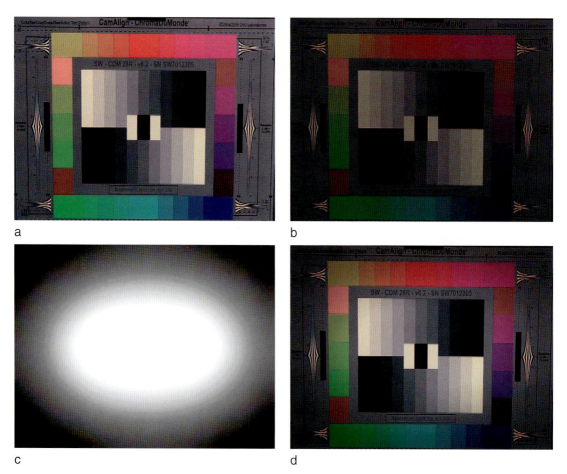

Fig. 5-22 **(a)** is the correct image. **(b)** is the darkened image. **(c)** is the matte that defines the vignette. **(d)** is the resulting vignetted image. Notice the shading around the outside of the image.

Fig. 5-23 Screenshot showing the timeline using Composite Mode.

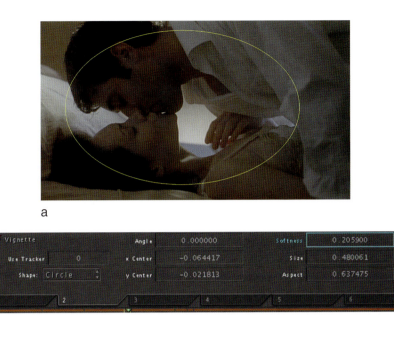

a

b

Fig. 5-24 The vignette controls from Color's Secondary Room. The yellow oval in the "A" image is part of the UI and will not show up in the final image. It simply shows you the outline of the shape that has been drawn.

Once you have at least a starting point for the shape and softness, you can choose the Control pulldown at the top right of the Secondary tab, near the HSL controls, and select whether you want to correct either the inside or outside of the vignette. You can choose to do both inside and outside corrections if you want to. I actually chose to lower the gain and midtones outside of the oval and bring up the chroma a bit inside the oval.

Fig. 5-24(c) is the image with a pretty strong vignette. We'll be seeing examples of vignettes in the color corrections that our panel of colorists execute in the coming chapters. I made this vignette pretty bold to emphasize what I was trying to do, but most of the vignettes that you'll see later in the book are much more subtle. These vignettes are very hard to show in print unless they're fairly obvious, which is the *opposite* thing that most colorists are trying to accomplish with vignettes.

Instead of a very broad oval that covers a lot of the image, you could also "aim" the center of the vignette to the focal point of the image. In Fig. 5-24(d), the correction remains the same as in Fig. 5-24(c), but the oval is centered on the kiss and the softness is expanded. The yellow lines are optional UI overlays that let you know the boundaries and shape of the vignette. You can see that this can be a very effective way of enhancing a shot.

c

Fig. 5-24 *(Continued)* **(c)** The image with a pretty strong vignette **(d)** The same correction, but with the vignette centered more on the faces.

d

Geographical Color Fix

You can also use spot color correction to solve a problem that exists in just a specific area of a picture or to enhance a specific area of a picture. For our example, call up the "ultralight_field" clip from the DVD.

This is not the best way to select the grass and/or sky, but it will work for the purpose of the tutorial. The best way to do this correction in real life is to use the same method that we used earlier in the chapter when explaining the FCP Limit Effect using the same clip. Let's continue with this method though so that you see how two different methods can be used to the same end result.

Figure 5-25(a) is very washed out, but it also looks like the top of the image needs to be treated in a much different way than the bottom of the picture, below the horizon. Normally, you would try to balance the picture and expand the contrast first in a primary color correction,

a

Fig. 5-25

but I'm going to take this right to a secondary color correction to make my point.

The first thing to do is to select the grass area with a window of some sort. I will do this correction in Color, so I will go into secondaries and enable a secondary and vignette. Choose a square shape and drag it out, positioning it so that the top of the resulting rectangle is roughly placed on the horizon, which is slightly off-angle. Color has an angle control that can be used to precisely align the top of the rectangle with the horizon. You can also add a slight softness to the rectangle.

For the purpose of this tutorial, we'll address a single frame of the shot, but the camera does actually tilt up over the course of the shot, so in a real-life situation, you would need to track the rectangle to follow the tilt (Color is capable of doing this) or add keyframes in a program that is not able to track so that the shot's horizon would stay lined up with your spot correction's horizon.

With the grass defined as the inside of the correction, you can adjust the contrast and colors of the grass alone, just as you would in a normal primary color correction. Originally, I started by trying to use the hue offset wheels to pull the grass toward green, but when I added a pretty heavy correction in the master lift, the saturation of my green color looked really bad. I reset my hue offset wheels and worked on contrast first. I chose to lower the master lift and slightly lower gamma and barely raise gain. With the contrast and tone set, I pulled the midtones away from blue just a little to improve the color of the grass. I also did similar, very minor corrections to highlights and shadows in the same direction. The darker overall shade of my grass correction helps focus attention up toward the ultralight. See Fig. 5-25(b).

b

Fig. 5-25 (Continued) Note the fine UI lines at the horizon of the ultralight shot which define the edge of the spot correction, or vignette.

Once the color of the grass is complete, switch the secondary control from inside to outside. With the sky, I started working on the contrast first. I brought down the master lift a lot. This popped the ultralight against the sky because it's the only really dark element in the top half of the image. I brought up the gain so that the clouds would "read" better against the blue of the sky and I brought down the gammas a bit to stretch the contrast between the sky and the clouds even further. Then I pulled the midtones toward blue pretty severely. The midtones really only affected the blue sky (remember that the grass is being protected from the midtone correction by the spot correction). I pulled the highlights, essentially the clouds, away from blue so that the clouds would be more cleanly balanced toward white. See Figure 5-25(c).

The result is something that could not be executed in a primary color correction, which is apparent when you see the wildly different corrections that went into the top and bottom of the image. See Figure 5-25(d).

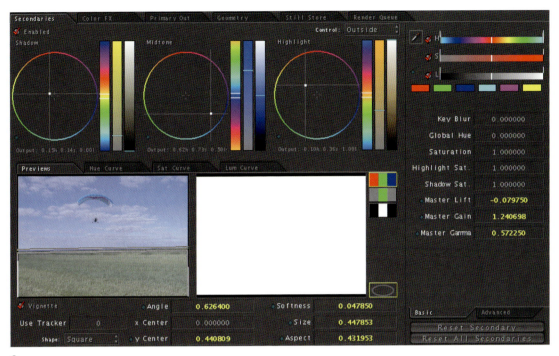

c

d   e

Fig. 5-25 *(Continued)* In (c) the qualification is the unchanged, but instead of correcting inside the qualification, we are correcting outside the qualification. Here again (d) is the image before the correction and the result (e).

User-Defined Shapes

Many file-based systems, like Color or Symphony, allow you to hand draw organic shapes to define their geographical areas on the screen. This is a very powerful tool that I both encourage and discourage you from using.

On one hand, these custom shapes are very valuable for at least two reasons: First, using squares and circles is obviously fairly limiting when you are trying to isolate a specific portion of the screen. Second, organic shapes are much less likely to be noticed as spot corrections. (You don't want *any* spot color correction to be noticed. That is a sure sign that it hasn't been done properly.) But even watching the best TV spots with a trained eye, you can see vignetting that has been done by a skilled colorist if you know what to look for. With a custom shape, it is very hard to see even a fairly extreme spot correction because the shape is not uniform. This is the same concept as camouflage in military and hunting use. A camouflaged person or truck is just as visible as any other person or truck, but the camouflage pattern works by breaking up the easily defined shapes that humans and animals are used to identifying as another human being or truck.

The only real down side to these custom shapes is that they tend to take a little longer and are usually a little less flexible in most applications when it comes to resizing, altering aspect, or rotating them. I don't want to say that you shouldn't do it the best way instead of the easy way, but you need to keep your deadline and budget in mind.

One of the most adamant users of these custom shapes for secondary color correction is veteran Chicago colorist Pete Jannotta: "I always prefer to draw (custom shapes) because even in da Vinci I don't use a fixed circle ever anymore. What I like to do is draw the shape and then move it around so I can see how the light is working. I don't care what the shape is, but if it's an oval, then it's fixed and I can't control it."

Using Spot Color Correction to Relight

One of the subsets of reasons to use a spot color correction is the ability to effectively relight an image in post production. This is not to cast aspersions on **directors of photography** in any way. They are under the same time constraints for lighting the scene that we are under for grading it in post, so sometimes what the director of photography *wants* to do just doesn't happen on the set.

When trying to relight a scene using spot correction, the use of user-defined shapes is very important because they can be shaped the way a pool of light might normally fall. Using these tools, you can remove **spill** where it wasn't wanted or add a little extra "punch" to a face or to eyes that didn't quite get enough light on set.

Color Vector with Garbage Matte

Sometimes it is impossible to qualify something with a color vector isolation alone and that is where the third method comes in, which is a combination of the color vector isolation assisted by a **garbage matte** (which is basically just another vignette in Color).

Let's go back to the first image we tried in this chapter, the Art Institute lions. Load the "art_institute_lion_proper" clip into your color correction application. Now try to select the lion again with a color vector isolation, or if you saved your isolation from the first example, then load it up. The best isolation that I could come up with looked like Figure 5-27.

Notice that the lion was pretty well selected, but I also selected some of the grayish green pedestal that the lion is standing on as well as some grayish green tones in the steps, under the arches, and in the eaves of the building. In the first example, we corrected the lion without further qualifying the isolated areas and we were able to do our corrections without damaging the rest of the image too much.

In this exercise, we want to get a much cleaner key and the only way to do that is to add a garbage matte so that will key out the rest of the isolation that we don't want. In Color, this is done by enabling the vignette portion of the same secondary in which the color vector isolation was executed.

Garbage Matte: A shape that is made to exclude or reinclude portions of an image that have been affected by some other procedure, such as a color vector isolation. Garbage mattes are commonly used in green-screen work to key out large portions of an image that are not properly included as part of the chroma key. Garbage mattes effectively clean up the garbage left by other procedures or processes. They tend to be fairly rough and are drawn quite distinctly clear of whatever boundary the other process is trying to select. So in the case of a color vector selection, the garbage matte selects a rough area around the color vector selection, which cleans up (deselects) any other unwanted portions of the image that had been selected by the color vector isolation. See Figure 5-26.

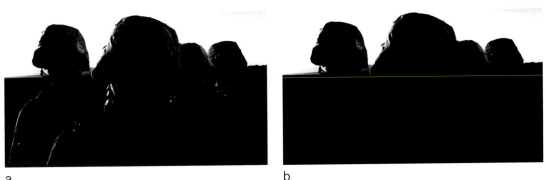

a   b

Fig. 5-26 **(a)** This is a matte created from luma of "MAR115H1" from Artbeats. Notice the unwanted highlight areas lower on the Marines' clothing. **(b)** This is the same matte with a garbage matte applied so that only the portions of the luma matte above the yellow line will be used for the qualification.

Fig. 5-27 This is the matte made by the qualification in the earlier tutorial. Some of the building is also qualified in this matte.

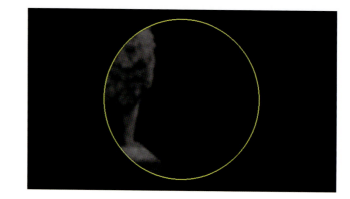

Fig. 5-28 This is the same matte as figure 5-27 with the addition of a vignette. The size and position of the circle is the default. You can see that it has further qualified the matte to only work inside the circle.

TIP

For those of you with the ability to do custom shapes, you do not need to add a lot of points. Adding lots of points slows down the processing time because the computer has to track every one of those points. It also makes moving all of those points trickier, even though in Color and many other applications, you can move groups of "lassoed" points together. You should be able to get very accurate shapes with fewer points using Bezier curves and controlling the handles.

If the secondary is enabled and you're looking at the Preview mode with the matte view selected (showing the matte on the second monitor), you will instantly see what the garbage matte does. See Figure 5-28.

Of course, that's not exactly what you want it to do, so we need to modify it a bit. If you are working in Color or some other application that allows you to draw vignettes or mattes with custom shapes, then you are in luck. If you are limited to only using geometric shapes, you'll still be fine completing the rest of this tutorial. Just use an oval and shape it, position it, rotate it, and soften it so that it isolates as much as possible without encroaching on the matte you already created for the lion. See Figure 5-29.

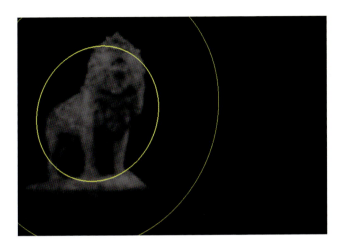

Fig. 5-29 The matte image with the circle garbage matte. The inside and outside softness of the circular garbage matte are defined by the yellow lines.

In Color, when you are in the vignette area and select User Shape from the Shape pulldown menu just below the vignette checkbox, you are instantly transported to the Geometry room where you have a larger image to work with to set your points. Just start clicking on the image of the lion in the Geometry room UI to create your shape. When you get back to almost where you started, choose the Close Shape button to the right of the lion image.

Once your shape is drawn, you have to use the Attach button at the top right of the UI to have the shape attached to your secondary correction. This is a necessary step because you can choose multiple saved or created shapes to attach to your correction. See Figure 5-30.

Fig. 5-30 The Color UI in the Secondary In Room showing a custom shape around the lion.

Then you can go back to the Secondary room and soften the edges of the shape so that there are no hard edges to the garbage matte. You can see the difference in the cleanliness of the matte by viewing the matte in the right-hand (non-UI) monitor while toggling the vignette checkbox off and on. See Figure 5-31.

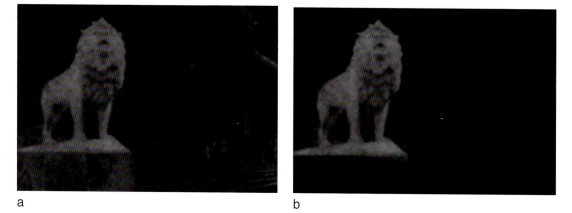

a   b

Fig. 5-31 **(a)** The original matte and **(b)** with the benefit of the custom user shape garbage matte.

The discernable difference in the final image is actually quite small. Remember that the original secondary correction without the garbage matte was to darken the lion and pump up the saturation. In small areas under the lion and in the eaves of the roof, this also darkened those areas and brought up the green cast. With the garbage matte in place, those areas are fixed. Was it worth the effort for the minimal gain? Only you and your client can say. I suggest that you try to make your qualifications as clean as possible, but sometimes, your schedule and budget will not allow it. You can certainly see the difference when you toggle between the shots with and without the garbage matte, but if you edited the nongarbage matte version into a show, then put in a second shot, and then cut back to the garbage matte version, there is no way anyone would see the difference.

Color's Secondary Curves

One of the interesting sets of secondary tools in Color are the Hue, Saturation (Sat), and Luminance (Lum) curves. These are unlike the curves that we discussed in Chapter 4. These curves allow you to select a specific hue with a click of a button and either rotate its hue, alter its saturation, or change its luminance value. A few pictures will be worth way more than the thousand words that it would take me to explain this further.

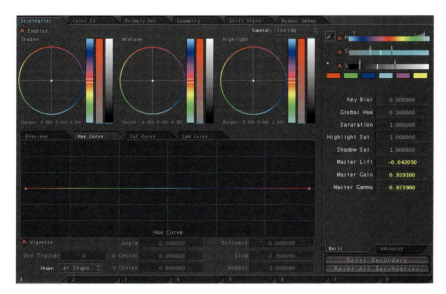

Fig. 5-32 The Hue curve in Color's Secondary Room. Color allows very quick adjustments to specific hues.

Fig. 5-33 The unaltered source image. Courtesy of Randy Riesen.

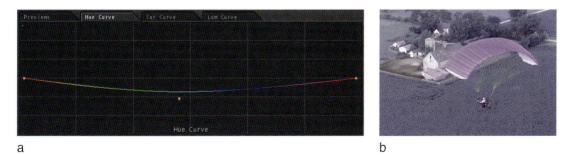

a   b

Fig. 5-34 The Hue curve adjustment (a) and the result (b). In the Hue curve, clicking on the point of the curve that corresponds to the hue of the ultralight's wing and adjusting it changes the hue of the wing.

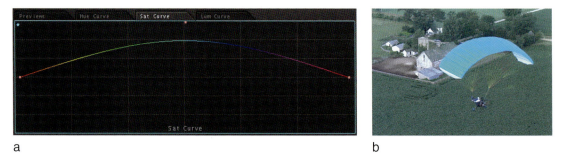

a   b

Fig. 5-35 The Saturation curve adjustment **(a)** and the result **(b)**. Adjusting the Saturation curve at the same point makes the wing more saturated instead of changing its hue.

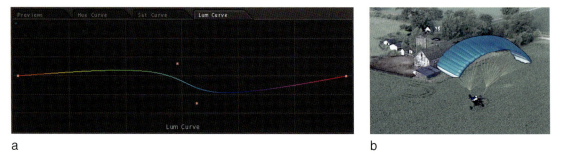

a   b

Fig. 5-36 The Luminance curve adjustment **(a)** and the result **(b)**. Adjusting the same point on the Luminance curve makes the wing darker. This required setting a second point to isolate the luminance correction on the wing from the other colors in the image that were similar.

Secondaries are Crucial

Knowing what to use secondaries for and how to decide what to isolate is really critical to good color correction. That is why Chapter 6 will finally bring in the full expertise of our expert panel of colorists. We'll have them walk you through a number of color corrections that use secondaries. We'll use that chapter instead of continuing with the form of the book so far, which normally follows a "primer" chapter with a "tools" chapter. The tools for each application are really either limited to tools that are available exclusively to a specific application or they are very limited to the color vector isolation and shapes drawing tools that have already been covered extensively in this chapter. So I now leave you in the capable hands of some very talented men and women as you explore secondary color correction with the *real* pros.

CHAPTER 6

Secondaries with the Pros

In the previous five chapters, we broke up color correction into various components or tasks, which makes sense when you are trying to learn something, but in reality, these tasks are not performed in isolation but in a more all-encompassing, holistic approach that includes revising work that was already done and fixing issues that actually developed throughout the color correction process.

Because of that, the following chapters, which are led mostly by our expert panel of colorists, will have a *primary* focus, like secondary correction or look creation, but will also include *other* elements, like primary correction, or may jump into other elements of the correction, because that's how the colorists actually worked on the images and to break up the tasks like in the previous chapters would be to take their entire thought process out of context.

I organized this chapter into two basic secondary concepts that we outlined in the previous chapter:

1. Vignettes (or spot corrections or windows).

2. Vector and luma qualifications (based on hue, saturation, and luminance [HSL] values).

Both of these methods actually create mattes inside of which the secondary corrections are done.

> Something to keep in mind as you see where each colorist took an image is that they were asked to be fairly "self-directed" in what they thought the image should look like. This is fairly unusual for a colorist, since a director of photography (DP) or director or producer is usually guiding the session and providing the colorist with context for the shot or a vision that had been developed prior to the shoot.

Vignettes

One of the methods of secondary color correction is vignetting or spot color correction. In a da Vinci suite, it would be known as Power Windows. Whatever the term, the tools allow for the correction of a specific geographic portion of an image that is usually defined or qualified by a geometric shape or possibly by a user-defined shape that is created by combining geometric shapes or by the use of Bezier or b-spline curves. See Figure 6-1.

Fig. 6-1 The yellow and white lines in this window describe a user-defined window, or vignette, in Apple's Color. Secondary color correction can be applied inside and outside of this shape. Image courtesy of Artbeats.

Apple's Color uses the term **vignette** to define any of these geographic corrections, but when most colorists are discussing vignetting, they don't mean *any* geographic correction, but the specific act of darkening the edges and focusing the viewer's attention on the middle of the screen or some other area of interest. Sometimes the technique is done with a defocus vignette that blurs the outside edges instead of, or in addition to, darkening them. See Figure 6-2.

Almost every colorist in this book used vignettes in their work, but for many of them, it seemed like they were almost a little embarrassed that they used them, despite the fact that vignetting is a tried-and-true technique that you can see in practically any national TV spot on the air. I asked veteran colorist Bob Festa of R!OT Santa Monica, in Santa Monica, CA, about this aversion to vignettes: "Well, I'm one of the original architects of one of the most abused techniques in color grading," Festa explained jokingly. "The beauty of it is that in any given shot you can't point to it and say, 'That's got a vignette on it.' It's a very subliminal, subconscious, 3D thing. And

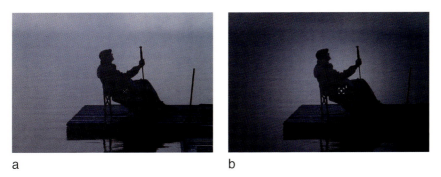

a   b

Fig. 6-2 **(a)** Source image without vignette and **(b)** vignetted image with very strong vignette effect. This is a much more obvious vignette than would normally be applied. Images courtesy of Artbeats.

quite frankly I used it as recently as 20 minutes ago. I'm not going to let it drop."

Bob Festa

When da Vinci announced their inaugural Master Colorist Awards, Bob Festa was the winner for the commercial category. Bob Festa is one of the most recognized names in color correction and is highly respected among his peers. His credits include virtually all of the world's best-known brands and spots, including the original Levis 501 Blues campaign. He has worked with some of the industry's finest directors, including Leslie Dektor, Bob Giraldi, Erich Joiner, Joe Pytka, and Jeff Zwart. His input has helped define many of the modern tools that colorists use every day.

Festa has a master's degree in public communication from Pepperdine University and honed his grading skills at Deluxe Laboratories, Action Video, Editel Los Angeles, Complete Post, and Hollywood Digital. For over a decade he's worked at R!OT Santa Monica.

For the colorists that used this technique in the sessions I watched, the vignetting clearly improved the final image, which I could confirm by disabling the secondaries with the vignettes in them. It makes the image seem to have more depth to it. If there are big bland areas, like a gray sky, it gives more texture to it, and it focuses the attention where it's supposed to be. Festa agreed with this assessment: "It's clearly more filmic. Maybe it's because early on in **Pandora**, people had to use square windows and a lot of people had a problem getting a good vignette with a square-based window. But in the round, oval-based world, I have no problem making it work within the confines of safe action in a tasteful way."

Another colorist who is unapologetic for using vignettes, despite chiding from some of his colorist co-workers, is Chris Pepperman of NFL Films:

"They think it's just darkening the edges. My idea of a vignette is: I don't want you to see it. I'm using it as an option like a DP would. I'm using it as a lighting tool. That's what I consider vignetting. Being able to help isolate your eye toward the specific product, person, or whatever you want in the picture. So that's why I use it all the time. I use vignetting on everything that I do in my commercial work. Whether it's a square or a circle or whether it's a shape that consists of a combination of shapes. [Da Vinci lets you combine geometric shapes in a variety of ways.] I always do it because when I look at a picture, I'm always trying to help what I'm looking at."

Vignetting the Ultralight Flyover Scene

Craig Leffel, of Chicago's Optimus, demonstrates this classic technique as part of his correction of the "ultralight field" shot (see Fig. 6-3 and 6-4). (You can follow along with these corrections by loading the tutorial scenes from the DVD into your color correction application or plug-in.) When creating the vignettes, some of the colorists chose to create the

Fig. 6-3 The uncorrected source image. Image courtesy of Randy Riesen.

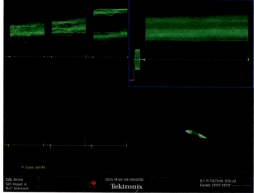

Fig. 6-4 Scopes showing the source image: the RGB parade (top left quadrant), the RGB parade expanded to show the black level (bottom left quadrant), the composite waveform (top right quadrant), and the vectorscope at standard zoom (bottom right quadrant). From Tektronix WVR7100.

shape and leave the edges sharp while affecting the secondary or setting the shape and size of the vignette. This sharp edge made it very easy to see exactly how much they were affecting the image. Other colorists preferred to set the softness on the vignette's edge *before* affecting any change so that they had a better sense for the way the correction would actually look when it was complete. Leffel puts himself in the first camp, saying, "I find it easier to change the shape before I change the softness of a vignette. But, I'm kind of in both camps. It depends on what I'm trying to do. If I'm trying to do something that's really extreme, then I don't need to see it, but if I'm trying to do something subtle, or I'm trying to just fix something, the more subtle it is, the more I like to have less softness so I can see what I'm actually doing instead of assuming it's working with the softness turned up. This one I'm gonna start hard just to see."

First, Leffel does a primary correction (see Fig. 6-5). This correction mostly involved the master black, gamma, and highlight levels. He also tweaked the highlight balance toward red and slightly moved blacks the same direction. (See Figure 6-5b) All colorists worked in FinalTouchHD, because Color was not yet released.

TIP

In addition to Craig Leffel, several other colorists graded this image. To read about all of the colorists' approaches to ANY of the images in this book, check out the folder on the DVD titled, "CC_Session_Text." Each text file inside is titled for the image that the colorists were grading. I included the transcripts for all of the sessions on that image.

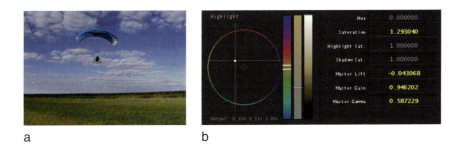

a   b   Fig. 6-5

He continues the correction with a secondary qualification on the grass. He grades inside and outside that qualification (see Figs. 6-6).

Leffel continues his correction. "Now that I've got an isolation and a sort of base-level correction, I'm doing an outside vignette, because in the original image, the sides are real flat. There's an even exposure across the whole thing. It's always nice to have a vignette there to blend out—not to do an *obvious* vignette, to darken the edges obviously, but to do a soft vignette. So, I brought down gamma and black and a little bit of gain, but not much. Mostly gamma. This image is mostly gamma anyway. There's not a whole lot of black and not a whole

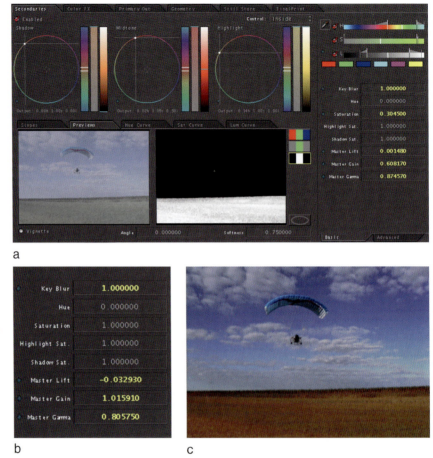

Fig. 6-6 **(a)** The correction inside of the qualification (white areas). **(b)** the small correction made outside the qualification (black areas), and **(c)** The image after a secondary qualification on the grass. Leffel wanted the grass to look like a field of wheat.

a

b

c

lot of white, so almost all of this image is easily manipulated with gamma."

While Leffel keeps the edge sharp on his vignette, he drops the level at the beginning and gets to a point where he needs to see the vignette softness closer to the way it will look in the end. "I'm going to make that vignette as soft as I can make it, and what this is going to do is just add richness to the whole image. We brought it down from what the original was. Now we're going to add even more richness. The interesting thing is going to be to see what happens when the ultralight flies. If you do the vignette soft enough, then the vignette doesn't become an issue with the motion. You don't really sense the vignette there. You just sense richness. The brighter center is just sort of a natural feeling, which is what I'm after." (See Fig. 6-7)

a

Fig. 6-7 **(a)** The image with a large soft oval vignette and **(b)** the statistics for the outside of the vignette. Notice that the subtle vignetting is difficult to see without examining the comers of the image.

b

Comparing da Vinci Secondaries to Color

For da Vinci colorists trying to get a handle on Color, Bob Sliga translates the Color paradigm into da Vinci terms:

> Your grade bin is kind of like your power grades. Secondaries are kind of like Power Windows *and* Power Tiers. Da Vinci comes with a Primary room and a Secondary room, which gives you circle and a square and a key that you can combine. When you have a circle or a square or a key, you have inside or outside color correction. That's as far as that goes. Then you get into their Power Tiers, and if we want to go outside of that one color, we have to copy it over and invert it. On Color, even though you're doing a thing that you would normally do in a Power Tier, we have outside and inside. Once da Vinci guys realize *that*, they're going to say, "Whoah, this is more powerful. This is easier to use."

Vignetting the Kiss Me in the Dark *Bedroom Scene*

Of all of the colorists who used vignettes to focus attention on the subject, the most intricate example was probably done by Mike Matusek, of Chicago's Nolo Digital Film. Matusek worked with several vignettes or windows to shape the bedroom scene from *Kiss Me in the Dark*. We'll walk through the entire correction, including the vignettes he creates at the end of the grade.

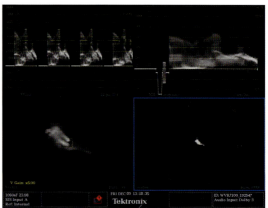

Fig. 6-8 The ungraded bedroom scene from *Kiss Me in the Dark*. Image courtesy of Seduced and Exploited Entertainment.

Fig. 6-9 Scopes showing the source image: the YRGB parade (top left quadrant), the vectorscope zoomed in 5× (bottom left quadrant), a composite waveform (top right quadrant), and the vectorscope at standard zoom (bottom right quadrant). From Tektronix WVR7100.

"I don't use the vectorscope much," Matusek mentions as he starts grading the image. "Before I start any shot I quickly glance at the waveform. See where the whites and the blacks are. I noticed that the blacks are a little warmer, so I thought I'd balance them. Sometimes I'll whack out the blacks just to give it a look, but I'll always try to start by balancing it. Overall I thought it looked a little washed, so I'm bringing the midtones down a little bit as opposed to crushing the blacks.

"On the **Nucoda** system that I work on, I'll zoom in and sample an area. So now I'm going to work on gain. The midtones are a little warmer than I'd like. I like playing off these little blue accents, these highlights," he says, pointing to her negligee. "So what I'd like to do is overall go a little cooler." Matusek simultaneously pushes warmth into the shadows and then adds blue into the midtones. "And I got some green out of the highlights, just because I didn't like that. I noticed that there is some green in the blanket or maybe there's some green fill and then I pulled green from those highlights, but the whole image starts to look magenta, because I'm losing green," Matusek explains, backing off of his green highlight correction.

Matusek switches between the original source and his correction. "See? That's getting a lot moodier." See Figure 6-10.

a

Fig. 6-10 **(a)** The final primary correction and **(b)** the FinalTouch UI showing the primary data.

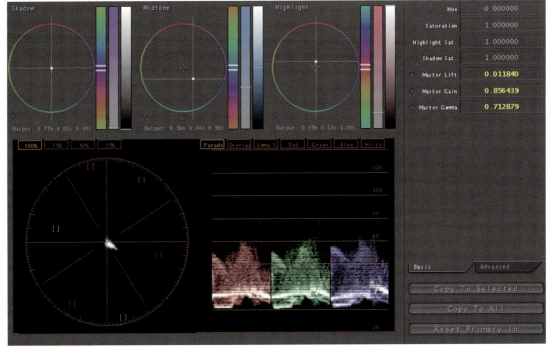

b

Kiss Me in the Dark

The short film *Kiss Me in the Dark* is a production of Seduced and Exploited Entertainment. It was directed by Barry Gilbert and the DP was Robin Miller. Gilbert has been working as a director and producer for several years on independent features and spots. Currently he works out of New York City.

Gilbert explains that this short film has its genesis in a feature script he was shopping. The aesthetic of the film was influenced by Gilbert's love of Ingmar Bergman films. Many of Gilbert's earlier projects were heavily reliant on dialog, so for this film, he sought out the challenge of making a film completely without dialog. If you want the context of the footage from the short as you are attempting to grade it, here is Gilbert's synopsis of the film:

> It's a woman who lives in a big, old empty house and apparently spends all of her time thumbing through old photos and watching videotapes of her and her dead husband. What we see rather quickly on is that apparently the husband is back in the house and comes and embraces her. But the issue is clouded when she wakes up and wonders if she was merely dreaming, and it becomes apparent that this is not an isolated incident, that this is a pattern. This is the night that she decides, after quite a few drinks, that she is going to settle the issue once and for all. She's wired the house and there are all these surveillance cameras and she has ordered some fancy night-vision goggles, which on one level is absurd, because if it was that easy, then everyone would have night-vision goggles. It's really a question for the audience. Is she privy to a ghost that wants to be found or is she so torn by her desire to reconnect with him that she's gone through these kind of sad attempts to rationalize. The point is that she's probably just as afraid of finding out that she's wrong than that there really is a ghost.

Matusek continues with his correction. "The thing that's a big pain in the ass is when you spend 10 minutes on a shot like this and hit play, and then the guy comes in the frame and screws up what you did, so what I would typically do is go through the whole shot to see what I'm getting myself in to." (See Fig. 6-11.) "So he does come in, but I notice that he doesn't really go in front of the pillow. What I notice is that my eye goes to this pillow (above her forehead) and even down here (the sheet under her neck and shoulders), so what I'd like to do is put a window here (on the pillow) and drop the

Fig. 6-11

exposure. Put a window here (foreground sheet) and drop the exposure. (See Figure 6-12) I really hate this highlight on the back wall, so I'd put a Bezier shape and bring that highlight down."

Fig. 6-12

I point out that he has to be careful because the guy drops down into the area he's planning on putting a vignette. Matusek says, "Exactly, so I'd put a general shape in there and really soften it and if I had to, I could keyframe it to stay where I wanted it to stay. First I'll put those other two windows, because I know they'll actually work."

Matusek explains that about half of the work he does is commercials and half is independent films. "The trend, I felt, was that in independent film it was more about setting the mood and emotion, and with commercials, it's about getting a really cool look to grab people's attention. Hopefully it's to help sell the product with the look having to do with the story of the spot, but mostly give it a hip, cool look and focus the attention on the product. And if you give it a really cool look, when you get to the product shot, make it look nice and pretty and bright. So basically commercials are a lot brighter, contrastier. Long form is a little bit moodier."

At this point Matusek adds a soft, low, wide vignette to darken the sheet below her body, bringing the highlights down to about half and the midrange down a little, commenting, See Fig. 6-13. "Now your eye goes to her and I still don't like that pillow, so I'll do one more window there." He draws a custom shape for the pillow and brings the master gain down. "I think I went a little too flat." He checks back and forth, toggling the vignette off and on before revising it by increasing the contrast inside the window. (See Fig. 6-14).

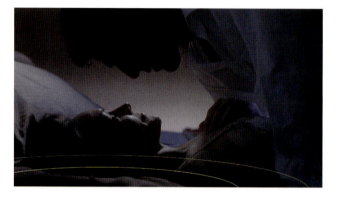

Fig. 6-13 Matusek's low, wide oval window darkens the bright sheet below her head and neck.

Fig. 6-14 The image with the vignette on the pillow. Only the Master Gain was brought down to about 75% inside the vignette.

Matusek continues, "There's nothing wrong with saying 'You wanna go darker with that? You wanna go darker?' But you've got to push it to the point where it looks pretty bad and then bring it back. Especially with clients. All colorists can see subtle changes in what they did. We're staring at the image for the whole time, while they're reading a magazine or they're on their laptop and they're looking up and down, so they miss those subtle changes. So it's good to show them, not extreme differences, but enough differences so they can see it."

Matusek then adds another vignette, bringing down the edges some more. "When you go back and forth, you kind of get a feel for the balance, like 'That feels a little top heavy.'" To fix the "top-heaviness" of the image, Matusek repositions the vignette lower in the frame, then toggles back and forth to check the correction. (See Fig 6-15b) "Here it looks a little bit overlit. Here it's a little more dynamic. There's more depth."

Matusek continues to evaluate the image to see how it can be improved. "Now that I'm happy with all this other stuff, this highlight [on the negligee on her breast] is bothering me. So now there're two things I could do. I can add a luma key on the highlights and defocus them. Or maybe just put another window and bring it down." Matusek adds another window, on the negligee, explaining, "By putting that window on her hand and her breast, your eye goes to her face." See Figure 6-15a.

When he is done with the vignettes, he summarizes what he did and what he looks for before he moves on to the next shot. "I kind of shaped it. First you start off getting the density of the image. Then I get the color balance where I want it. Then the mood and where you want to put the gamma and the midtones. Then I kind of shape it. And now I'll go back to my primary and maybe I'll go even cooler with it, just for the heck of it and see what it looks like." See Figure 6-16.

a

b

Fig. 6-15 (a) A vignette on the negligee. Only the Master Gain was brought down to about 70% inside the vignette. (b) An overall vignette was added to focus attention and give texture. The outside of the vignette has the Master Gain lowered to about 50%.

a

b

Fig. 6-16 (a) The original source image from Seduced and Exploited Entertainment's *Kiss Me in the Dark* and (b) Matusek's final correction.

Mike Matusek

Mike Matusek is the principal colorist at Nolo Digital Film in Chicago, IL. Nolo specializes in digital intermediates for features and creative color grading. He has extensive experience as a telecine and digital intermediate (DI) colorist, grading commercials, feature films, and documentaries. While he has experience with da Vinci's 2K color corrector, he has done most of his recent grading on the Nucoda Film Master.

Commercial projects include clients like Disney, Nintendo, McDonalds, Kelloggs, GoDaddy.com, Sears, and Bally's Total Fitness. Feature films include *Drunkboat*, *The War Tapes*, *Kubuku Rides* (the first film from Steppenwolf Films), and *Crime Fiction*. Matusek is a graduate of Southern Illinois University.

Spot Color Correction

In addition to using shapes to vignette a shot to focus attention to a specific area or to create depth in flat areas, these same tools can be used to isolate specific areas of a picture to do traditional secondary color correction, like some of the first windows Matusek used in the last example.

The conventional wisdom with this technique is that it is often better to try to create the qualification in some other way that doesn't depend on basic geography because if the shot moves or images in the frame move in or out of the geographic area, then the correction probably won't work, though sometimes tracking the vignette can help.

In the next correction, Neal Kassner, of CBS's "48 Hours," uses a spot correction to isolate the sky correction from the grass correction. Another option for this correction may have been pulling qualifications on the blue sky, the green grass, and the clouds. But with the simple shape to qualify at the horizon combined with the ability to track the correction as the camera moves, the spot correction is quick, easy, and effective.

Fun with Windows

Larry Field, the colorist on FOX's "24," was reminded of a trick he'd done with a Power Window on his da Vinci color corrector. "On one of my shows I needed a sunrise, so we picked a spot behind a mountain and I grabbed a Power Window with a pretty broad soft edge to it and created a pinpoint, and dropped another window and graded off that and basically produced a sunrise using Power Windows."

Vignette to Create Day-for-Night Shot

NFL Films' Chris Pepperman used vignettes to create a day-for-night look in the MichAve_pumpkinlights.mov" scene in the "Tutorial_footage_and_files" folder of the DVD. (see Figs. 6-17 and 6-18).

Fig. 6-17 The source image. Image courtesy of Randy Riesen.

Fig. 6-18 Color's built in scopes with the source image (top left quadrant), a traditional vectorscope at standard zoom (bottom left quadrant), Color's 3D vectorscope (top right quadrant) and an RGB Parade (bottom right quadrant).

Normally, in a day-for-night shot, you would want to avoid shooting the sky, because even if you darken down the entire shot, the contrast between the sky and the rest of the image is usually a clear giveaway that the scene was not shot at night. To bring that contrast under control, Pepperman used several vignettes throughout the image. But he started the process with a primary color correction that cooled the highlights and lowered the Master Lift and Gamma levels, as seen in Figure 6-19.

"So the first thing I'm going to do is create a circle. I'm going to take it down below the pumpkins and I'm going to rotate it, and now I'm going to stretch it. I'm situating this window where I can now work on the outside of it, and I really want to knock down the sky even more. I'm gonna really crush the you-know-what out of it." As he does this, he notices something that bothers him. "Can you see the noise in there a little bit? So what I'm going to do is come up

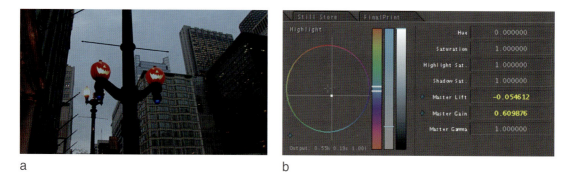

a   b

Fig. 6-19 **(a)** The primary correction and **(b)** the primary data from the FinalTouch UI.

on the black levels to get rid of that noise and leave the black levels alone, because there are some blacks here in the building. I'm going to bury [the highlights] and add even more dark blue." But as he does this, he sees another problem develop. "I don't like what it's doing here. I should be able to track more of that blue in there. And I see some posterizing going on."

Because of these issues he backs off the more extreme correction that he was trying to do before continuing. "So the next thing I'm going to do is soften that out. But I want to almost see the curvature of the vignette, because I want to put some texture in the sky. I want it to be almost organic. I don't want it to look flat like you're keying something in. I like having it darker to lighter. It gives it more of a true appearance." I comment to Pepperman that the vignette he's created looks like something a DP might have done with a filter. He'd been working outside of the vignette he created, but switches back to the inside to work on the lower part of the frame.

"Now inside the vignette, I might bring up the black levels a little bit. I'm going to push a little more blue to give it a perception more of night. Now I don't want to contaminate the blacks too much, because I don't want to change the color of the building either. Now I'll start to bury the blacks again so you can really almost see the shadow on that. Now I really like that, but I still think we can push it more. So I'm going to go back outside the window and now I'm going to bring the midrange down and the whites. Now I'm just going to make it a little more blue. And now I'm going to drop the window down. See Fig. 6-20.

"Now, what I'm going to do is an isolation appearance. This is something I like to do." Pepperman creates a custom user shape for the next vignette, defining one of the buildings. "What I'm doing is, I'm brightening the building to give it the appearance that the lights are on." Pepperman creates this illusion by raising the highlights and crushing the blacks inside the vignette. "I'm going to make sure that the blacks are deep, so it doesn't look like it's got a spotlight on it. And the midrange might even

a

Fig. 6-20 **(a)** The first secondary correction. Corrections were made inside and outside the qualified area made by the oval vignette. **(b)** The data for the outside corrections to the secondary,

b

c

Fig. 6-20 (*Continued*) (c) the data from the inside corrections to the secondary.

help that. Now, that looks pretty good. Now I'm going to soften it. So I like that." See Fig. 6-21.

As his next step in the correction, Pepperman plans to bring up the blacks on the building to the left and raise the highlights. "I'm going to use the trackballs to clean up the blue and now I'll soften it." See Figure 6-22. "And then I just want to do one more thing." Pepperman creates a custom shape in the middle of the frame and darkens it. "Now it doesn't look like it's darker on the edges. You've got a darker feel in the middle too." See Figure 6-23.

"Now if I really wanted to, I could isolate the pumpkins and bring them up. I don't like the way they clip. I would brighten them back up to where they're clipping. Like they would in real life. Because when it's clipped like, that but it's low, it just doesn't look right. So if I brighten the pumpkins up, this picture would say day-for-night much better. It would simulate it much better." As he blows out the pumpkin lights, the shot looks much more realistic as day-for-night. "But you can start to see the illumination or the halo around the building, so we need to tighten that up." See Figure 6-24.

Fig. 6-21 **(a)** This image has the second vignette added to the top right building. **(b)** Note the triangular window and the changes to the master levels to create the impression that the lights are on bright inside the building.

a

b

Fig. 6-22 (a) This image has the third vignette added to the leftmost building. **(b)** The data from the secondary, including the shape of the window.

a

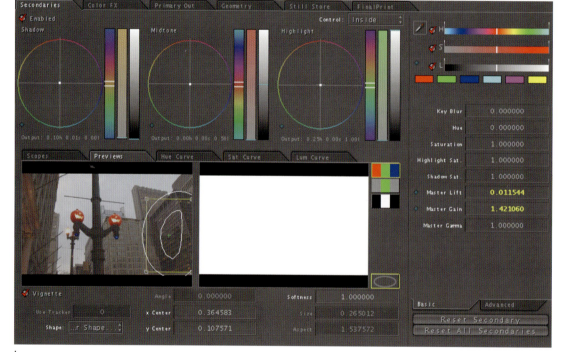

b

a

Fig. 6-23 **(a)** This image shows the effect of the fourth secondary vignette and **(b)** the data from the fourth vignette.

b

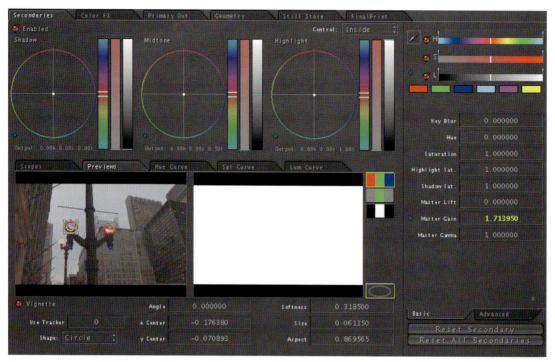

a

b

Fig. 6-24 (a) The data from one of the pumpkin lights. (b) The data from the other pumpkin light.

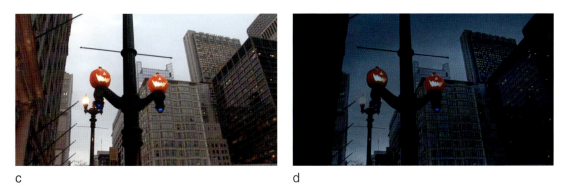

c   d

Fig. 6-24 (*Continued*) **(c)** The starting point for the image. **(d)** The final correction including the last two pumpkin light vignettes.

Vector and Luma Qualified Secondaries

One of the reasons to use secondaries is because balancing an entire tonal range—highlights, midtones, or shadows—is not specific enough to fix more isolated color casts within that range. When that happens, secondaries allow the colorist greater precision to manipulate more specific ranges of color. One example of this is in the scene from *Chasing Ghosts* that I call "Banker's Light." See Figures 6-25 and 6-26.

Fig. 6-25 The source image is a 2K film scan converted to HD, from the feature film, *Chasing Ghosts*. Image courtesy of Wingman Productions, Inc.

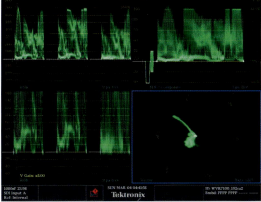

Fig. 6-26 Scopes showing the source image: the RGB parade (top left quadrant), the RGB parade expanded to show the black level (bottom left quadrant), the composite waveform (top right quadrant), and the vectorscope at standard zoom (bottom right quadrant). From Tektronix WVR7100.

Janet Falcon, formerly a Miami-based colorist who is now at Shooters Post in Philadelphia, liked the challenge of bringing this scene to life and used secondary color correction to execute her vision. She starts with a basic primary correction (see Fig. 6-27), then moves on the secondaries.

"The highlighted areas in the shirt don't have much green in them," she begins. "It's the midtone shadow areas that have more green. If I just take green out of the highlights, that'll go farther away. I just want to take green out of the lower-lit areas (of the shirt)." Falcon pulls green out with a secondary qualification based on the greens of the shirt. She pulls some of the green out, but when she does, she sees that her qualification of the green needs to be tweaked to better get all of the green out of the shirt without affecting the green tint in the window over the detective's shoulder. She explains her qualification: "I like green. A lot of people don't like green. Normally, what I would do is qualify a color, the green, based on a combination of luminance and chrominance. That is why I am trying to pull up the bottom end of the luminance qualification to eliminate the darker

Fig. 6-27 (a) The primary correction and (b) the data from the primary correction in FinalTouch UI.

a

b

green of the door from the qualification. I then try to focus the qualification primarily on the stronger parts of the color I want to change and let the qualification fall off on the less saturated areas of the color. That way, when the correction is applied it has more of an effect on the areas that need it most and just a minor effect on the areas that need it less. I personally don't want to affect [the green in the window of the door] unless the client or somebody told me to get rid of the green in the window." See Figure 6-28.

a

Fig. 6-28 (a) This correction pulls some of the green out of the more midtone areas of the shirt. (b) The data, including the qualification for Falcon's first secondary.

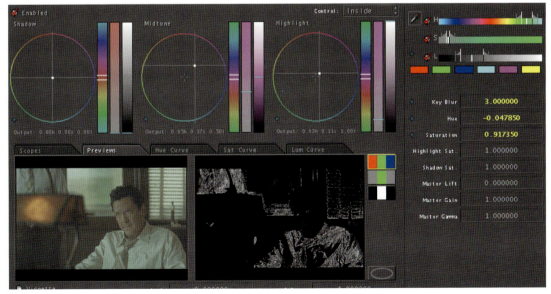

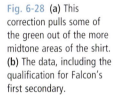

b

When I ask why she doesn't simply use a vignette to save the green light in the window of the door, she responds, "Usually it's easier if you can do something without windows, because you never know where you're going to end up later. Maybe we'll come back to this shot later and he'll be up and standing in front of that or moving around, walking. So to the extent that you can do it with a color vector qualification, you never have to follow it with a window and track it. So I always try to do everything first without a window, and then if you have to put in a window, then put in a window. And depending on what this is for, I might put a vignette on him to focus attention on him. Falcon sets up a new secondary with a circle, softens it, and corrects outside of the circle (see Fig. 6-29).

I point out the different "camps" of colorists who prefer adding softness to the vignette early or later. Falcon walks the fence on this decision, though she seems to land in the "soften early" camp. "I like to get the window positioned the way I think I'm going to want it, and then I go back and forth. For me, they all go together. The amount of color correction; the shape of the window; the softness of the window. All those things play together. I know a lot of other people do it the other way. They'll put the color correction in first and then do the luminance key. I know Kevin Shaw does that." (Kevin Shaw is a prominent color correction trainer and consultant.) "If he wants a luminance key of the sky, he'll make a color correction in a circle, then create a luminance key, and bring that correction into the luminance key. I create the key as close as I think I can get it and then I color correct it. Then I go back and touch up the softness and the positioning. I do a lot of back and forth. I know I work differently than other people. I've seen people do it the other way but I'm not comfortable working that way." Falcon tweaks the aspect and rotation of the circle to include his face and some look room and darkens outside of it. Then she pulls a secondary HSL key on the highest chroma part of the banker light. "I think it helps to knock that light down a little bit." I can tell she's not quite happy with her correction because she's unfamiliar with using FinalTouch/Color.

"I like to be very, very, very specific about what I affect and what I don't affect. Some people aren't that specific. I'm kind of neurotic about it. Like, his face looks like he's sick. It's kind of pink here and green here, and that's because I didn't get a perfect isolation on the pinker parts of the face. I got some of the pink out, but I also got it out of some of the places that I didn't want to affect," Falcon mentions as she points to the detective's forehead. "And in here, not enough, she continues, pointing at the darkened side of face. So he ends up looking kind of blotchy, but in the end it's better." See Figure 6-30.

a

Fig. 6-29 **(a)** This image shows the effect of the correction to the outside of the second vignette and **(b)** the data from the second secondary correction.

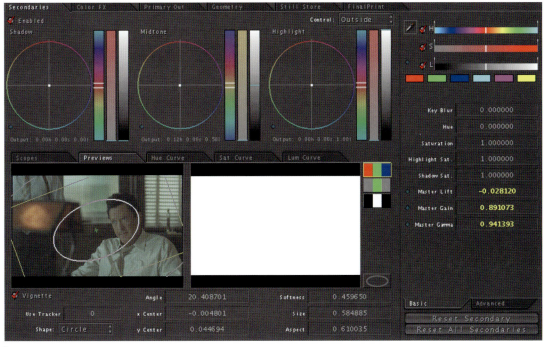

b

a

Fig. 6-30 (a) The completed correction, including a third secondary to reduce the intensity of the glow in the banker's light. (b) The data from the third secondary showing the qualified area.

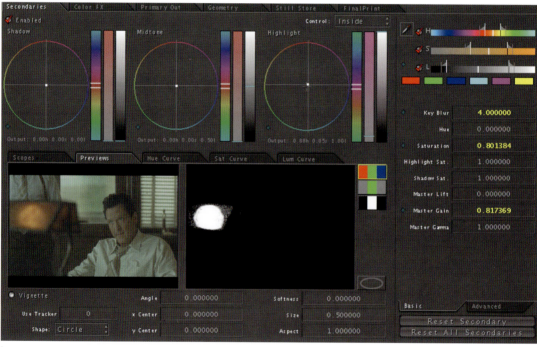

b

Janet Falcon

Janet Falcon graduated from Tulane University in 1987. She worked at Teleproductions, Inc. in New Orleans. In 1988 she went to work as senior colorist at Limlite/Edefx in Miami and then moved to Manhattan Transfer - Miami before landing at Shooters Post in Philadelphia in 2002.

Her commercial reel includes work for clients like Volkswagen, Chevy, Miller Beer, Reebok, Time/Warner, and Campbell's Soup. She has also graded music videos for The Baha Men and Wyclef Jean among others and has been the colorist on full-length feature DIs such as *Shadowboxer* with Cuba Gooding, Jr., *Teeth*, and *Perfect Weekend*.

Secondary Corrections Can Focus Attention

Larry Field of Level 3 Post in Los Angeles, CA, used a vector qualification to place the attention where it was needed in the scene I call "MusicVideoGirl.mov." See Figures 6-31 and 6-32.

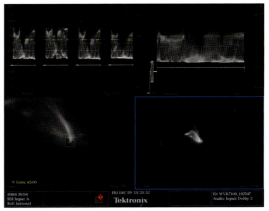

Fig. 6-31 The ungraded source image. This image is from a flat transfer from 35 mm straight to HD Quicktime by Bono Labs. Flat transfers are done so that blacks are slightly elevated and highlights are not clipped giving the colorist the most options after the transfer. Image courtesy of Vanderpool Films and Charles Vanderpool.

Fig. 6-32 Scopes showing the source image: the YRGB parade (top left quadrant), the vectorscope zoomed in 5× (bottom left quadrant), the composite waveform (top right quadrant), and the vectorscope at standard zoom (bottom right quadrant). From Tektronix WVR7100.

Before he begins, Field jokes about the general look of music videos, saying, "So no one's afraid of contrast in a music video. What I would do if [the strong color of the floor] was a concern, would be to grab a color isolation on just that color and desaturate it after everything else was balanced and that would send your eye to her better. But first I want to start at a position where everything is where we want to be instead of starting with just that color and everything else is out of balance. I start basically with primary color correction. Do the contrast and the basic feel first. It doesn't matter who you're with or where you're at; people are gonna enjoy the image a lot better once the primaries are balanced, and you're in the ballpark where you need to be (see Fig. 6-33). Then you can start playing in the secondaries—effects, windows, keys, masks. That stuff is always secondary to me. It's always after I have it balanced and I have an idea of where I'm going and what we're doing. Then use a secondary to pick the narrowest range of the floor so it isn't affecting anything else and desaturate it and maybe swing toward red a little bit to blend in with the shadows more. With the secondary, look at the matte to see what part of the picture you're affecting (see Fig. 6-34)."

a

Fig. 6-33 (a) The scene after the primary correction. This is reconstructed from watching a videotape of the session. **(b)** The data from the reconstructed primary correction.

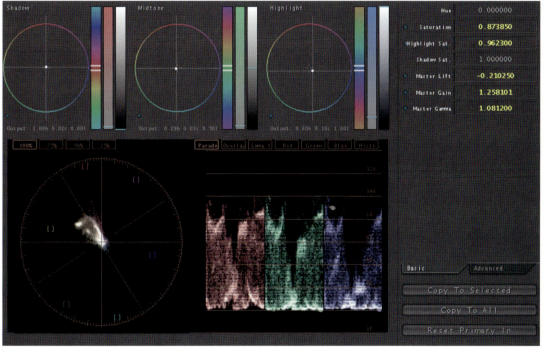

b

Fig. 6-34 **(a)** Field just talked through this secondary correction during the session. I reconstructed it later using his instructions. **(b)** The recreated secondary data.

a

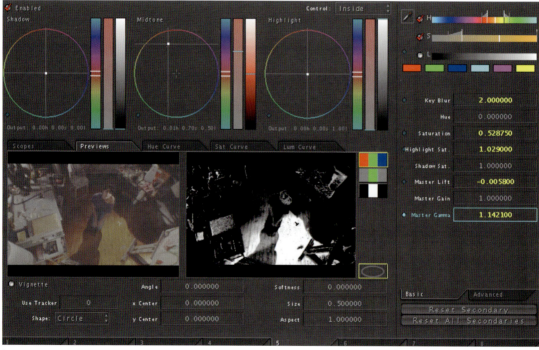

b

Using Secondaries to Match

We have an entire chapter devoted to matching shots (Chapter 9), but here we'll point out several ways that secondaries can help resolve tricky matching problems. Robert Lovejoy from Shooters Post in Philadelphia used just about every type of secondary qualification as he did his match of the "Art_Institute_proper" scene (see Figs. 6-35 and 6-36) with the "Art_Institute_blue" scene (see Figs. 6-37 and 6-38). These images are in the tutorial folder of the DVD.

Fig. 6-35 The source image of "Art_Institute_proper" scene.

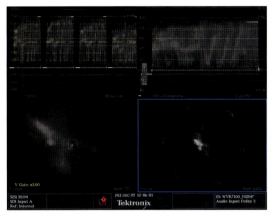

Fig. 6-36 Scopes showing the source image: the YRGB parade (top left quadrant), the vectorscope zoomed in 5× (bottom left quadrant), the composite waveform (top right quadrant), and the vectorscope at standard zoom (bottom right quadrant). From Tektronix WVR7100.

Fig. 6-37 The source image of "Art_Institute_blue" scene.

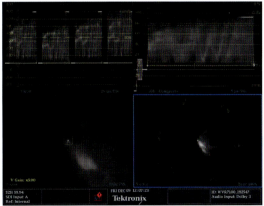

Fig. 6-38 Scopes showing the source image: the YRGB parade (top left quadrant), the vectorscope zoomed in 5× (bottom left quadrant), the composite waveform (top right quadrant), and the vectorscope at standard zoom (bottom right quadrant). From Tektronix WVR7100.

Like most colorists, he started with the basics before moving to secondaries. Lovejoy explained his opening steps. "I'm balancing blacks, balancing whites, and spreading my tonal range. I'm looking at the steps and the building façade." He sets up a split screen between the correctly shot image and the cool image and then positions the split down the middle of the lion. He starts by trying to match the base that the lion is standing on, adding some red to the midtones. See Figure 6-39.

Fig. 6-39 **(a)** The "cool" lion corrected with a primary correction and **(b)** the data from the "cool" lion primary correction.

a

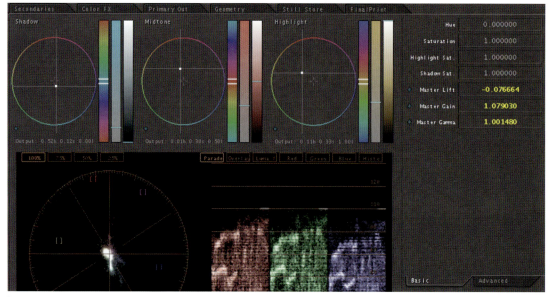

b

His primary correction to the cool image turns the sky a freakish color. This is where secondaries come in handy to fix problems created in the primary correction. Lovejoy qualifies the sky in the upper right corner with a luminance-only matte, then desaturates the highlights within the qualification, taking the sky back to pure white. See Figure 6-40.

a

Fig. 6-40 **(a)** This secondary pulls the sky back to white and **(b)** the data from the secondary correction of the sky.

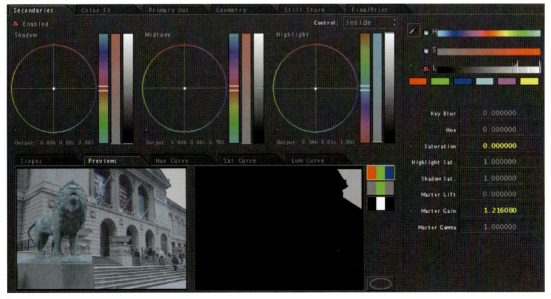

b

Instead of simply trying to match the "base" scene with the "cool" scene, Lovejoy also improves the "base" scene, then grabs a still of the improved "base" scene and wipes between it and the cool version he's trying to match. Instead of relying on scopes, he's using just his eyes, the video monitor, and years of experience. "It's very close. There are subtle differences in the lion. Secondary could be my friend on that." See Fig. 6-41.

To create his secondary correction on the lion, Lovejoy combines two qualifications. First he qualifies the lion using an HSL key. His HSL quali-

Fig. 6-41 **(a)** This is the "Art_Institute_proper" semicorrect image with a primary and **(b)** the data from the primary correction on the "base" image.

a

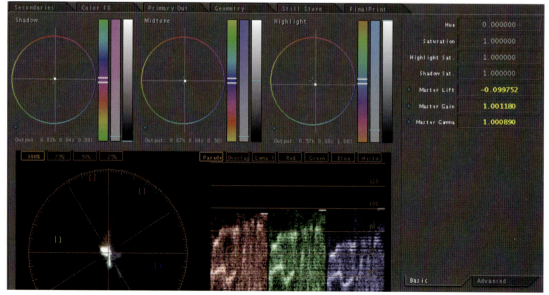

b

fication goes a little broad, selecting some portions of the image beyond the lion, so he adds a circle vignette around the lion as a garbage matte. With the lion qualified, he lowers the saturation of the lion. "It's hard to get a perfect match out of two widely divergent sources. You can see here that the base [that the lion stands on] is cooler." Using the Tangent Devices CP-200-BK panel, he warms up the midtones and highlights within the secondary qualification, ending up with a very close match (see Fig. 6-42).

a

Fig. 6-42 **(a)** The second secondary correction, desaturating the lion to make the match and **(b)** the data from the second secondary correction.

b

Robert Lovejoy

Bob Lovejoy graduated from Syracuse University in 1969 and became a combat photographer in the Vietnam War. He has worked at Devlin Videoservice and Magno Video in New York City, Century III in Boston, and Modern Video in Philadelphia before joining Shooters Post more than a decade ago to drive their Spirit Datacine. Lovejoy has worked on music videos, feature films, and national spots.

Shooters Post is located steps away from the Liberty Bell in historic downtown Philadelphia. In addition to working with advertising agencies and production companies, they have a cinema services company, DIVE, that provides visual effects, DIs, and titles for feature films. They also coproduce The Food Network's "Dinner: Impossible."

Secondaries Use Is Changing

When I first started learning about color correction, the prevailing wisdom was that you "saved" your secondaries. In other words, you wanted to just use a secondary color correction for something that really needed it. However, that was the wisdom when additional secondaries were either nonexistent or came as options at a *very* high premium. Bob Sliga and I discussed how this wisdom is changing with products like Apple's Color, which allows what would have been considered as 16 or more secondaries in a color corrector from the 1990s. According to Sliga,

> The secondary in Color is not the same as traditional secondary in film-to-tape transfer. You can go back to the days when we didn't really have secondary color correction, when we could only grab the six vectors and change saturation and hue and maybe luminance a little bit. That was the typical secondary color correction where you could isolate a color, [that is,] up until da Vinci changed the game in secondary color correction, by isolating a color by using a luminance key or an HSL key or by putting a window around something, which wasn't traditionally called a secondary, but they called that Power Tiers.

> In Color, the Secondary room is not just picking colors. We can use it as eight separate levels of full-up color correction. We're creating a color as opposed to just enhancing it and that is how the game has changed. Having eight secondaries—I think I've filled them up *once*, where I've run out of room. If you're that far down, either (A) the shot was totally mis-shot, or (B) the effect you're trying to create was "you better be paying big money per hour," because if you're using all eight windows and secondaries per scene on a feature or on a commercial, that's a long-time color correction. Does every job need all the complexity? No. But it's good to have the headroom if you need to be able to take something or push something a different way or a different color. I think the colorist that learns these tools and is more flexible and thinks "outside the bun" will be effective longer.

And, in addition to using the Secondary room as a true secondary, it's also possible to use the secondaries as "layers" of primary correction, where you don't even bother making a qualification before doing adjustments. This allows you to easily enable or disable the various layers as you perfect your grade.

Using a Luma Key to Build Contrast

Bob Sliga shows how to use secondaries to create a unique, high-contrast look using the "Football HD" scene from Artbeats'_SP123H1 Sports Collection (see Figs. 6-43 and 6-44).

In addition to the traditional method of stretching out the tonal range in primary color correction, it's possible to create even greater contrast by grading inside and outside of a luminance key.

First Sliga takes us through the traditional method, starting with some primary-type corrections that he decides to do in a secondary. He examines the source footage and begins. "If you go to our original picture, it's balanced out pretty decent. So the Primary room would be the basic, just starting it out, getting it in the ballpark. I'm just looking for a clean black, and I've got one. Now this is a little warm, so we could bring the red gamma down, but the truth of the matter is, that if we graded film to look like what it should be, people would not like their film. I mean, everyone loves things warm." Sliga makes a primary correction, but it is so slight that it is hard to perceive, especially on the printed page.

Since the original image is balanced and in a good place, Sliga moves to secondaries to modify the original, using secondaries like layers of primaries without any qualification (see the "Secondaries Use Is Changing" box above). "Now I'm just going to pull the gammas down like this. Really compress the blacks. I'm gonna crank up some more

Fig. 6-43 The source footage. Image courtesy of Artbeats.

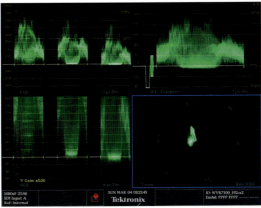

Fig. 6-44 Scopes showing the source image: the RGB parade (top left quadrant), the RGB parade expanded to show the black level (bottom left quadrant), the composite waveform (top right quadrant), and the vectorscope at standard zoom (bottom right quadrant). From Tektronix WVR7100.

contrast by raising the highlights. I don't care about these highlights," Sliga explains, pointing to the white tape on the center's fingers. "I'm creating an effect. I'm blowing them out. I can pull the blacks down even further if you want. But you can see as we pull the blacks down that it's going to kind of naturally funnel in. That's why sometimes I really won't do that. That's why I do a lot more with the gamma. Pull that saturation back down. Maybe warm the gammas back up a little bit." See Figure 6-45.

Fig. 6-45 **(a)** The secondary correction with no qualification at all. **(b)** Note the numbers under the color wheels.

a

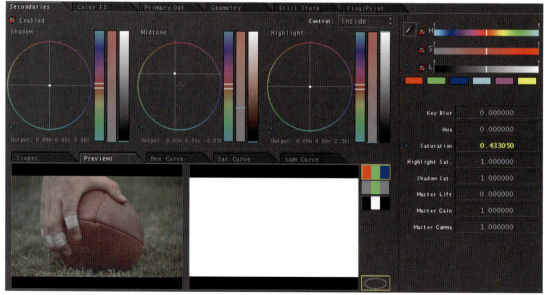

b

Switching gears from the more traditional method of building contrast, Sliga attacks the image by using the secondaries as they're designed to be used—*with* a qualification. "Now let's use it as more of a secondary tool. We're going to create a luminance key." Sliga sets the luminance key so that basically half of the image is black and half is white. Then he decides to work on the outside of the selection, which is the black part of the qualification. He brings both gain and gamma down. "By creating a luminance key, I've kind

a

Fig. 6-46 **(a)** The secondary correction on both sides of the luminance qualification. **(b)** The data from the outside of the secondary

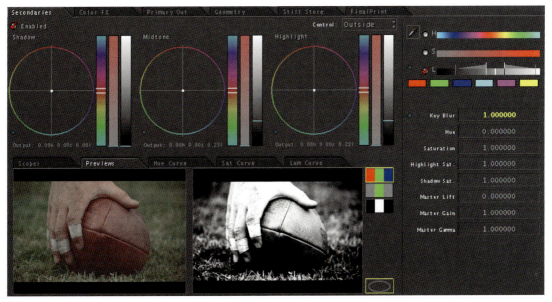

b

C

Fig. 6-46 (*Continued*) **(c)** the data from the inside of the secondary. Note the numbers under the color wheels of both (b) and (c).

of created some contrast naturally without even raising the whites. I didn't make the blacks black. I just darkened the gammas down and pulled the luminance value of that down. So now I can actually go back and choose inside and kick him back up, bringing gain up." See Figure 6-46c.

Conclusion

You can see that the ability to use secondaries to fix problems and delve into the details of the image is an exciting area to explore. In the following chapters, you'll see more examples of the use of secondary corrections as the colorists show you how to use them to improve images, further the story, match shots, and create cool looks.

Please follow along with these expert colorists using the footage in the Tutorials footage folder on the DVD. Remember, color correction is a subjective art form. Follow along, but let your own eye guide you. This is a great time to experiment and make mistakes since there's nothing at stake and no one is watching over your shoulder. Also, for an even wider vision of how different colorists work, there is a folder on the DVD that includes text files of the transcriptions of the colorists sessions. I have edited these and grouped them according to the various tutorial scenes, so instead of one or two "takes" on a given scene, you may be able to get as many as a dozen!

CHAPTER 7

Correcting Shots

Many colorists disapprove of the term *color correction* because so much of their talent extends well beyond simply "correcting" bad color. But the truth of the matter is that when working on many images, the first order of business *is* "correcting" the scene. Also, for many aspiring colorists, an even larger part of their jobs will be trying to correct bad video images. So this chapter is devoted to making bad images look okay, making decent images look good, and taking good images over the top.

Three More Grades of the "Banker's Light" Scene

Pete Jannotta, one of the most veteran and respected names in Chicago postproduction, is a colorist at Filmworker's Club. Pete chose to work on the same scene ("Ghosts_Bankerslight") from *Chasing Ghosts* that Janet Falcon tackled in Chapter 6 (see Figs. 7-1 and 7-2). He provides a detailed explanation of how he approaches this image mostly in primary, with forays into secondaries that are a nice transition from the previous chapter.

Jannotta evaluates the image, explaining, "My feeling would be that I'd want to make more out of this banker's light being warm and then leave some green on the outside. I also feel like this is plain too much green, even if it is fluorescent-lit and we want to have that office feeling, so I know that's in the midtones—most of it." Jannotta starts to push warmth into the banker's light using the gamma trackball, explaining, "If anything interacts, like the black gets pulled up a little out of whack, then adjust it. I did not do what I said to do first and that is to get the brightness and contrast kind of set where I want it." Jannotta completes the basic primary correction and continues.

"Now, this is starting to feel a little better already." When he cuts back and forth between his current correction and the source, he sees something that he didn't see before. "I went too magenta with it. I went overboard. I feel like my monitor and my vectorscope are telling me two different things." Unlike most of the other colorists, Jannotta did his corrections with my standard 17-inch Panasonic LCD HD monitor instead of

Fig. 7-1 "Ghosts_Bankerslight" scene from *Chasing Ghosts*. Image courtesy of Wingman Productions, Inc.

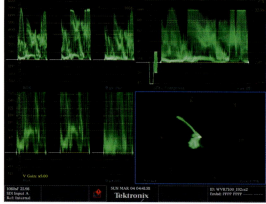

Fig. 7-2 Scopes showing the source image: the RGB parade (top left quadrant), the RGB parade expanded to show the black level (bottom left quadrant), the composite waveform (top right quadrant), and a standard vectorscope image (bottom right quadrant). From Tektronix WVR7100.

eCinema's grading monitor. In my monitor, Jannotta is seeing magenta but the vectorscope is not showing magenta. "But assuming that the monitoring is set up properly," he explains, "no matter what the vectorscope says, this (pointing to the monitor) is the end. But these (pointing to the RGB parade and vectorscope) always help me get there."

Jannotta continues to evaluate the image. "He's got a really interesting face and I think there's too much distracting around him to be focusing on him, so I like less saturation, because it would be more realistic I think for it not to be very saturated. It's not a real super colorful situation, but rather than green . . . it's more like drab office lighting. You can still feel some green, but, I like that better.

"Now what I think I want to do is get him to be more the central focus." I ask if secondaries are the way to accomplish that. "Yeah. And it looks like my blacks are up too high. It looks milky in here." Jannotta points to the pants under the banker's light and the edges of the banker's light. "When I look at the RGB parade, it looks like it's kind of high, and blue-black is kind of low, and that looks better when I fix that. It's always when you see something there [on the RGB parade] and you balance it, then you look at the screen and you say, 'Yeah. That's it. That did do it.' Sometimes your eye helps and sometimes the scopes." Jannotta also dials out some saturation and compresses the midtones while stretching out the highlights. "Make more out of it. Make him a little more interesting. I feel like I'm seeing a little blue in the lowlights, so I'm taking that out." See Figure 7-3.

"Okay. So now I'm going to go and do a secondary," Jannotta explains. "I'm going to vignette and I'm going to draw a window." Jannotta indicates the shape he wants with his hands on the monitor before using custom shapes in Color's vignette tool to create the shape.

The shape is vaguely triangular but is similar to a short, wide oval. I ask why an oval wouldn't be acceptable since it's less effort. Jannotta responds, "I always prefer to draw them because even in da Vinci I don't use a fixed circle ever anymore. What I like to do is draw the shape and then move it around so I can see how the light is working. I don't care what the shape is, but if it's an oval, then it's fixed and I can't control it. I could do an oval, but what if I want to give his tie a little more light? If I make a user shape, then I can pull that section down, because I'll have

a

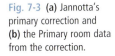

Fig. 7-3 **(a)** Jannotta's primary correction and **(b)** the Primary room data from the correction.

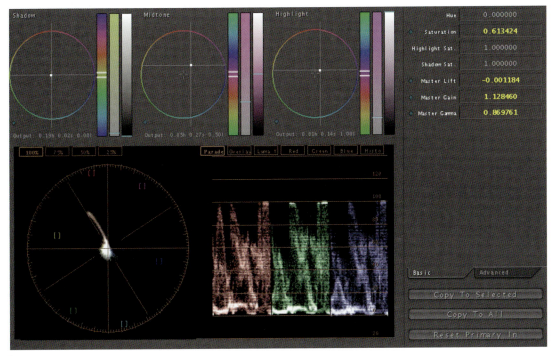

b

it set up. I'm always wanting to be able to move the shape around as if you were pointing a light."

In the discussion of whether to soften vignettes before or affecting them after, Jannotta falls far into the "soften first" camp. He explains, "If you get all done and you have it hard, and then you feather it and you don't have what you want, then you have to go back and do it anyway. That's why I soften it first and then I decide if I want to add more softness or take some of the softness away. But I always like to see it start [with softness]." See Figure 7-4.

a

Fig. 7-4 **(a)** The final correction with the secondary vignette. **(b)** Secondary room data from the inside of the vignette.

b

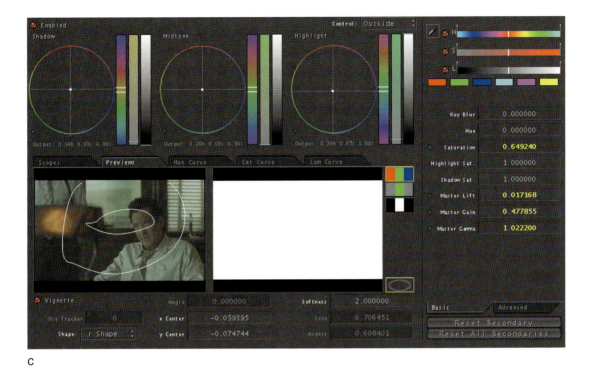

c

Fig. 7-4 (*Continued*) (**c**) Secondary room data from the outside of the vignette.

Neal Kassner of CBS also grades the "Ghosts_Bankerslight" The first thing I want to do, as my background is in **painting cameras**, I want to balance the blacks, the whites, and then the midtones. So the first thing I want to do is look for something dark in the frame—in this case it's the pants over there on the left—and I'm going to move the primary color corrector around until I begin to null it out somewhere in there," he explains as he works with the shadow trackball.

Kassner continues, "Now his shirt is supposed to be white. If it helps sell the story, I might leave it a bit greenish. In my normal work, we don't want to see that green, because it's news and the object is to enhance visual reality without distorting it. So what I'm going to do in that case is to take the green out of his shirt," Kassner explains as he uses the highlight trackball to balance out the shirt.

As he does this, I ask what he's watching. Kassner responds, "I'm watching the vectorscope primarily. Normally what I would do is I have my waveform monitor set to magnified and it's an overlaid display, so I can watch the colors null out. At this point what I would want to do is cut between the graded image as it is now and the raw image and see where I am." See Figure 7-5.

Definition

Painting Cameras:
Painting cameras, sometimes called *shading cameras*, is the act of balancing all of the cameras in a multicamera shoot so that all of the cameras match. During a live broadcast, this sometimes also requires making adjustments to the brightness or iris of the camera.

Chasing Ghosts

The footage of Sony Picture's *Chasing Ghosts* came courtesy of Wingman Productions, Inc. and the director of the feature, Kyle Jackson.

The story behind the movie is an interesting one. When Jackson and his producing partner, Alan Pao, were looking for a company to do the digital intermediate (DI), they couldn't find anyone who would work within their deadline and budget of $125,000. So they hooked up with the DR Group in Hollywood, CA (who coincidentally helped with equipment for this book) and they learned about a fledgling company called Silicon Color that had created color correction software for DI on a Mac G5.

Chasing Ghosts became the first feature film to use FinalTouch2K and when it was done and word got out about the DI for the movie, many other indie producers wanted them to do the DI for their films as well. That's when the producing/directing team decided to open a postproduction house called Tunnel Post and started doing DIs based on their workflow for *Chasing Ghosts*. In the year and a half since they set up shop, they've done the DIs for 30 feature films.

According to Jackson, "The workflow hasn't changed a lot. On *Chasing Ghosts* we scanned in — at an outside facility, though, since then we bought our own scanner — at 2K, then used Final Cut Film list. We wrote a simple Excel macro to translate those film lists into a text file that FinalTouch can read in and then go through the process of grading for 40, 60, 80 hours depending, while we're doing titles and effects stuff at the same time. Then we're rendering to video deliverables, film out, Web previews, and trailer all at once instead of having to go through inter-positive (IP) and then video transfers and downconvert. It saves a lot of money in the end."

The colorist for *Chasing Ghosts* was Teague Crowley, who still works with Tunnel. For more on the film's look, check out the sidebar on *Chasing Ghosts* in Chapter 8.

Kassner continues, "So now, what I might want to do as well is, since there's a lamp in the foreground, that's going to motivate some light in his face, so I want to brighten things up just a little bit. And this is where Power Windows (a da Vinci trademark tool) or a mask would come in handy."

Kassner goes into secondaries and adds a small soft circle vignette over the lamp, explaining, "So I'm going to crank down the gain here, to counteract what I did to bring Michael Madsen (the actor) up. And this obviously is a judgment call as to how much is too much. Then we go back and forth to the before and after just to compare the luminance of the lamp." (See Figure 7-6)

After switching back and forth between his current correction and the uncorrected source, Kassner determines that he needs to soften the vignette on the lamp even more. "I don't want to go too far, because I don't want it to affect his face particularly. Now I'm going to cut back

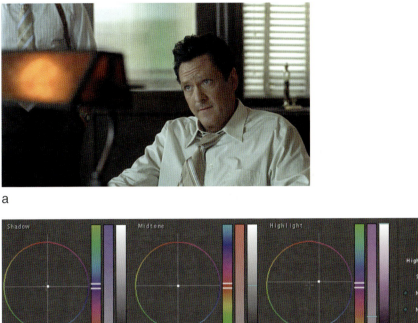

a

Fig. 7-5 (a) Kassner's primary correction and **(b)** the data from the Primary room.

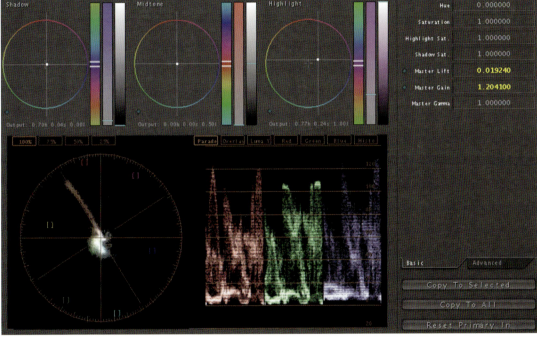

b

Fig. 7-6 (a) This secondary brings down the light luminance inside the vignette and slightly pulls highlights away from green outside the vignette. **(b)** The data from the inside of the vignette. The outside data is just a slight highlight correction away from green.

a

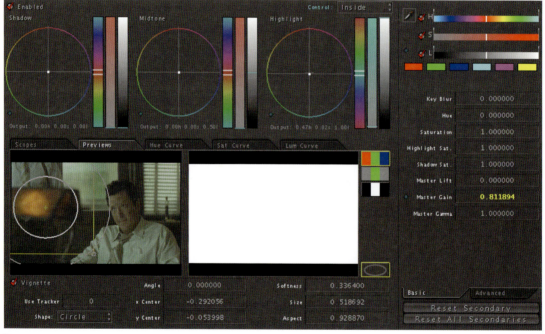

b

and forth between them. It's still there if you know what to look for, but if you're not doing a side-by-side comparison, it looks better. I like that. There's still a little bit of yellow left in his shirt . . . well a little more green and yellow."

Kassner chooses to fix the color on the outside of the lamp vignette instead of going back to primaries. "I'm watching the vectorscope primarily. Normally what I would do is look at one of my waveform monitors which is set to 5 times horizontal magnification; since it shows all three color channels overlaid, I can watch the colors null out to pure black or white as I move the trackballs around. It doesn't have to be pure white. And actually his skin tone is going a little bit reddish, which is not bad, but maybe a little bit too red. So what I want to do now is pick a red secondary." Kassner qualifies the face with a red color pick and a vignette before he rolls the midtone trackball away from red. "I just want to make his face look a little tanner." See Fig. 7-7.

a

Fig. 7-7 **(a)** The final correction with the addition of a secondary to pull some redness out of the skin tones. **(b)** The data from the inside of the qualification, pulling midtones slightly more yellow.

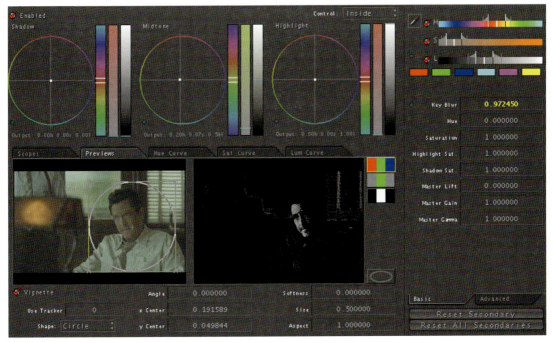

b

Kassner continues with a helpful tip. "I do a lot of switching between graded and ungraded. It helps me see what changes I need to make to improve the shot. Some people like to use a split screen. In my previous work as a live-air video operator in a control room I didn't have split-screen capability. I had what we called a 'match switcher' that allowed me to cut back and forth among cameras and the other sources in the production switcher, making adjustments to match their 'looks'. The quicker you cut, the more you can see color or exposure differences; that's the way I grew up learning, so that's what I do here."

I ask Level 3 Post colorist Larry Field to take the same "Banker's Light" image in a different direction: more straight sitcom. "Well to do that I'd defer to the scopes," begins Field. "Make sure the blacks are balanced. One reason I like at least one of my parade scopes expanded out is so I can really see that black balance coupled with the expanded vectorscope. Then the next thing is to neutralize the shirt and white balance and bring his shirt away from green." As he pulls the scene toward a proper balance, he seems to be looking primarily at the zoomed-in vectorscope. "I'm kind of looking at everything simultaneously. One of the bad things that happened to this shot as I corrected it was the background started going magenta, which is natural since I'm try to bring his shirt from green. If we need to neutralize the shot, I can then affect that area separately if I need to. And everything's interactive somewhat, so I'm looking at all my scopes at one time." See Figure 7-8.

Fig. 7-8 (a) This image was recreated by watching the videotaped session with Field and re-executing the grade. This is the primary correction.

a

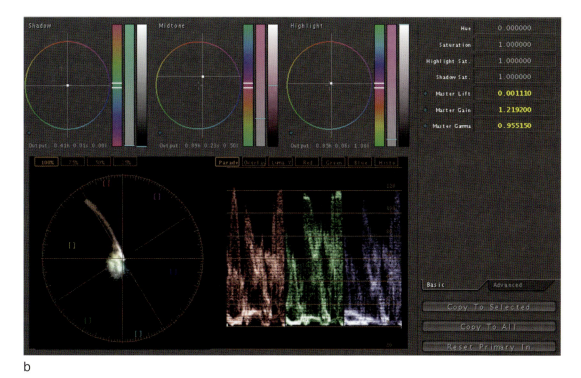

b

Fig. 7-8 *(Continued)* **(b)** The recreated data from the Primary room.

I ask him about his use of the RGB parade scopes in trying to achieve color balance. "I'm looking at RGB. I'm also looking at black in the middle of the vectorscope, as well as white, and also separation on the chroma side of the split waveform, but again, all at one time."

Field is not happy with his correction yet, since it's veering toward magenta. Instead of continuing with the correction, I ask him to simply explain what he would do next. "I think it's that window up there where you can see things are going magenta," Field mentions as he points to the vectorscope. "That looks pretty hot up there, so I'd put a key on that," he explains, pointing at the window over the talent's left shoulder. "Then I'd bring it to neutral. Or I can use the Power Window with a soft edge. Or I could put a Power Window over his shirt and white balance the window out. A few different techniques, all of which would work."

Fig. 7-9 (a) This is my grade following Field's suggestion to pull a key on the window (and shirt), eliminating even more of the green, then adding a garbage matte to the HSL (hue, saturation, and luminance) qualification to bring the windows down in Master Gain. **(b)** The Secondary room data on the inside of the HSL qualification plus a garbage matte on the windows.

a

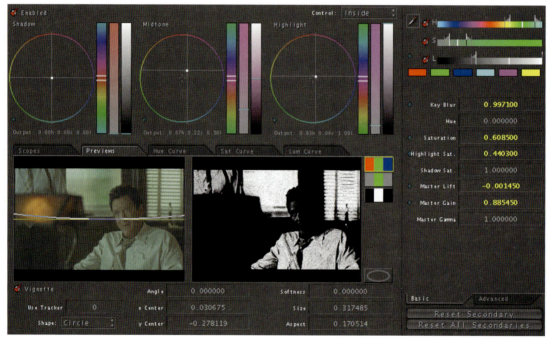

b

Saving a Shot with Bad Color Cast

Neal Kassner, colorist for CBS's "48 Hours," was drawn to the challenge of the "flowerbench" scene (see Figs. 7-11 and 7-12). "Obviously it's very washed out and it's very green. There's some whites there. There's actually some blacks as well. So I'm going to crank down the black level and then bring the gammas down a little bit as well. There's a lot of green in

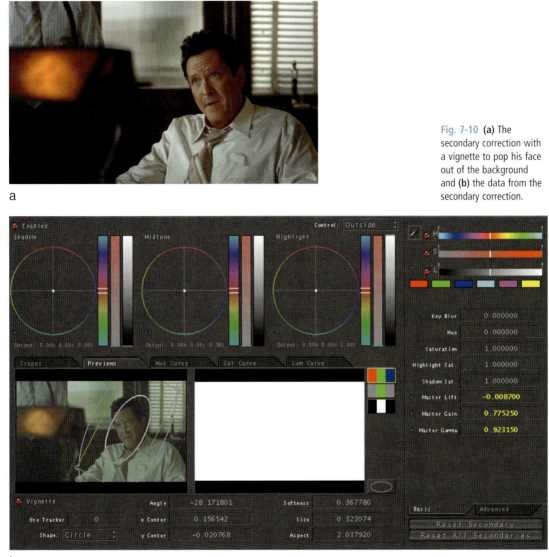

a

Fig. 7-10 (a) The secondary correction with a vignette to pop his face out of the background and (b) the data from the secondary correction.

b

the blacks there, so I'm using the primary color corrector and watching the vectorscope to a certain extent. I'm just going to walk this in."

By using the expression "walk this in," I assumed he was using the vectorscope to get the blacks into the middle. Kassner responds, "Well, kind of. That's what I started to do, but the foliage in the shadow areas is not really truly black. There's still supposed to be a green cast to it, so

Fig. 7-11 The original source image.

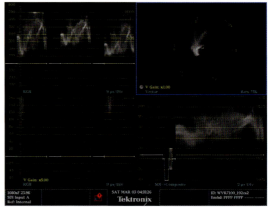

Fig. 7-12 Scopes showing the source image: the RGB parade (top left quadrant), the RGB parade expanded to show the black level (bottom left quadrant), the vectorscope (top right quadrant), and the composite waveform (bottom right quadrant). From Tektronix WVR7100.

now I'm going to go by eye until it looks a little bit better. Then maybe bring down the master blacks again. Now I can attack the whites. There's a nice, big, fat, white post there that I can use to get a white balance on essentially." Kassner looks at the standard composite waveform monitor and watches as the trace that represents the white area "compresses," indicating that it is getting more neutral. See "Kassner's Balancing Tricks" box below for more on this technique.

Neal Kassner

Neal Kassner's first brush with fame was in college when he lit the audition reel for his class-mate, Al Roker, while they attended Oswego State University in upstate New York together. After college he worked as an electrician on such feature films as *Superman* and *Hair*.

Eventually he was hired at ABC Television where he matched multicamera shoots for shows like "World News Tonight" and "Nightline," as well as on soap operas "All My Children" and "One Life to Live." In addition, he did fill-in roadwork on "Monday Night Football."

In 1981 he joined CBS Television and worked for 14 years as a video operator and technical director. That was when he began building toward a career in color correction, starting in 1995 with the news magazine "Eye To Eye With Connie Chung" and several documentaries for CBS News. He also graded for "60 Minutes" and "Sunday Morning" before starting work on "48 Hours", where he's been ever since. Kassner considers the highlight of his career to date to be the documentary "9/11", the Naudet brothers' first-person account from inside the World Trade Center on the day of the attacks.

Kassner continues, "Now I'm going to bring up the gain in there because that's the hottest thing in the picture. This has also altered the color cast of everything else. It's actually made things a little more yellow. So, I'm going to back that off in the blacks. I'm going to do this by eye instead of by the scope because this is one of those places where you could do it via the scope, but you're going to end up with an uninteresting looking picture. So I'm just going to play around with it until I see something that looks good."

He moves on to the gammas. "Now I'm playing with the gammas just to kind of even out the midtones a little bit because they were still a little bit yellow looking. Now I want to increase the overall saturation. The magenta really pops. And maybe just bring down the overall gamma a little bit to make it pop a little bit more. Now of course because it's all interactive, whatever you do in one area may affect the others, so I'm going to go back and tighten up the whites. So this is where a magnified H display would really help me dial that in nice and tight. But that's close enough for here." See Figure 7-13.

a

Fig. 7-13 **(a)** Kassner's final correction, and **(b)** the data from the Primary room.

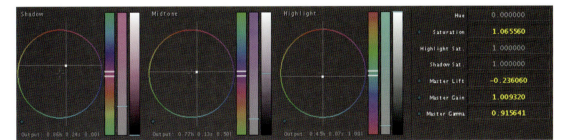

b

Kassner's Balancing Tricks

One of Neal Kassner's favorite tricks for balancing whites and blacks was developed long before he became a colorist. His previous career involved "shading" cameras for multicamera shoots. (See earlier definition in this chapter for Painting Cameras.) That practice is similar to color correction, but takes place with multiple live cameras *before* the shoot, and continues to some extent *during* the shoot.

Kassner blows up the composite waveform *horizontally* to five times normal zoom. Then he positions the waveform so he can see an area of the screen that he believes has white or black in it. Remember, the composite waveform in flat-pass mode, or YC waveform, displays not only pure luminance values, but reflects chroma as well, which is represented by the excursion of the trace. What does that mean? Well, if the line that represents black or white is thick, then there's chroma or color in it. If the line is as narrow as you can get it, then the color has been eliminated.

Kassner expounds on this idea with another one of his tricks for balancing shots. "Now here's a cheat that I use and I don't think anyone else uses it. In the da Vinci, I use a Power Window to isolate the black or white areas of the picture. So if I make a Power Window and center it over a black area of the picture, I get a truly black area in the shadows. Then by repositioning the window to a white area, I can do the same kind of thing. So now I've got a rough white and black balance. From there, I can trim as necessary. Isolating that helps because sometimes in the waveform display, the area that you're trying to sample just gets lost in everything else that's in there. It's hard to separate out a white shirt against a blown-out sky."

This trick is possible in Color by going in to the Geometry room and zooming in to an area you believe represents white or black. With the overlay waveform monitor active, or better yet an external composite waveform in flat-pass mode, adjust the highlights or shadows to flatten the trace as much as possible. This can be done with the hue offset wheels or with the red, green, and blue channel controls in the Advanced tab. See Figure 7-14.

a   b

Fig. 7-14 **(a)** shows part of Color's Geometry Room UI with a small black area indicated, sending only what is in the selected area out to the scopes. **(b)** shows the vectorscope and composite waveform for only the color from within the box in 7-14a.

Four Trips Down the "Alley"

I call this scene the "Alleyway" shot from *Chasing Ghosts* (see Figs. 7-15 and 7-16). On the DVD this clip is called "Ghosts_alley.mov" and is in the "Tutorial_footage_and_files" folder. What follows here are three different colorists' takes on this same shot. Actually almost all of the colorists who took part in the book took a shot at this image, but the three who were the most descriptive about what they were doing as they corrected it were Chris Pepperman, Mike Most, and Greg Creaser.

NFL Films' Chris "Pep" Pepperman takes the first shot at the "Alleyway" scene: "So when I look at something like this, what comes to my mind is that it's definitely a flat light. There's some clipped areas in the building that, regardless of what we do, we're not going to bring back, simply because that's the way it is on tape. I'll explain that to the client. But I won't necessarily say that right away because I don't want to start right off the bat by saying, 'Well, I can't do this.' Mostly I try to say, 'I can, I can, I can,' and if I can't do it, I'll say, 'I can' . . . slowly," Pep jokes.

"Right now, I'm bringing the blacks down to 0, and I want to bring the video level completely out of clip." Pepperman uses the term *video* or *video level* throughout his session, referring to gain or highlights. He points at the RGB waveform monitor as he lowers the gain. Then he continues, "I'm assuming I'm out of the clip now. What I'm saying is that I'm not

Fig. 7-15 The source scene from *Chasing Ghosts*. Image courtesy of Wingman Productions, Inc.

Fig. 7-16 Scopes showing the source image: the YRGB parade (top left quadrant), the vectorscope expanded 5× (bottom left quadrant), the composite waveform (top right quadrant), and the standard zoom on the vectorscope (bottom right quadrant). From Tektronix WVR7100.

Definition

Peds: This is a typical abbreviation for pedestal or blacks.

electronically clipping it. And once I establish that I'm not, I'm going to come back up a little bit. Now, I'm a little flatter than what I want to be, but I don't want to clip anything now, because I want to be sure my reds, greens, and blues are balanced. Now, just by looking at the picture, take the overall video and **peds** and start to swing that on the warmer side. And as I do that, I'm liking what I see."

As Pepperman sets the levels, he's careful to keep the video levels just under 100 IRE. "We clip at 100% here," he explains. "At Manhattan Transfer, we used to clip at 103% or 104%. Some colorists like to see all of the detail that's in the film element. I like to see what's important, what's relative in the film. Meaning, if something looks good to me and the background is clipped out, then I don't care about the background clipping out. I care about somebody saying 'That's visually pleasing to me.' And that's what film is about. As far as I'm concerned that's the beauty of film, being able to do those things. And that's where the art of color correction is different. I always try to look at the picture, interpret what's the most important part of the picture in that image, especially when it's commercial work and I want your eye to go there."

Pepperman continues, "For me, what is this picture all about? It's all about him talking. So visually, as you're watching this, you're not going to be watching the background. You're not going to be looking at the building. You're going to be looking at him. So let's make him the subject. Let's make him the priority. Let's make him look good. Whatever happens in the background happens. Now with the tools we have, I balance him, make him look good, *then* I work on the things that surround him. So I start with the primary subject and then I work my way around the picture and decide what else is important to me. So right now, all I'm concerned about is him. Right now, I want to make him look good. So now I'm going to start to brighten him up again, and I'm going to start adding some warmth, because I still feel that it's cooler."

Pepperman explains, "Now I feel like the warmth in the midrange would help. As I'm looking at this, I'm starting to see red in the blacks so I don't want to bleed too much, but I like the skin tone in him." At this point, Pepperman cuts back and forth between the current correction and the original source footage.

Pleased with his progress, Pepperman continues, "Now, I'm taking into consideration the fact that he's in a shadowed area. So you're not going to want it to be real bright. I typically don't use high and low **sat**. Only when I'm dealing with very rough film. What I mean is very underexposed or overexposed, because sometimes I feel like I have to add warmth overall to the picture, but sometimes it affects the peds. So then I have to clean the peds up, so that's when I use that tool. But primarily, I wouldn't use that." See Figure 7-17.

Definition

Sat: This is a typical abbreviation for saturation, especially when describing the application's controls for saturation. For example, "I lowered the high sat so the clouds would go white."

a

b

Pepperman continues, "So, here's where it becomes subjective. If a DP wants it on the cooler side, I'd add more coolness. If he wanted it warmer, I'd add some warmth. But I would like this a little bit on the warm/neutral side. Now the second thing that I would do is I would isolate about three-quarters of the picture. I would build a window around him and her and knock the background down. Because what I want to do is bring that clip down and I also want to add some depth, some midrange to the building in the back, and try to give it a little more guts. The background I would consider as thin and I want to try to help that out. The way I would do that . . . well there are a couple of ways, but the easiest way for me quickly is just to build a window around him, grab the outside of that window, and start coming down see what would happen. So I'm going to position the circle around him and her and soften it. Now I want to affect the outside of the window."

In the continuing saga of correcting with sharp or softened edges on vignettes, Pepperman lands in the "keep it sharp so I can see it" camp: "All I'm doing right now is going down as far as I can to see what the background looks like. And I'm liking what I see, because it's bringing those subtle details. I like the coolness temperature on the building. I like the fact that the midrange is really helping it out. And I like the fact that I'm seeing the areas of the picture that were clipped before. And I would typically build a circle just about where it is right now. And I tend to go a little deeper with my shapes as far as overall correction, and as I soften it, I'll make the decision of whether I need to add something or take something out. So what I'm going to do now is, I'm going to go back inside the circle. And I just want to clean up the black areas a little bit."

Pepperman lowers the low saturation setting inside the window as he explains his change from his earlier stance, "I typically wouldn't use low sat or high sat here, because you can build yourself into a corner. Because what happens with a da Vinci is that the color correction that you apply to the scene will go to the next scene. I just don't like painting myself in a corner that way."

Finally, he softens the edge of the vignette and moves it up a bit from where it had been. "Now I want to go inside the circle and increase the video a little bit. And I want to come up on the peds a tad. I want to go to the point where I don't see emulsion anymore, what we consider emulsion in the blacks, but I still see detail." See Figure 7-18.

Next, industry veteran Mike Most, of Miami's Cineworks Digital Studios, takes on the "Alleyway" scene: "The whole thing is timed a little cool for my tastes, so once again I'll go through my usual. And I'll look and see if there's anything that warrants being white, and in this case it probably does. In this case I wouldn't be afraid to let some of the white areas clip. Normally you try to hold those in check if you can. But in point of fact, the grayscale of this, if I start pulling it up, the picture just looks flat. So I probably want it down where it was, and yet I want his face to look right. So I can do that either with a window, or more likely, I'll do it by just clipping the white areas and then fixing the flesh tone a little bit. The reason I prefer to do it that way is simply because it gives me a little more kick. I mean, he's clearly in a shadow anyway so you don't want him too bright. But there's nothing up there (pointing to the sky in the top left) that you need to see, so I would just kind of let it go."

Fig. 7-18 **(a)** The secondary correction with the vignette. Corrections were made inside and outside of the vignette,

a

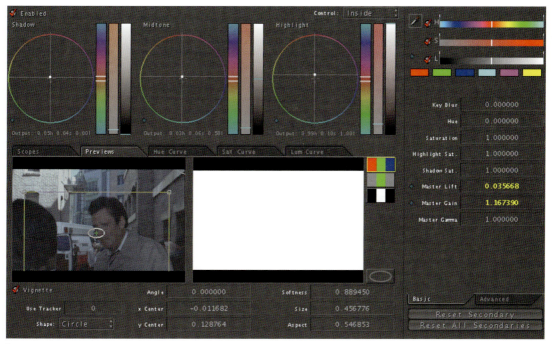

b

c

Fig. 7-18 (*Continued*) **(b)** The data from the inside of the vignette, **(c)** the data from the outside of the vignette.

Fig. 7-19

Fig. 7-20

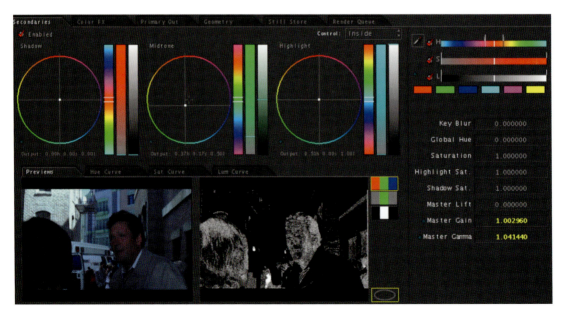

Fig. 7-21

Mike Most

Mike Most has an extensive background in both color correction and visual effects. His color correction credits include "L.A. Law," "Murder One," and "NYPD Blue." He has also served as visual effects supervisor for shows like "Ally McBeal" and "Charmed." Currently at Miami's Cineworks Digital Studios, he supervises visual effects.

Now Most leaves the Primary room to hone in on the flesh tones in the secondary room. He qualifies the skin tones with hue only and pulls the skin tones toward green, adding a little to both Master Gain and Master Gamma. Joining me at the session with Most was Roland Wood, founder of FinalTouch, which later became Apple's Color. *Chasing Ghosts* was the first feature graded on FinalTouch and Wood used the footage to do demos and training with hundreds of colorists around the world. He was impressed by Most's correction, saying "That's the best correction I've ever seen on that shot. And I've seen this shot done a lot."

Most takes the compliment with typical modesty, "Well, you notice that I haven't used any windows. I tend to use windows for two reasons: I have a real problem—I have a blown-out sky or a blown-out window—something very specific; or creatively, like I did in the other shot where it was clear that to emphasize where the key was hitting and to emphasize the shadows would improve the shot. But on something like this, I know guys who would try to do a window around the hot area."

Greg Creaser, a Los Angeles, CA, freelance colorist who specializes in grading digital intermediates, shows his take on the "Alleyway" scene as well. "I'm attacking the midtones again right away because it's an opened-up image. I mean there's a lot of range in there. Midtones are going to be fine for the brunt of it. He's looking a little cool to me. Let's give him a little more flesh tone back. Somewhere in there. The highlights may be a little bit hot. There's a couple ways to attack that. We could pull them down here," he says, referring to the highlights in primaries. "Then pull the midtones back up. Not much we can do with that hotspot. That would be another key situation. Or you maybe want to throw a shape in there to knock it down if your eye is getting drawn to it. If we want a little more bite in there, we can dip the blacks a little bit more. I think this image can handle it. Bring the midtones back up just a little bit."

Creaser continues, "Now let's check out before and after. It's just kind of normalized. I'd like to see a little more bite to the image, but I'd be a little afraid of the hair going away. Sometimes, if I'm grading a film (for DI), I'd use a pixel picker to see where we were in our 10-bit data. Since we're working in HD, I would leave it where it is or we'll get ghosting in the blacks, which is what would happen if you force it too far. I like it." See Figure 7-15 again for the original source and Figure 7-22.

Fig. 7-22 **(a)** Creaser's final correction and **(b)** the FinalTouch UI data from the final correction.

a

b

Creaser cuts back and forth between the source and his correction. "We lessened the contrast just a little bit and gave it a normal look. They're in the shadow so they wouldn't have a lot of contrast here."

I ask Creaser what clues or hints he sees in the picture to decide help him what an image should look like. He responds, "He's in the shadow, even though he's lit of course. It'd be flat light, because he's not getting any kick from highlight of the sun. So the first place to attack this would be lessening the contrast, because I felt it to be a little bit too much in the original. It doesn't look correct that way. I mean, if you were standing there looking at this guy, would it be that contrasty? I don't think so. So you back it out just a little bit and it looks a little more natural. And we didn't kill it and we took the blue out. When you're working on film, you can be a little more bold on things. But if you're working in 8-bit video, you have to watch it."

Three Passes Over the Barn

Now three colorists approach Randy Riesen's documentary scene of an ultralight flying over a barn (see Figs. 7-23 and 7-24). On the DVD, this is the "ultralight_barn.mov" file in the Tutorial folder.

 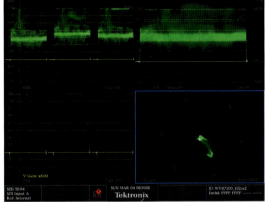

Fig. 7-23 The uncorrected BetaSP-originated source image for the "ultralight_bam" scene. Image courtesy of Randy Riesen.

Fig. 7-24 Scopes showing the source image: the RGB parade (top left quadrant), the expanded RGB parade to see the black balance (bottom left quadrant), the composite waveform (top right quadrant), and the standard vectorscope (bottom right quadrant). From Tektronix WVR7100.

Randy Riesen

It's a brave thing for any good cameraman to offer his stuff up to be color corrected in front of the world. Luckily, Riesen is confident enough of his considerable skills with a camera to allow me to go through hours and hours of his personal footage looking for a few seconds of less-than-perfect footage.

Randy Riesen has shot in Chicago for more than two decades. In addition to shooting numerous music videos for bands like the Smashing Pumpkins and the John Mathie Band and serving as DP for countless documentary projects, he has also racked up an impressive number of credits shooting for more than 25 of the country's top national shows, including "Investigative Reports" with Bill Kurtis, "Entertainment Tonight," "America's Most Wanted," "The Daily Show," and the "Jane Pauley Show." He has also shot spots for Leo Burnett and Twitch Films.

Riesen works at Big Shoulders Digital Video Productions.

First up on this video-originated scene is Mike Matusek, of Nolo Digital Film in Chicago, IL. "I guess there're two approaches to this shot. What I would do here, because I like the highlights on the barn, is to warm it up and give it a golden-hour kind of look. Again, since golden hour is more about the highlights being golden, I'm going to go to the gain controls, because right now they're kind of bluish white. At golden hour, there's much more contrast between the shadows and the highlights, so I might crush the blacks a little bit. When you crush the blacks, you're saturating the blacks. When you increase the gain, you're saturating the highlights, which is good for this image because it's washed out." However, with most images, this increased saturation is something that you would need to counteract, especially when dealing with footage that requires extreme changes of blacks or gain. See Figure 7-25.

Matusek continues, "So now what I would try to do is grab these highlights individually, because I'm trying to push more warmth into the highlights. What I'm doing is whacking out the midtones a little bit, and they're getting a little too yellowy and ugly, so I'd probably grab those (white of the buildings), blur them, and get that magenta out of there."

At this point, Matusek enables a secondary and pulls an HSL key on the buildings' facades. "So instead of pushing artificial warmth into it, I'll desaturate it a little bit and warm it up like that. So it goes from that pink to a little more white, but there's still some warmth in the highlights. It looks a lot more lush than it was," he concludes. See Figure 7-26.

Mike Most takes the next shot at the "ultralight flyover" scene. He explains his approach: "Usually when I'm tackling a shot that I know to

Fig. 7-25 **(a)** Matusek's primary color correction imparting a golden-hour look and **(b)** the data from the Primary room.

a

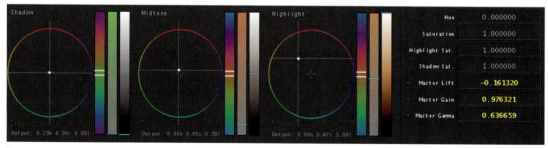

b

a

Fig. 7-26 **(a)** The secondary correction to move highlights from pink and **(b)** the data from the Secondary room.

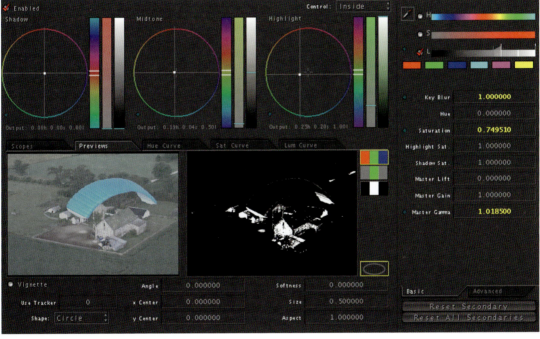

b

have all kinds of problems, I try to give myself something to latch on to. I mean, I'm seeing dark shadows in the trees that I can probably boost the contrast of a little bit. I'm seeing white on a barn that I can try and grab, and it's also on the parachute a little bit. So I'm going to try to use that for a rough white balance. I'm seeing green on the bottom that I probably can't get through primaries alone, so I'll try to get that through secondaries. And once again, boosting contrast will help me separation-wise. You don't want to go too far on your whites, because you're just throwing away detail, and ultimately you're going to need some of that detail. Crushing the gammas a little bit would not be a bad thing. There's going to be a little bit of green in the blacks. If you look at the parade display that's exactly what I have."

I notice that although he'd pulled down the blacks quite a bit to increase contrast, he brought them back up a bit after looking at the RGB parade. Most explains his change of heart, "Yeah. You play. You don't always know exactly where you're going to go. Sometimes you do, but sometimes you don't. You see what you've got and then you figure out what you want to do. So in terms of my starting point, I'm pretty much there." See Figure 7-27.

With his primary correction complete, he moves to secondaries, explaining, "I'll try to pull something that's green here. What you see as green isn't always green. I mean, it's more yellow than green, but what I'm going to try to do is find the center of most of the grass and trees." Most qualifies a green area that mostly selects the trees behind the barn,

Fig. 7-27 **(a)** Most's primary correction and **(b)** the data from the Primary room. The original FinalTouch grades were brought in to Color for screenshots.

a

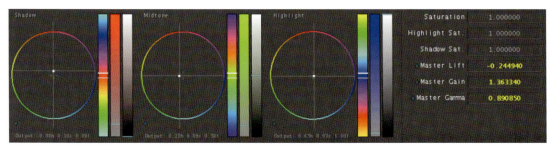

b

then adds a little key blur before starting his adjustment of the qualified area. "I'll try boosting the saturation to the keyed area, then I'll try
swinging the hue around. See what it gets me, if anything—swinging it
away from yellow. At that point you can go back to the primaries because
you've got the secondary on. If you increase that toward yellow you're
going to get more green, because you've got a secondary working on top
of it. Like I say, it's all about separation and contrast, so now I've got
something that may not be the kickiest-looking picture in the world, but
it's a lot better than what I started with." See Figure 7-28.

a

Fig. 7-28 (a) The
secondary correction on
the foliage and **(b)** the
data from the Secondary
room.

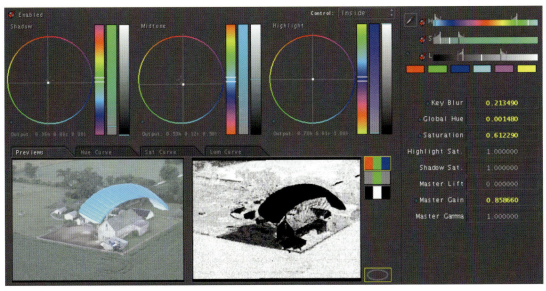

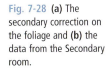

b

Most talks through his other options. "The other thing I might do is go into another secondary. I hate using multiple secondaries. I honestly do, because I think it's a crutch. I think you've got to get things separated by balance before you start going into secondaries, but when you've got something like this that had so little contrast on the original and so many colors as a result that are overlapping each other, that's about the only excuse I can think of for using multiple secondaries. And so what I would probably do here is try to go in and grab another secondary and maybe start with a cyan grab on the parachute and see what happens. Try and separate out the parachute completely, so that I'm only working on the parachute." Most qualifies a beautiful secondary isolating the parachute. "Right in there seems to get it. Blur the key a little bit. Then what I can do is try and swing that away from the greenish cyan back toward a blue. It just makes it stand out more. Not sure I can do much with the saturation, but I probably can in the primaries, now that I have it separated. Once again swinging it more toward a pure blue than the cyanish blue that we were getting before. That creates separation." See Figure 7-29.

Bob Sliga also makes a pass at the "ultralight_bam" image. Before Sliga starts to balance out the image, I ask if he likes to use the expanded, or zoomed, RGB parade waveform display that so many of the other colorists liked to use when balancing blacks. "No. I use the vectorscope for that. I mean, you can. Every person does it a little differently. But it gives me the ability to see what I need to see here," he explains, pointing at the center of the vectorscope, which has been zoomed in four times. "I'm looking for a nice tight ball there. That gets me where black is black, but we're still so far blue balanced," he says, looking at the shadows of trees above the farm.

"Now I'm going to richen this up something like that," he says as he lowers the gamma and then warms it up. Then he pulls blue out of highlights and touches on the shadows briefly. "I **time** more on the richer side—little heftier blacks, heavier gammas just to give you more pop through it, letting the highlights blow out. It's just the theory that if you don't like that, it's very easy to time back." See Figure 7-30.

At this point, Sliga goes to the Saturation curve in Color's Secondary room and cranks up the green point. "You'll see that the green and yellow secondary color correction will blend together." Since not everyone has access to Color's Saturation curve tool, I ask Sliga to walk me through doing the correction without it. In response to the challenge, Sliga creates a qualification based on green that picks the grass and trees. "Once we have that qualification we aren't limited to anything. We can change the gain, the gamma. Very powerful." Sliga makes the grass a nice green

a

Fig. 7-29 **(a)** The secondary correction on the parachute and **(b)** the data from the Secondary room.

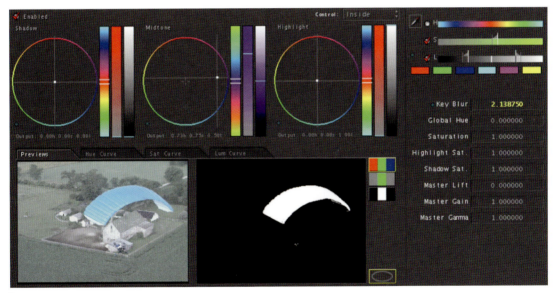

b

a

Fig. 7-30 **(a)** The primary correction only and **(b)** the data from the Primary room.

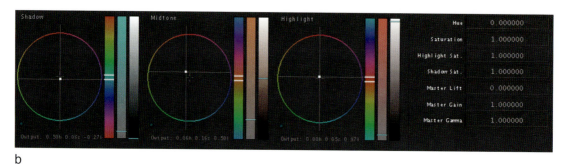

b

color before adding, "And now let's go outside, and if we want to, make it more contrasty." Sliga brings up the gain outside of his green qualification before showing the difference his secondary correction makes (see Fig. 7-31). Sliga also pulls a qualification on the parachute wing for a final tweak (see Fig. 7-32).

Sliga's original Saturation curve alteration essentially selected a green color along a color bar with the entire range of hues then allowed him to raise or lower the saturation of *just* that vector or hue. The other Curves in Color's secondary room work similarly, but instead of raising or lowering saturation, the Hue curve allows a specific hue to be swung to a different hue and the Luma curve allows you to raise or lower the luminance of a specific hue. See the "Color's Secondary Curves" section at the end of Chapter 5 for more.

a

Fig. 7-31 (a) The secondary correction on the foliage and **(b)** the data from the Secondary room.

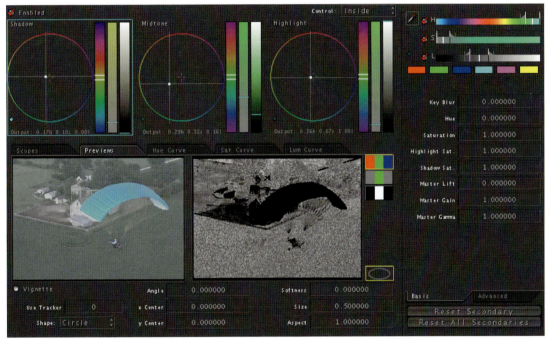

b

Fig. 7-32 (a) The secondary correction on the parachute and (b) the data from the Secondary room.

a

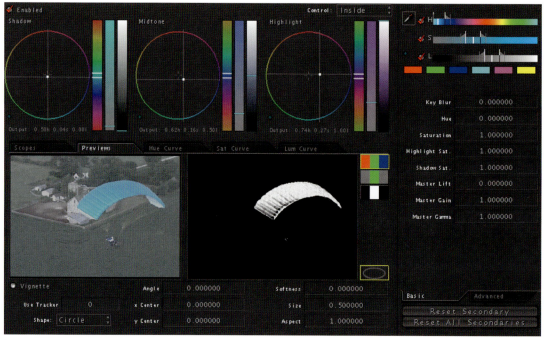

b

Building Up a Weak Piece of Video

Figure 7-33 (see also Fig. 7-34) is an image that I guess I should be embarrassed to say that I shot. It was done as a "one-man-band" interview for a documentary I produced about my family's 1977 bicycle trip across the United States. The subject is my brother Brian. It was shot around 1995 on BetaSP. We will be returning to this shot in Chapter 9, "Matching Shots," since this interview started in bright daylight and went into twilight. So in that chapter, we'll discuss how to match the interview footage from earlier in the day to the footage shot near dusk.

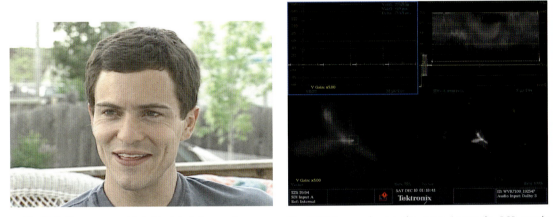

Fig. 7-33 The uncorrected BetaSP-originated source image.

Fig. 7-34 Scopes showing the source image: the RGB parade expanded to view the black balance (top left quadrant), the vectorscope blown up 5× (bottom left quadrant), the composite waveform (top right quadrant), and the vectorscope at standard zoom (top right quadrant). From Tektronix WVR7100.

For this chapter, Chris Pepperman tries to turn the washed-out footage into something broadcastable. "The first thing I'm going to do is take the blacks and the midtones and start crushing at the same time. So the midrange is going to give you all the facial tones."

I tried to gauge how low Pep would take the blacks and midtones, asking him, "So you're taking it down until you see some noise that you don't like, then you stop?"

"Exactly," he confirmed. "When it gets too crushed. Right there, it's too crushed. So now I'm going to bring the midrange up a little bit to where I like it. Right there. And I'm going to bring the black levels back up to where I like it . . . right there."

As Pep takes the blacks and midtones from one extreme past the proper point and back into a comfortable range, he follows the same "focusing" analogy that I've espoused in previous chapters. "Now I've got to balance. I'm going to overall balance the image. And what I'm doing is looking at the vector and the waveform and I'm touching the peds, the gammas, and the video, and I'm just balancing everything." As he gets closer to what he wants, his eyes move from the scopes back to the picture monitor as he tries to find a pleasing skin tone. "I'm seeing that it's still a little blocked up now, so I'm going to come up on the peds." He confirms that by "blocked up" he means that the blacks are too dark. "So now I'm coming up so I can see all of his hair." Pep's visual clue that the blacks were blocking up came when the hair above Brian's forehead started to lose detail. "I'm looking at the front lock of hair. I'm not looking at his eyes because his eyes are going to be darker. He's not getting fill light into his eyes, so if I were to bring up his eyes, everything else is going to go. Like his eyes are good there, but it's too flat. So I'm looking at his hair, his eyebrows, and that tree in the back. So I'm kind of liking where that is right now. I'm also liking overall balance. I might warm it up a tad in the skin tone." He cuts back and forth between the original and his current correction. "So we're seeing a significant difference. Now let's get in to the nitty gritty." See Figure 7-35.

Leaving the Primary room, Pep creates a secondary and enables a vignette, creating a tall oval shape around the subject's face. "Now I'm going to go outside and I want to crush just the midrange and the blacks, leaving the highlights alone right now. And now bringing the highlights down a little bit to where I can see detail in everything. Now I'm going to bring the midrange down, down, down. Now I'm going to bring the black levels up. I'm just seeing...it's a feel, ya know?"

As I watch Pep dial in his correction, I assume that one of the indications he's using is the amount of "grit" and noise that begins to appear

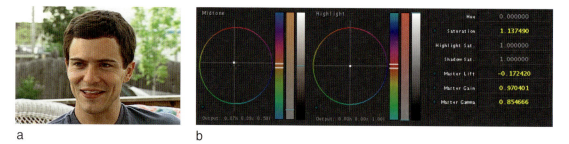

a   b

Fig. 7-35 **(a)** Pepperman's primary correction and **(b)** the data from the Primary room.

in the trees. "That's exactly what I'm trying to do. I don't want to see any noise but yet I want to see detail. And I want your eye to go toward him obviously. So I'm just playing around with the background right now so I don't get any noise. And now I'm just cranking down the video levels, and I'm cranking down the blacks too. I really like that. So what I want to do now, is just open my window (vignette) a tad, move it down, and now soften it." His vignette almost perfectly describes the subject's face, hair, and neck. "Now I love it. The only thing that's bothering me is the sky. The sky looks like it was clipped and brought down. It doesn't look natural to me. So all I'm going to do is stay on the outside and brighten up the gain a little bit until it starts to look natural. Just about there, so it looks like a bright day and it doesn't look like it's clipped and brought down. It's bright back there, so it's going to clip. *Let* it clip! Take it up to 100. Maybe even a tad bit more. Now the last thing I'm going to do is go back inside and just bring up the blacks, because I want to see where I have them. Then I want to bring them back down to right about here."

Pep and I discuss the boundaries he was reaching as he tried to determine the black level. On the low side, the blacks were creating "grittiness" and noise, but when he brought them up, the blacks became muddy. "That's when I brought it back down," he explains. "Always going past the sweet point and then coming back. It's like rack focusing. You have to go past, so you know to come back. Same thing here applies. Once again, if I was to do anything else here, I might go back to primary and try overall saturation and add just a tiny bit."

a

Fig. 7-36 **(a)** Pepperman's secondary correction, bringing out the face

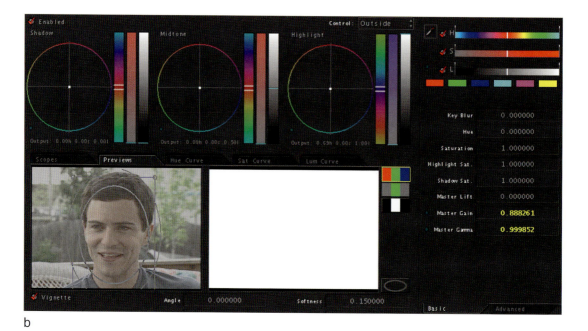

b

Fig. 7-36 (*Continued*) (**b**) the data from the outside of the secondary vignette.

Using Many Tools to Fix a Shot

Using another of Randy Riesen's ultralight documentary images, Bob Sliga uses just about "every tool in the shed" to tweak a shot that isn't bad to begin with (see Figs. 7-37 and 7-38). This file—"ultralight_unload. mov"—is in the Tutorial folder of the DVD. Before taking too many clues from this experienced Color operator and veteran colorist, you may want to take another look at the boxed text "Thinking about the Budget" in Chapter 2.

To begin his correction, Sliga checks the highlights to see if there's anything that he can "unclip." He decides that there's not much that can be done to rescue detail in the highlights, so he starts balancing the blacks in the image using the shadow trackball on the Tangent Devices control panel. After balancing them, he takes the blacks down to around 0 IRE before he warms up the gammas using the red channel gamma level adjustment in the Primary room's Advanced tab. Then he brings the reds in the blacks down again using the red channel lift slider to compensate for the interaction with the gamma adjustment. See Figure 7-39.

With the image "in the ballpark," Sliga moves to secondary corrections. But for Sliga, his use of secondaries at this point is more closely

Fig. 7-37 The uncorrected BetaSP-originated source image. Image courtesy of Randy Riesen.

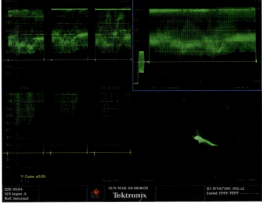

Fig. 7-38 Scopes showing the source image: the RGB parade (top left quadrant), the RGB parade expanded to see the black balance (bottom left quadrant), the composite waveform (top right quadrant), and the vectorscope (bottom right quadrant). From Tektronix WVR7100.

a

Fig. 7-39 **(a)** Sliga's primary correction is minimal due to his workflow of using secondaries as additional layers of primaries. **(b)** The data from the Primary room. Note the info under the wheels and that he did some corrections in the Advanced tab with individual color channels.

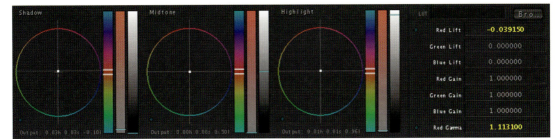

b

akin to another layer of primary correction because he doesn't qualify anything before he starts tweaking. "This jacket has a nice little high-light of blue on it, so I want to keep that. We're going to use that to our advantage a little later. We're gonna richen this up," Sliga states as he pulls down the gammas. "And warm this up a little," he continues as he pulls the gamma wheel toward red, then raises highlights back to close to 100 IRE (see Fig. 7-40).

Sliga attempts to "green" the grass a little bit using the Hue curve, but undoes the correction. Then he pulls a luminance matte on the sky and

Fig. 7-40 (a) The secondary correction and (b) the data from the Hue Curve Tab of the Secondary room.

a

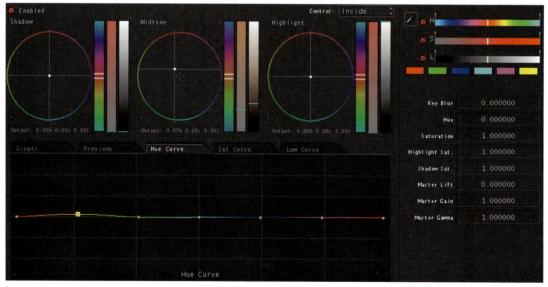

b

pushes the highlight wheel toward blue. "Then let's go outside of it and warm it up a touch." Sliga selects outside of the qualification and pulls the gamma wheel to red. The grass is quite reddish/yellow/green at this point. "So we've gone from there to there," he says, checking the original shot against his correction. "Feels like it's nice and warm and the sun is low." See Figure 7-41.

At this point, Sliga leaves Color's Secondary room for a foray into the Color Effects room. "Let's do a highlight blur. So we're going to need an alpha blend, we're going to need a blur, and we'll need a key. So I generally drag black and white into scale and just adjust the scale creating a highlight key." Sliga drags a blur to the output of the scale node and blurs it, then connects that to the key channel of the alpha blend node.

a

Fig. 7-41 **(a)** The inside of the second secondary correction to pump up the blues in the sky and jacket. **(b)** The data on the correction from the inside of the qualification

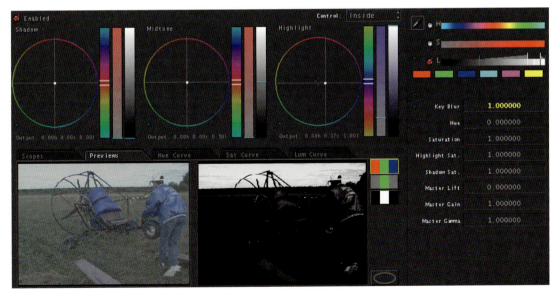

b

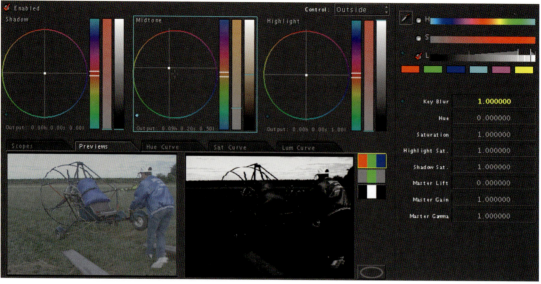

c

Fig. 7-41 (*Continued*) **(c)** the data on the correction from the outside of the qualification, warming the midtones.

"Now we have another blur here, and we'll take this blur up big time. If I drag the blurry image into the light section of the alpha blend, which is source two, then press alpha blend, it's going to blur the highlights. But if we drag it to the other input of the alpha blend node, it'll blur the shadows." See Figure 7-42.

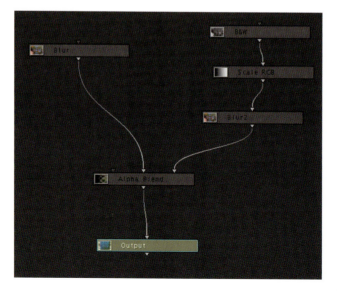

Fig. 7-42 Sliga's process in the Color Effects Room.

Grading with Curves in Primary

As I mentioned earlier in the book, Terry Curren was one of the few proponents of using Curves, which are now available in Color's Primary In Room. But when I was interviewing colorists for the book, I was using Color's predecessor, FinalTouch, which did not have Primary Curves. For the correction that Curren does here (see Figs. 7-43 and 7-44), he worked out of his suite at Alpha Dogs in Burbank, CA, on an Avid Symphony Nitris, but you can follow along with his work method in any application that has Curves.

Curren begins by explaining his working setup. "I generally work with two scopes up. I use a vectorscope laid over a luminance waveform and then I also have the RGB parade waveform. I go for the black and white levels first out of the two. And since I don't have four scopes to look at, I tend to watch the RGB parade to see if my blacks are in balance instead of the center dot on the vector."

"My first step would be to get down to black with at least one of the colors, whichever is the lowest," Curren explains as he uses the Master curve to drop down blacks overall. "Then bring the others down. In this case the blacks are a little green. I can instantly look and see the bulk of the image is here," he says, as he points to the bottom of the RGB parade. "I can see that in the picture too," he says, pointing on the monitor to the dark water.

Fig. 7-43 The original uncorrected source image.

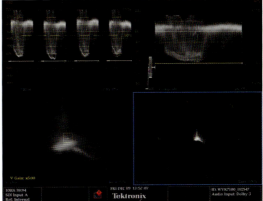

Fig. 7-44 Scopes showing the source image: the YRGB parade (top left quadrant), the vectorscope expanded 5× (bottom left quadrant), the composite waveform (top right quadrant), and the vectorscope (bottom right quadrant). From Tektronix WVR7100.

Curren continues, "The gamma needs to be bumped, so I can grab that and I'm bringing up the gamma and not the blacks or the top any. I can see that the overall picture has a blue tint to it. For most scenes, in the gamma on the RGB parade it goes like that," he says placing a pen across the RGB parade shapes in the gammas showing a slight downward angle from the R to the B side of about 10 to 15 degrees. "In other words, it's not equal red, green, and blue in the middle. But the RGB here is straight across the gammas. So I can see that the blue gamma is high and reds are a little low. That warms the image up a bit. If I wanted to, I could go into the secondaries and pull out some of the green in the water or make it *really* green."

Curren's screenshot of his Curves correction (see Figs. 7-45 and 7-46) shows his primary correction in the center and the source image on either side. The master saturation has been increased, but all other color correction was done with the four Curves. This correction took under 30 seconds for Curren to walk through.

Curren continues exploring the scene called "Treesclouds" using the Curves in his Symphony Nitris (see Figs. 7-47 and 7-48). "So this is why I'm in Curves so much. For me, I want to bring out the gamma in this to get more life in the picture—make it pop more. Now, there is a lot of

Fig. 7-45 Curren's Curves correction.

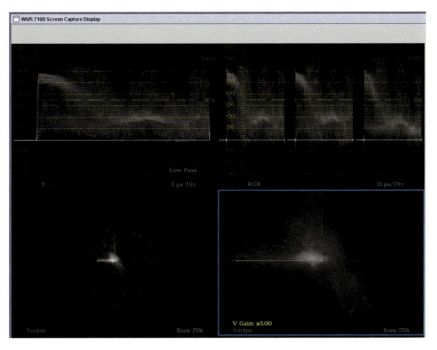

Fig. 7-46 Scopes showing the corrected image: the composite waveform (top left quadrant), vectorscope at normal zoom (bottom left quadrant), the RGB parade waveform (top right quadrant), and the vectorscope at 5× zoom (bottom right quadrant). From Tektronix WVR7100.

Fig. 7-47 The original source image.

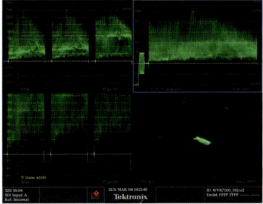

Fig. 7-48 Scopes showing the source image: the RGB parade (top left quadrant), the RGB parade expanded to show the black balance (bottom left quadrant), the composite waveform (top right quadrant), and the vectorscope (bottom right quadrant). From Tektronix WVR7100.

blue in this. Of course, it's a blue sky, but there's also a lot of blue in the blacks, too," he demonstrates, pointing to the bottom of the RGB parade. "The red black is down there, the green is a little higher, and the blue is up here. Generally, I see the gammas weighted the opposite way," he says, demonstrating the angle again. "But right now it's weighted this way," he comments, showing that the angle is the opposite of the way he wants it.

Curren continues, "You can tell by looking at it that it's a very blue picture. So basically, what I've done is, I've brought up the gamma, I pulled some blue out, and I've added a little red (moving the high/midtone blues down on the curve and the high/midtone reds up barely). Then if this was a commercial, they'd probably want the sky to pop more, so this is where the secondaries would come in for me, in the skies, to bring them out more. Just drive the sky more blue while holding blue out of the clouds. That's where I really find myself using the secondaries the most, is on skies. Sky looks great like this as a dark blue, but usually it's much brighter. So if you can grab it and bring the luminance down on it without affecting the rest of the picture, that's really nice." See Figures 7-49 and 7-50.

Curren does another correction of some Randy Riesen footage with Curves in Symphony (see Figs. 7-51 and 7-52). "Again, I'm going in to

Fig. 7-49 The Symphony color correction UI. The center image is the final.

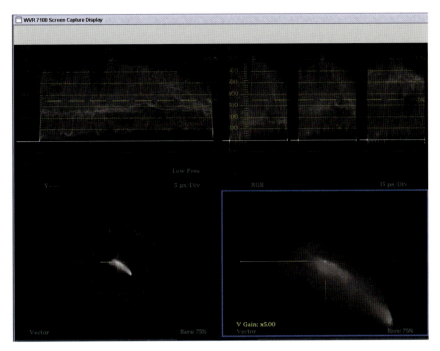

Fig. 7-50 Scopes on the final correction: the composite waveform (top left quadrant), the vectorscope at normal zoom (bottom left quadrant), the RGB parade waveform (top right quadrant), and the vectorscope at 5× zoom (bottom right quadrant). From Tektronix WVR7100.

Fig. 7-51 The original source image.

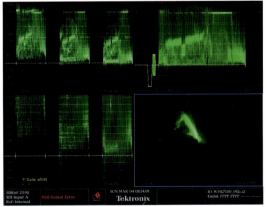

Fig. 7-52 Scopes on the source image: (a) the RGB parade, (b) the RGB parade expanded to see the black balance, (c) the composite waveform, and (d) the vectorscope. From Tektronix WVR7100.

pull up gamma," he says as he uses the Master curve about one-third up from the bottom. "I'm going to bring the highs down lower because they're clipped anyway. I find when they're already clipped, I like to get them down below 100 IRE. It seems to not be as offensive. Obviously the picture is blue, but I can see, looking at the bottom of the RGB parade, that both the green and blue are much higher. So in the reds, I can bring up the gamma and I can bring both the blue and the green down in the blacks," Curren explains. So basically, I've pulled all the blue cast out of it. But, you might not want that, because this is downtown city, which is always kind of blue in the middle of the day, because you never see the sun until it's directly overhead. So, again, this all depends on what was wrapped around it. So left to my own devices, this is where I would go because it's the closest to normal," Curren concludes. See Figures 7-53 and 7-54.

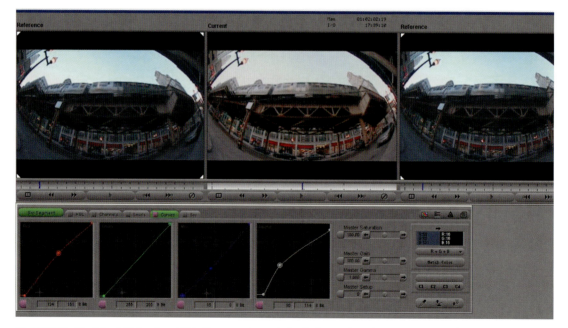

Fig. 7-53 The UI of the Avid Symphony Nitris. The center image is the final correction. The two images on either side are the starting point.

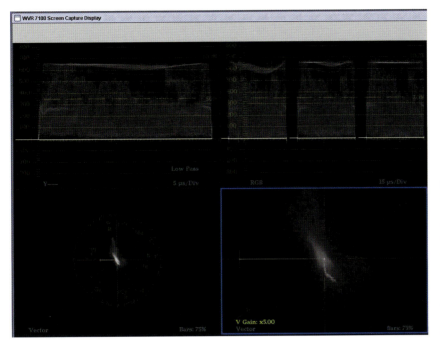

Fig. 7-54 The scopes for the final image: the composite waveform (top left quadrant), the vectorscope at normal zoom (bottom left quadrant), the RGB parade waveform (top right quadrant), and (bottom right quadrant) the vectorscope at 5× zoom. From Tektronix WVR7100.

Terry Curren

Terry Curren is a principal and editor at Alpha Dogs in Burbank, CA. He hosts a popular series of gatherings in Los Angeles known as the Editor's Lounge.

He began his career in the early 1980s by directing, editing, and producing music videos as well as a successful direct-to-video feature film, *Interview with Terror*. In 1986, he began work at Matchframe Video, a Burbank-based postproduction studio, where he spearheaded the creation of the studio's edit bays while perfecting his editing and color correction skill set under the tutelage of top-tier da Vinci colorists.

With the introduction of Avid's Symphony online nonlinear editing system, and its powerful color corrector, Curren saw a golden opportunity. He proceeded to hone his color correction and effects skills with this new toolset until he became a respected colorist in his own right.

Seeing the future, Curren started Alpha Dogs, Inc. in 2002. They are currently providing audio and video finishing and graphic design on a wide variety of formats from feature films to television, documentaries, and commercials.

CHAPTER 8

Telling the Story

Most of this book has been a fairly one-sided discussion from the perspective of the colorist. As I've pointed out before though, color correction is a very collaborative art form or craft. One of the main collaborators, the originator of the image itself, is the director of photography (DP). In addition to my conversations with colorists, I also spoke to several DPs, including David Mullen, A.S.C.

In this chapter, we're going to discuss how the colorist helps to tell the story, which is arguably one of the most important points of color correction. How does the colorist get the viewer into the story using color and keep the viewer's attention and focus in the story? What can the colorist add to the visual process that was started by the director and DP?

Mullen begins: "The majority of movies today are shot in a style that could be called romantic realism. Sort of naturalistic lighting and photography, but naturalism pushed to kind of its most dramatic or interesting. So we try to make things look realistic, but manipulated for the mood of the story. Sometimes when I'm breaking down a script, I'll list the obvious visual devices that the script seems to call for, then I ask myself if those are clichés and whether the *opposite* is really what the film needs. It's like the Hitchcock thing where he liked to set a murder scene in a sunny field with flowers, just those kind of opposite choices. But this is all stuff you have to talk about with the director. Sort of bounce these ideas off of them. Sometimes they want kind of off-the-wall suggestions that kind of spark new ideas, but generally there are certain cultural associations like warmth for passion or coldness for badness or isolation or something like that. It's not always true."

I've read interviews with directors from northern Europe who feel that cold colors are pleasant and relaxing and warm colors are aggressive and disturbing. You can pick a symbolic style for the film in terms of color and contrast, and as long as you clue the audience as to what your symbolism means . . . I mean it's sort of like a code, when someone comes up with a code in the spy business, they also have to come up with a key to break that code so the person at the other end can decipher that code. So you can decide that red symbolizes something or blue symbolizes something, and as long as the audience is told in the beginning what that structure is, they sort of accept it for the rest of the film. When you look at *Little Buddha*, Storraro has all of the scenes in Seattle in very cold, blue-gray colors, and wherever possible he tries to have the scenes set at twilight with deep blue light out the windows. So there's always a blue accent in the frame somewhere. And all of the scenes in Tibet are very golden. And sometimes you can flip those two ideas.

I remember in the film *Delores Clayburn* where they shot the modern scenes on Kodak film with a blue uncorrected tungsten look and the flashbacks all on Fuji film with a warm saturated color scheme. Now one could say that you could shoot the flashbacks on Kodak and shoot that saturated and the present on Fuji and make that desaturated and cold. Maybe the present should be saturated because that's the colors of real life and the past is manipulated and desaturated to suggest a distant memory where the colors are missing. But as long as the filmmaker has a kind of structure, it doesn't mean that everyone has to use the same palettes for everything. So that's how I break down a script. I think of it as a sort of series of color and contrast arcs that match the plotline of the story. Some stories are structured in what I'd call and "A/B" comparison and other stories are structured in an "A to B" arc. So some visual designs of a film are a character starts at one point and ends at a different point, so you try to create a gradual change throughout the film. And other films more intercut the lines of two characters, or one world versus another world, so your visual structure is more of a back and forth thing. And there are some films that have no visual arc in terms of color and contrast.

You just try to create a single, solid world that has a consistent structure and look to it: a cold, desaturated look, let's say. A film like *Letters from Iwo Jima*, let's say, which has a consistently almost black and whitish look to it. A relentless kind of look. They don't lighten it or darken it that much from scene to scene to scene, so it's kind of meant to be oppressive; 'cause the world there was oppressive and it never really changes. So, there isn't one way to approach a film, but mental games that you can use to spark ideas, basically. Sometimes I play a game of opposites, you know. I think of all the opposite ideas for a scene: wide angle or telephoto, blue versus red, fast movement versus slow movement, static shots versus moving shots, lots of cuts versus very few cuts. And I break down a scene and try to think which one of those ideas is most appropriate.

> ### David Mullen, A.S.C.
>
> David Mullen has worked as a cinematographer on numerous feature films and television episodics, beginning in the early 1990s. His feature work includes *Twin Falls Idaho*, *The Hypnotist*, *Northfork*, *D.E.B.S.*, *Shadowboxer*, *Akeelah and the Bee*, *The Astronaut Farmer*, and *Solstice*.
>
> He was nominated for the Independent Spirit Award for Best Cinematography twice for *Twin Falls Idaho* (2000) and *Northfork* (2004). He was also nominated for a Chlotrudis Award for Best Cinematography for *Northfork*. He became a member of the American Society of Cinematographers in 2004. In 2007 he was invited to join AMPAS.

I asked Bob Festa if he felt that there are visual clues to a story that the audience expects: "I think so. I think generally if you look at American cinema, Americans are trained on some really stupid levels. They see a dark-blue picture and they know that's evening even though it's day-for-night. I think those types of associations are pretty popular. But I work in a primarily commercial and music video environment, so I'm pretty much product driven. So if you look at the types of things I do that tell the story, they are generally based around selling the product. So the things that I might do and I might be influenced by are things that heighten or bring to the surface the product focus. So I might use traditional dodging and burning techniques to bring the product up and not really be so concerned about the general tone because I'm here to sell things."

I argue that commercials need their stories told even faster than films, and that if the story of the commercial is "your life sucks until you use our product," do you start the spot cool and desaturated until the product arrives, then have the images go warmer and more pleasing once the product saves the day? "I think in my world where I've got 30 seconds to tell a story, that's a little too vague. I think I practice it on a small scale, but nine times out of ten I'm going to blow the product up and stick it in front of your nose and hit you over the head."

Level 3 colorist Larry Field explains one of the ways he works with color to promote the story in his work. "With '24,' if one of the main characters is doing something bad, we'll make it a very gritty and aggressive look to go with the action."

So the question is: What should the shot look like to tell the story?

Mullen responds: "Everyone wants context. Without context, you can make a billion different choices, but as soon as you know the context of the shot, it narrows the choices; to me, to know whether that scene is late in the day, or whether a character turned off half the lights in the office, so this office is not as bright as it normally is. So if they haven't seen the shot where the character turns off the lights, they might try to match the look of the office from the last time they saw the office in the movie, so you need the kind of story context in order to make the final decisions on stuff. Especially since some cinematographers shoot a kind of flat image and then create the look later, the DP definitely needs to be there to give an idea of what the intent of the scene was."

CBS's Neal Kassner agrees: "You've got to know the story, because color is part of the storytelling tools." Kassner related several stories about how he had corrections go off-track because he sometimes started grading before he understood the story.

Color Changes the Story

When Shooters Post colorist Janet Falcon looks at the Artbeats' image of the Marines in the desert (see Figs. 8-1 and 8-2 and file "Marines_MAR115H1" from the Artbeats folder in the "Tutorial_footage_and_files" folder on the DVD), she believes that the image could tell two different stories depending on the color scheme. She says, "I look at this and I think, 'It's the desert and it's hot,' and it came up really warm, so without any direction, my feeling is that it should be brownish, goldish, not so blue-sky."

Fig. 8-1 The source image Courtesy of Artbeats' "Marines HD Vol. 1" Collection.

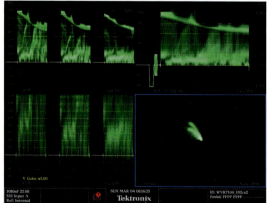

Fig. 8-2 Scopes showing the source image: the RGB parade (top left quadrant), the RGB parade expanded to see black levels better (bottom left quadrant), the composite waveform (top right quadrant), and the vectorscope (bottom right quadrant). From Tektronix WVR7100.

Again, for Falcon, it's all about context. "That's just a judgment call, if I had to start somewhere," she explains as she desaturates the image. "That's what I'm trying to go for—this tobacco look. I could be wrong. That's why clients are important, because you need somebody telling you—like that story you told me about—where something's supposed to go," says Falcon, referring to a story I told in my other color correction book, *Color Correction for Digital Video*, about how Bob Sliga was working on an image before the client arrived. It was a beautiful image of a woman in a flowing dress under a green tree carrying milk jugs toward a big red barn. With no input from the client, he began by turning it into a pretty "Kodak moment." But when the client arrived, he told Sliga that the woman was supposed to be ill, so Sliga switched gears and took the saturation out and changed the warm look to something more cool and depressed.

Returning to the image of the Marines, Falcon continues her assessment, "I mean it doesn't look like a happy moment. It looks like a more serious moment." With the context of being a serious moment, I ask Falcon what she would do. "You think less saturation. More contrast probably," she thinks out loud. "Serious moments don't have to be low color, but I think it definitely helps to convey a message." See Figure 8-3.

Definition

Tobacco refers to a common filter used by directors of photography either on the lens or on lighting instruments to create a brownish/yellowish light similar to sepia approximately the shade of this small colored square.

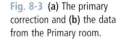

a

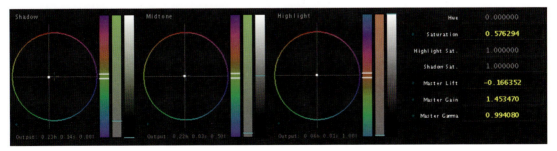

b

Fig. 8-3 **(a)** The primary correction and **(b)** the data from the Primary room.

She adds a vignette and darkens the edges. The darkened vignette serves several purposes for the image: It focuses the attention on the Marines, it gives some depth and texture to an otherwise flat, burned-out sky, and it also creates a degree of tension by claustrophobically "surrounding" the soldiers (see Fig. 8-4).

With the vignette done, she qualifies an HSL key on the bright skin tones, blurs the key, and pulls the saturation out (see Fig. 8-5). "Let's

Fig. 8-4 **(a)** The first secondary correction gives texture to the sky and focuses attention on the Marines and **(b)** the data from the outside of the first secondary correction.

a

b

a

Fig. 8-5 **(a)** The second secondary correction qualifies and brightens skin-tone highlights and **(b)** the data from the inside of the second secondary correction.

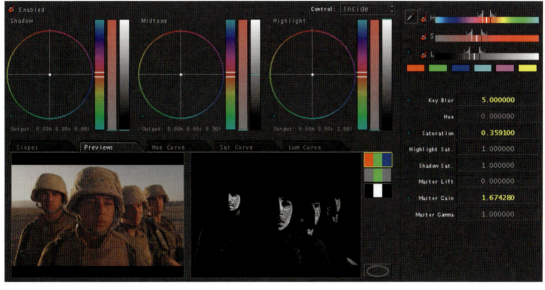

b

see if we can do a luminance key to the sky." She pulls a key and blurs it. "I'm trying to make it look like a nuclear holocaust. Now if I lift up the blacks it gives it a Pro-mist-type look. And I was trying to get some yellow in there, but I think it's just clipped out. Okay, there's my nuclear holocaust." See Figure 8-6.

For another look at the same Marines image we join Falcon's colleague at Shooters Post, Bob Lovejoy. Lovejoy worked quickly

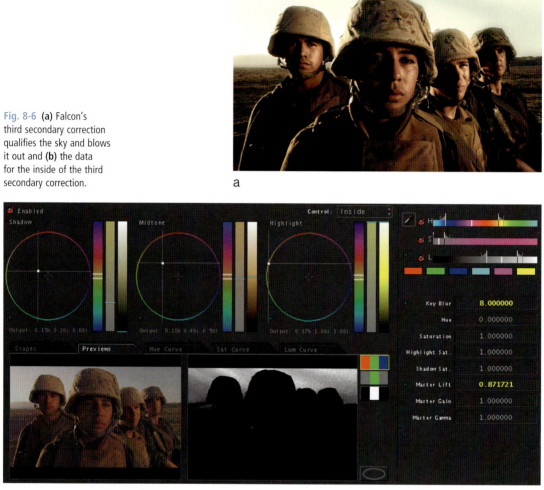

Fig. 8-6 (a) Falcon's third secondary correction qualifies the sky and blows it out and **(b)** the data for the inside of the third secondary correction.

a

b

and barely spoke as he went through this correction, saying only, "This one speaks to me. Often in the absence of direction, I just let the picture take me. It's a subconscious process." In addition to the primary correction (see Figs. 8-7a and b), I believe this image also shows the effect of a color effect that was placed on the image to give it the blown-out look. Due to a bug, I couldn't get the primary correction to show without the color effect (see Fig 8-7c). See Figures 8-8 and 8-9 for the secondary corrections.

a

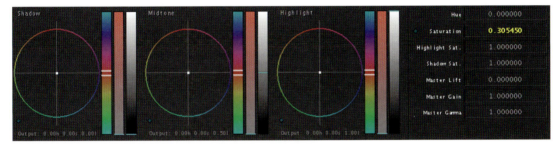

b

Fig. 8-7 **(a)** The primary correction and **(b)** the data from the Primary room. **(c)** The color effect tree. The blur was set to about 1.5, the scale was set to about 2, and the Nattress Plug-in "G_Blend" was set to blend as a "screen."

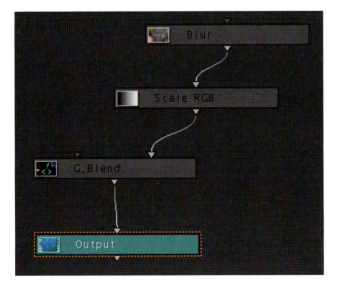

c

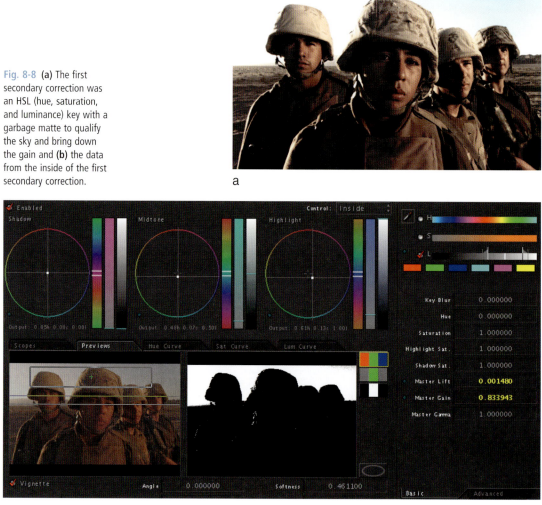

Fig. 8-8 **(a)** The first secondary correction was an HSL (hue, saturation, and luminance) key with a garbage matte to qualify the sky and bring down the gain and **(b)** the data from the inside of the first secondary correction.

Talk Like a Director of Photography

One thing to note as Falcon was describing the Marines image was that she often referred to terms to which DP could relate. The creative arts are filled with jargon and specialized language and colorists and DPs are no exception when using these terms. The trick in becoming an effective communicator and collaborator is to learn the language of your collaborator, which in this case is the cinematographer.

a

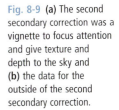

Fig. 8-9 **(a)** The second secondary correction was a vignette to focus attention and give texture and depth to the sky and **(b)** the data for the outside of the second secondary correction.

b

Specifically, Falcon mentioned the words "tobacco" and "Pro-mist." Both of these are filters that a DP could relate to. Cinematographers like photographic terms so learning these terms is a valuable thing. Often, instead of referring to a general sense of how bright something should be, cinematographers will describe something specifically in terms of f-stops, saying, for example, "That needs to be a stop brighter." Or sometimes they'll discuss an image in terms of the film negative, like

"That image seems a little thin," meaning overexposed and not contrasty enough.

Understanding color in terms of some of the filters that a DP uses is a valuable skill. While some filters vary in color, you should be familiar with some of the popular colors and filters and what effect they have on an image.

David Mullen, A.S.C., explains that the relationship can go both ways: "I find that the more I sit in on color correction sessions, the more I can talk to colorists on their level. I don't tell them how to turn the trackballs on a da Vinci, but generally when you're looking at a scene you're either adding or subtracting primary or secondary colors, so I tell the colorist, "That warm light needs a little more magenta in it." Or, "It's warm, but warm with a yellow bias." Or, "It looks like the shadows have a little cyan in them." If you talk in terms of red, green, or blue—a little more or a little less—it sort of gives them a good idea of what you want. If you start talking to them in terms of colors that don't have any photochemical or electronic sense, if you say, "I want that light more turquoise with some chartreuse color cast or burgundy," then everyone's going to start to wonder, because we *sort* of know what those colors are but we don't sort of all *agree* on what those colors are. And there's another tendency for cameramen to use photographic terms, like filters, like "That's a coral filter." Well a colorist may not have any photography background and they might not have ever seen a coral filter and even coral filters don't match each other from manufacturer to manufacturer, so it can be a meaningless term when you get into the color correction space. I've seen cinematographers say to colorists, "I shot this with an antique white filter and you got rid of all of it." And I'm like, "What's an antique white filter to a colorist." You have to talk to them in terms of colors that *they* understand, which is red, green, blue, cyan, magenta, and yellow. When you start getting things like brown that's a very tricky color to create in post, and my theory is that brown is really warm minus saturation."

Another popular reference for cinematographers is the way film is processed, for example, bleach bypass, pushed or cross-processed, or which film stock they want it to look like. We'll discuss those in more depth in Chapter 10.

The Story Is the Script

Los Angeles, CA, freelance digital intermediate (DI) colorist Greg Creaser takes on the same scene from *Kiss Me in the Dark* that Mike Matusek covered in Chapter 6 (see Figs. 8-10 and 8-11). Creaser believes the story is so important that he likes to read the script before he works on a film.

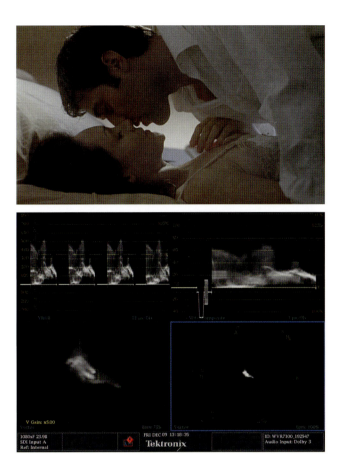

Fig. 8-10 The source image. Image courtesy of Seduced and Exploited Entertainment.

Fig. 8-11 Scopes showing the ungraded source image: the YRGB parade (top left quadrant), the vectorscope blown up 5× (bottom left quadrant), the composite waveform (top right quadrant), and the vectorscope (bottom right quadrant). From Tektronix WVR7100.

"I think story is really important. I know any time I'm going to grade a film, if I'm doing a digital intermediate (DI), I'd either like to read a script or at least see a cut of the movie before I do it to know what's involved or to know what the genre is, because I think that has a lot of say on the color as well. I think that's really a key," states Creaser.

He doesn't have that option as he starts grading the bedroom scene from *Kiss Me in the Dark*, so he has to make up the story as he goes. "If I was the DP on this, I'd want more of a mood so it'd be definitely warmer. And I would probably dip right into the shadows with this and probably the midtones; probably want to drop it down a little bit density-wise." (Note that Creaser uses the photographic/cinematographic term *density* to describe the brightness of the image. Density is also the term used by the original colorists—negative timers.)

"I'm just going to look at the highlight color and see if pushing it to the warm side makes it nicer. I think that makes more sense," he says as he checks back from his grade to the original image. "That's a little cyan for me," he comments, then switches back to his grade. "That's a little more in the mood. I'd leave it there to start with for the client." See 8-12.

I point out that pretty much all of the colorists who worked on this image warmed up the shot and darkened it. Creaser adds, "I think that's what makes a good colorist. I think being able to have that interaction, being able to help the client make creative decisions—a lot of time they maybe don't. I've heard from clients about being in a room where they didn't get what they wanted and they kind of didn't even know what to do with a shot themselves, so it's kind of helpful if you help them with that a little bit."

The Director Speaks

Kiss Me in the Dark director Barry Gilbert describes trying to color correct this image himself (see also *Kiss Me in the Dark* boxed text in Chapter 6).

With the husband kissing her we've established that she is lonely to the point of perhaps being obsessive in her attempts to recapture her memories with her husband. And we've made it clear to the audience that this person is dead and that she is a grieving widow. We see her fall onto her side in bed and cover her face in her hands, then we cut outside and see the lightbulb on the porch. Then we see her house through the surveillance monitors and the light goes out. Her eyes flutter open and he appears in the frame and they kiss. I really wanted to crush the blacks and get him to emanate out of the shadows. I spent more time coloring that shot than any shot in the movie. If there was any shot that I wish that I'd had the power of full-scale correction (he originally graded it in FCP), it was that one, because I found it very challenging to crush the blacks without having the color range, because I was working in DV. To have a nice skin tone and crush the shadows without it looking ghastly, I just couldn't do it. I wanted to have that shot be as shadow-filled as possible, and that was difficult. This is the first project that I'd shot that was all about shadow. The projects I'd shot before were all comedies and very poppy and that was quite easy to color because the neg was good so it was really just a matter of taking what you had and plussing it.

Emphasize Elements to Further the Story

Filmworker's Club colorist Pete Jannotta sees an interesting storytelling challenge in the shot from *Chasing Ghosts* of a basement corridor in a museum (see Figs. 8-13 and 8-14 and the Tutorial file, "Ghosts_basement.mov").

"The first thing I would do is make sure I'm getting as much out of the bottom as I can," Jannotta begins, digging into the blacks with the Master

a

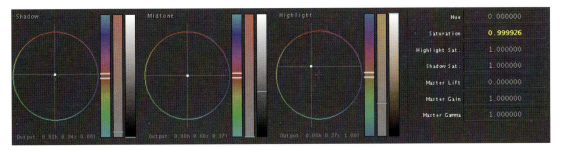

b

Fig. 8-12 (a) Creaser's final correction and (b) the FinalTouch UI of the data from the correction.

Fig. 8-13 The ungraded source image of the museum basement scene from *Chasing Ghosts*. Image courtesy of Wingman Productions, Inc.

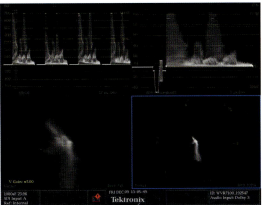

Fig. 8-14 Scopes showing the source image: the YRGB parade (top left quadrant), the vectorscope expanded 5× (bottom left quadrant), the composite waveform (top right quadrant), and the vectorscope (bottom right quadrant). From Tektronix WVR7100.

Setup control. "Stretch a little gamma out of there, pull the whites down to make sure that whatever I can get out of the top, I'm getting. But I know if nothing comes down where it's clipped, it's clipped . . . clipped on the source material." Jannotta points out that the fluorescent tubes in the image are clipped. "But for shadow detail, depending on how much noise it generates, I would always try to pull up whatever is hidden toward the bottom, just so I know what's in there. Except, for this shot, stretching it isn't going to do me any favors. Just set black on the baseline and compress the gamma. Push all the stuff from middle black down, toward black," Jannotta explains, "because when I'm looking at this shot, it's asking for much more mystery than the way it comes up, to me. And I don't particularly care for it green. I see it more cold to neutral, and I see him more lit up. Make more out the flashlight stuff and less out of the side walls. And less out of this up here for sure," he says, pointing to the ceiling detail.

Jannotta continues, "I'm just looking at the vectorscope now and pulling the vectorscope away from yellow, without making it overly blue, which it looks like it's getting. I constantly go between looking at the image and looking at the vectorscope . . . and the waveform."

The Director Speaks

Kyle Jackson, the director of *Chasing Ghosts*, gives some story and look direction:

We wanted to create a kind of a noir look, letting it fall off, letting it be kind of an ENR skip-bleach kind of look. It's supposed to look like New York, but we shot in LA.

The basement scene was supposed to be an old museum that had long since been shutdown. High contrast. We wanted to show that the place was long abandoned.

Throughout the film there're basically four looks. There's the police station look that should apply to that "Banker's Light" shot. It's a look that we went for any time Michael Madsen's character was alone at his house or in the police station. It should be kind of a smoked tobacco look. Like a refined cigar. Then the exteriors kind of did their own thing because they were less controlled because of the budget. So that was just trying to give it a grit. Then there are a bunch of flashbacks that are super contrasty and grainy with Gary Busey and Michael Madsen. The SWAT scene was just a basic exterior. But it should look like New York. The green cast to the film was the result of a bad film scan.

That bad scan is one of the reasons that Tunnel Post bought their own film scanner.

Pete is getting comfortable with where he's taking the image, except for the wall in the foreground, but he decides to attack that in secondaries instead. "Maybe push a little blue in the grays, this way. Because that's mostly the middle of the grayscale," he says, pointing to the shadowed foreground wall on the right side close to the camera. "Also I see that this blue waveform (indicating the RGB parade scope) is, or was, a little more compressed than the other two channels in that area," he adds, indicating the shadows. "So that's a pretty good spot for just a general balance I think. Let's see if I can put a little more blue into it, because I don't mind if he's a little cold. Then maybe compress the grays a little bit," Jannotta continues, moving the gamma lower. "I want to make it look a little more mysterious." See Figure 8-15.

"What I'm thinking I would do in secondary is take that green . . . isolate that greeny/yellow stuff and take it down," Jannotta says as he goes into secondary and selects the bright highlight on the right foreground wall with the eyedropper, then customizes his selection. "Now I want to bring the saturation down in that area. I didn't like the green stuff. Now I want to take that matte and make the gain come down. That's what I want. So I'm just seeing what I can do with contrast in that matte. So I'm just seeing what I can do that looks natural." See Figure 8-16.

a

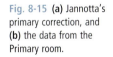

Fig. 8-15 (a) Jannotta's primary correction, and (b) the data from the Primary room.

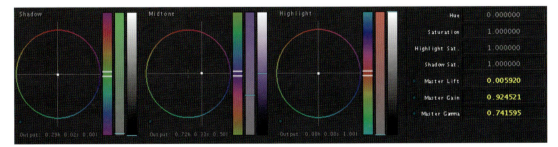

b

Fig. 8-16 **(a)** The following corrections do not really show up well in print. The first secondary correction lowers the glare on the wall and hides detail in the shadows and **(b)** the data from the first secondary correction.

a

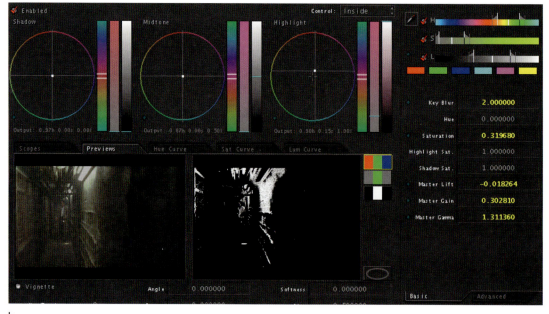

b

I notice that as he's trying to dial in his correction, he's being constrained in where he can take it by some funkiness that's happening in the highlight on the wall under the fluorescents. "Yeah. I'm seeing edges that I don't like, but I'd like to bring it down. I want to snap him out and make more of this light made by his flashlight spilling on his clothes and that light," he says, pointing to the pool of the flashlight on the floor. See Figure 8-17.

Jannotta also wants to diminish the detail in the image above the actor's head. He decides to do this with a window, or vignette. Jannotta

a

Fig. 8-17 **(a)** The second secondary correction focuses on the flashlight, **(b)** the data for the inside of the second secondary correction,

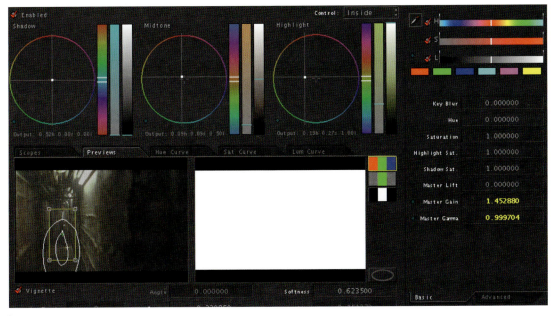

b

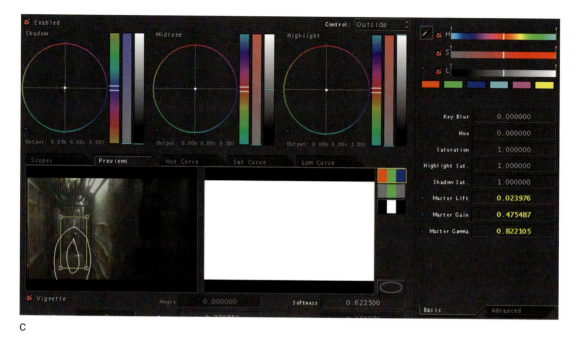

C

Fig. 8-17 *(Continued)* **(c)** the data from the outside of the second secondary correction. The (a) images from here to the end of Jannotta's final grade are a little dark in print, but held detail well on the screen.

draws a custom vignette shape and softens it. "I would make him a little warmer. But first I want to change the shape so that it covers less of the top of him and is bigger at the bottom where the flashlight pool is. So my thought is to keep his head cooler, and it will be more interesting if more of the warmth comes from the bottom," he explains. See Figure 8-18.

"I'd like to keep his head cool and it's too dark up there," Jannotta continues as he plays with the original shape to better define the beam and pool of the flashlight. "So I'm just trying now to see if I can—even though it's not like a flashlight beam—try and have it feel more like a source light. I'm pulling out the softness on the bottom, because I really want to feather that bottom."

Jannotta creates another secondary vignette. "What I think I'm going to do now is get his head with a triangle kind of thing. So they'll be overlapping, but this one on top is going to be so I can light up his head a little bit, but keep it cool. I like the way that shot feels now."

Continuing with his definition of the image using secondaries, Pete draws an upside down dome along the top middle of the picture, selecting the bright practical lights near the top of the frame, then pulls the highlights down, explaining that he didn't like emphasis on the bright lights over the actor's head. "That looks more interesting to me. To me this

a

Fig. 8-18 **(a)** The third secondary correction focuses some attention on the face and **(b)** the data from the third secondary.

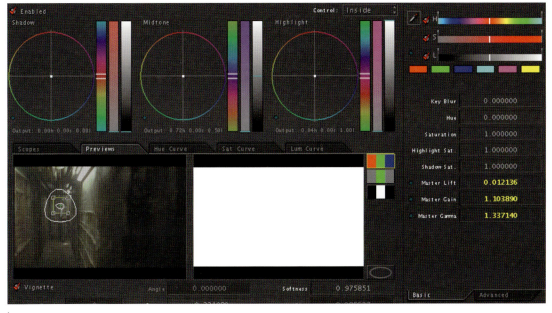

b

tells the story better. This guy's looking for something . . . . He's looking for trouble. It's all about being in a dark scary place with a flashlight. So I brought all of the shadow detail down and it becomes more about him and his flashlight." See Figure 8-19.

I stepped in briefly to save Jannotta's grade for him, but before I did, I moved the timeline to a more representative frame of the grade. "So you grabbed a thumbnail at a better place? I do that all the time," Jannotta says approvingly.

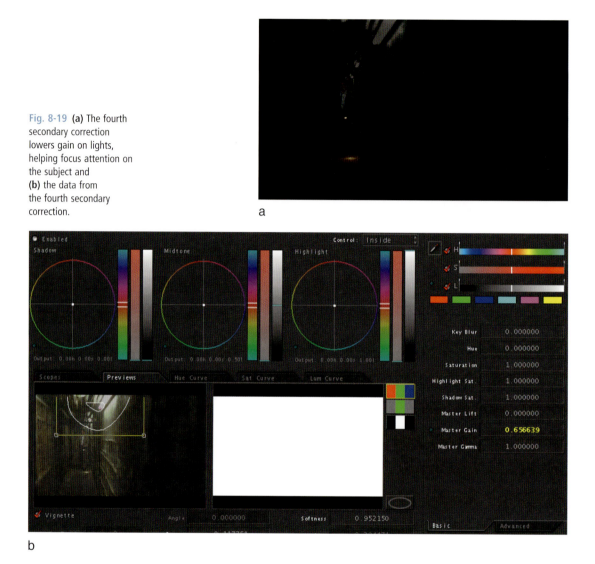

Fig. 8-19 (a) The fourth
secondary correction
lowers gain on lights,
helping focus attention on
the subject and
(b) the data from
the fourth secondary
correction.

a

b

Imposing a Story on the Boxer

Nolo's Digital Film's Mike Matusek and NFL Films' Chris Pepperman both decided to create their own story around the Artbeats' image of the boxer (see Figs. 8-20 and 8-21).

Matusek begins, "So you wanted me to pick something and make up a story. I just saw *Rocky*, so I'm going to say that this guy is training for the big fight. He looks like a mean guy, so I don't know if he's the villain or if he's the hero, but I'll say he's the bad guy. So I would want to give

Fig. 8-20 The source image. Image courtesy of Artbeats.

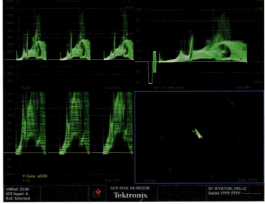

Fig. 8-21 Scopes showing the source image: the RGB parade (top left quadrant), the RGB parade expanded to see the black balance (bottom left quadrant), the composite waveform (top right quadrant), and the vectorscope (bottom right quadrant). From Tecktronix WVR7100.

it a kind of unsettling look, so first I started off by crushing the blacks, basically giving it more contrast. I went a little green with it—desaturated—trying to give it a more menacing look Obviously it was lit to be contrasty, because of the difference between dark and light, so I'm just playing on that contrast and seeing how far I can push it. If I crush the blacks too much, I'll lose too much detail."

Matusek checks back to look at the original image. "So that's where it was. Looking a little muddy. I think I crushed it down too much. I think this is a better place for it, but maybe go back to the greens and see what that looks like. Again, this guy's the villain, so give him a more menacing look. Try going a little more warm with it in the highlights. Give it a different look. Basically I started off going kind of dark with it." See Figure 8-22.

Matusek continues, creating another look, "Then I decided I liked it brighter. So the highlights are somewhat clean. I guess they're a little green." See Figure 8-23. Continuing his exploration of the image, Matusek tries something else. "Then I decided to go warm with it. I think that's a better fit. It has more contrast anyway. And this one (bright and warm) has the most grittiness to it I think." See Figures 8-24 and 8-25.

Chris Pepperman also worked on this image and had this take on it. "So the first thing I think about is what this picture can look like. And I see this guy in an element that is real gritty. I see that it's a monochromatic, almost black and white with a little bit of color and a very hard

Fig. 8-22 (a) The image was done with just a primary grade and (b) the data from the Primary room.

a

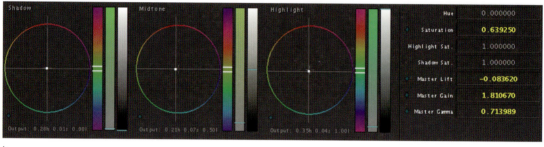

b

Fig. 8-23 (a) The image was done with just a primary grade and (b) the data from the Primary room.

a

b

a

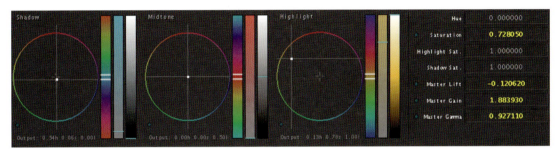

b

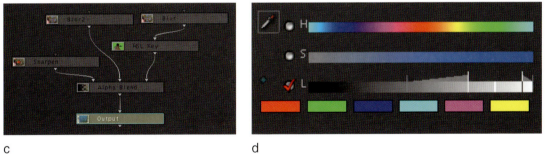

c   d

Fig. 8-24 **(a)** The image with just the primary grade and **(b)** the data from the Primary room. **(c)** The color effect tree for highlight glow; both blurs are set to 5 and the sharpen is set to 2. **(d)** The data from the HSL key in the color effect tree.

Fig. 8-25 The final image with the primary correction and color effect.

shaft of light coming through, and he's training very hard. He's getting ready for a fight and he's really intense about it. So how can we tell a story with color? I'm going to start by doing what I typically do and that is adding contrast. I'm going to see what I can work with clip-wise. So I'm coming down on highlights and I'm coming up on setup to see where my detail is," Pepperman explains as he adjusts both tonal ranges simultaneously with the dials around the trackballs that control Master Gain and Master Setup.

Pepperman continues, "All I'm doing is seeing what my parameters are. I know what it's going to look like clipped. I'm really seeing what I have in the image. So now what I'm going to do is just add a little bit of contrast to it and start letting the light fall off where it wants to be."

I explain to Pepperman that the image has already been touched by a colorist. "I was just going to say, balance-wise, it's almost there. There's not much to balance."

But I prod him to take the image further by pointing out that we're telling a story so the balance isn't necessarily important. "Right," he agrees. "And that's just what I was doing. I'm fine tuning the balance where I am comfortable. So I really want to see that smoke. I really want to see that highlight. So I'm going to start kicking the highlights. I don't care if his back blows out. As a matter of fact, I *want* his back to blow out. I want you to see this really hard, edgy light screaming and kind of cutting him out of the background. And I just want to bury the blacks to where it's not going to hide anything but it's where it wants to be, which I'm going to say is right about there," Pepperman states as he looks into the shadow areas to see if he's losing any important details. "There's nothing back there, so I'm going to get rid of it completely. So I'm going to take the black levels all the way down to about here."

Pepperman continues to explain, "So that's where I'm going to start. So the next thing I'm going to do is take the color almost all the way out, then I'm going to come back in a little bit. So I'm liking where I'm going, but I'm still not happy with the contrast."

Pepperman explains an important point, "When you add contrast, it also affects the saturation, no matter how separated it is. Anytime you build heavy contrast, you're going to have to come back on the saturation if you want to stay consistent. Meaning if you create something that is this green and you like that color, but then you stretch that signal and make it more contrasty, inherently that green is going to get more saturated, so you have to pay attention to that. So I'm going to add more contrast and I'm going to come down on the midrange a little bit. So I like that. Now what I want to do is accentuate that shaft. I want it to be really warm light. I want it to look like it's late August. Like it's this hard, hot, humid day. This is how I envision it." See Figure 8-26.

Pepperman enables a secondary and a vignette and creates a shape diagonally across the screen in line with the shaft of light. "Now I'll go inside and kick it up a notch." The highlight on the fighter's neck really starts to look good. "Keep coming, keep coming. I want to see how far we can go with this. That's what it's about. Now I want to warm it up," he says as he pushes warmth into just the highlights and midtones (see Fig. 8-27).

"So that gave me what I wanted," he concludes. "That was pretty easy actually. Let's talk about what I did. First I checked to see where my range was. Then I added contrast. Then I desaturated it. Then I created the window. I brightened the inside. I went back and darkened the outside. I kept going back and forth until I got the ratio that I wanted between outside and inside the vignette. Then I applied overall primary warmth to it."

As he explains his finished process, Pepperman decides to add a few more touches. "Now let's just say I like the warmth in the highlights, but I want to grab his skin tone and mess around with his skin tone. So now I'm going to go to another secondary." Pepperman grabs an HSL key based on the fighter's skin tone and plays with it. "Finding that key is all trial and error. That's really what that is," he states as he adds a vignette to the same secondary, creating an oval to garbage matte the skin tone and eliminate the punching bag, which is also a skin-tone color.

Hue	0.000000
Saturation	0.242150
Highlight Sat.	1.000000
Shadow Sat.	1.000000
Master Lift	-0.149480
Master Gain	1.221860
Master Gamma	0.976468

a   b

Fig. 8-26 **(a)** Pepperman's primary correction is largely a drop in saturation since the image was already nicely color corrected by Artbeats. **(b)** The data from the Primary room.

Fig. 8-27 (a) This secondary is the one that really imparted the look. (b) The data from the inside of the vignette and (c) the data from the outside of the vignette.

a

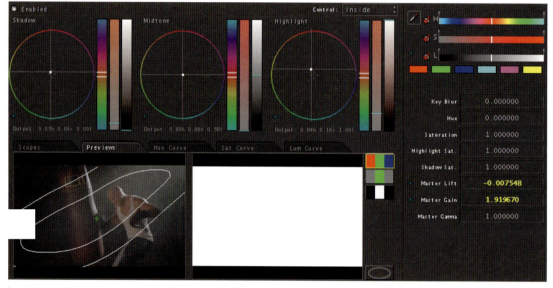

b

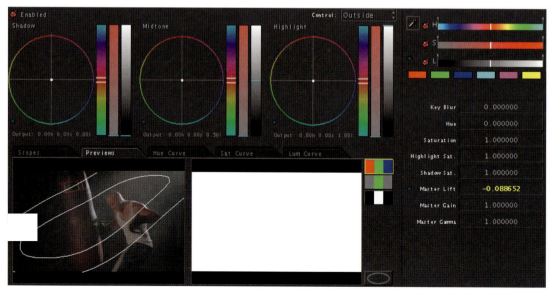

c

With the skin tone qualified, Pepperman starts to tweak. "I'm actually trying to eliminate the red in his skin tones without affecting the high-lighted areas of the smoke. So as opposed to doing an overall correction, I'm trying to see if I can grab that skin tone without affecting anything else and just desaturate it. I liked where I was overall, I just wanted to desaturate his skin tone a tiny bit. So I really like what I've done here. I like this feeling of it's hot, it's warm, he's sweating. And that's where I really wanted to be." See Figure 8-28.

Well, not quite. Still seeing yet another tweak, Pepperman continues his correction with an additional secondary. "Okay, I want to try one

a

Fig. 8-28 **(a)** This secondary correction is a slight desaturation of the skin tones and **(b)** the data from the second secondary correction.

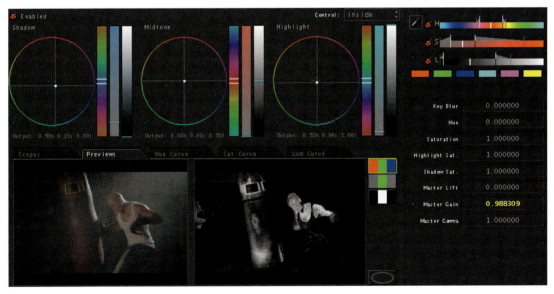

b

more thing. I like this a lot but I just want to see the blue in his pants a little bit more. So why don't we do this. Let's go into yet another secondary." Pepperman draws a square, resizes and rotates it, and positions it over the fighter's shorts. "So right now I'm opening it up to see how much I have, and I want to add a little artificial blue," he says as he pushes blue into the shadows of the square vignette, then softens the shape. "That's much better." See Figure 8-29.

Fig. 8-29 **(a)** This secondary correction is a minor tweak to the color of the boxer's shorts and **(b)** the data from the third secondary correction.

a

b

In an effort to save time with the colorists and have them touch as many images of interest as possible, we didn't follow all of these corrections through the entire process that would be needed to truly finish them. In this case, each of these windows would need to be tracked to the motion of the shot.

Conclusion

For me, the thing that stands out in this discussion of color correcting to help promote a story is that the colorist really needs a strong sense of the story to focus the direction of the corrections. Without context, as David Mullen mentioned, the creative choices are unlimited. Context helps to focus those creative decisions.

There are several books that attempt to define the emotional clues that color delivers. Patti Bellantoni's *If It's Purple, Someone's Gonna Die* (Focal Press, 2005) is a prime example of this school of thought. Another excellent example is Bruce Block's *The Visual Story* (Focal Press, 2001).

I don't believe that defining hard-and-fast rules about what specific colors *always* say is valid due to cultural differences and trends and fashion, but the colorist definitely has a strong storytelling capability through the use of color and contrast in the collaboration with the other storytelling artists on a film as they attempt to influence and engage the audience.

As an exercise, watch a few films and try to determine if there is a story-based reason why the director, DP, art director, and colorist are using certain colors and how they are using contrast and tonality to help tell the story.

CHAPTER 9

Matching Shots

This chapter is devoted to one of the basic colorist tasks: matching shots. This is one of the *least* subjective areas in which a colorist must be proficient. Either the shots match or they don't. You'll see that there are numerous strategies and tips to make these matches easier but that the more experienced you become, the more you simply rely on your eyes. But until then, learning to match shots is a valuable skill and training method in learning to force a very specific look on a shot with a clearly definable and quantifiable result.

There are four matching scenes in this chapter. The first pair of matching shots includes a shot of the lion in front of the Art Institute of Chicago. One was shot with proper white balance (though fairly warm) and one was shot balanced blue or "cool". The second pair of shots includes an interview clip and a b-roll shot that need to cut back to back. The third pair includes two clips from the same interview that was shot outdoors as lighting conditions changed.

Matching the Lions of the Art Institute

Craig Leffel, of the Chicago, IL, postproduction house Optimus, starts us out with his take on the match (see Figs. 9-1 through 9-4).

He begins by analyzing the images and correcting the "base" image (see Fig. 9-1): "I'm looking at these shadows (pointing to the black areas above the three colored banners), since they're the darkest shadows that I can see the fastest. This (pointing to the shadowed archways above the doors) is also a good place to see texture; to see if I'm cranking the blacks too hard or too harshly, this stuff will look pretty awful pretty fast. I'm trying to get the blacks not to look milky and trying to get some richness, but richness with separation. Just adding contrast to an image and just crushing the blacks is not the same as trying to get tonal separation and get richness. Especially when I'm working off something that I know is a piece of tape, I try to separate out as much dynamic

Fig. 9-1 The "base" shot, though it's a little warm.

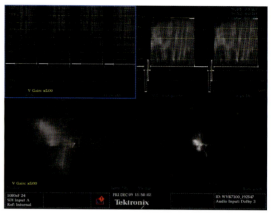

Fig. 9-2 Scopes showing the source image: the YRGB parade (top left quadrant), the vectorscope zoomed 5× (bottom left quadrant), the composite waveform (top right quadrant), and the vectorscope (bottom right quadrant). From Tektronix WVR7100.

Fig. 9-3 The "cool" shot.

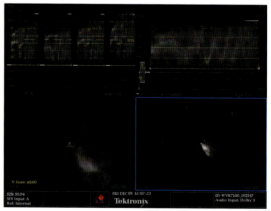

Fig. 9-4 Scopes showing the source image: (a) the YRGB parade, (b) the vectorscope zoomed 5×, (c) the composite waveform, and (d) the vectorscope. From Tektronix WVR7100.

range as I can. The way I discern that is by the black to midtone relationship and then the midtone to highlight relationship. And to me, when you start out—it's one thing where you finish—but where you start, it's nice to have as much range between each stage of black, gamma, and white as you can without any clipping, crushing... just get as full a tonal range as you can. Imagining it's a photograph and trying to see every bit of the tone from 16 steps of gray that you can or more. Kind of a **Zone System** kind of a thing. Whenever I'm doing an image I'm always thinking about, not literally the Zone System, but that's pretty much how I judge an image."

With the base image looking the way he wants (see Fig. 9-5), Leffel grabs a still to begin working on the match. Very quickly, without referring to the scopes, Leffel has a pretty close match.

Leffel ignores the fact that the sky in the "cool" image is radically off, knowing that he'll deal with that later. He switches from the split to cutting back and forth between the still store and the correction. "I have a blue shift in my shadows if you look at the bottom of that lion. The color of the building is right, except the contrast is wrong. You can also see the blue in the shadows in the doorways and in the guy's jacket on the stairs. However, in a case like this of a misbalanced camera, there's gonna be a tradeoff of what compromises you're willing to make in order to make *most* of the image feel good."

Definition

The Zone System: A photographic concept espoused heavily by famous landscape photographer Ansel Adams. The system was designed to be used for the initial negative exposure right through the final print. It is a system designed to properly expose prints by envisioning, describing, and targeting the exposures of certain tonal "zones." There are several books on the subject including Adams' original *The Negative: Exposure and Development*.

a

Fig. 9-5 **(a)** Leffel got the "base" image to a place he was comfortable with and **(b)** the data from the Primary room.

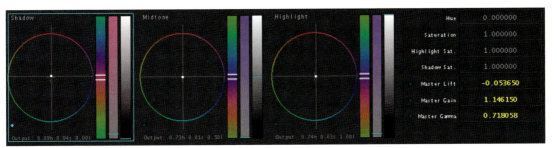

b

Still Store

Any good color correction application or system should have some method of storing and recalling visuals to which you can refer. There are a number of important ways to use a still store. Several colorists grabbed stills throughout their corrections so that they could judge whether the direction they were heading was improving the image or not. Others grabbed stills of shots they were trying to match exactly or of scenes in which they were trying to maintain continuity. Also, the still store can be used to maintain consistency over long-form programs.

Learn to use the still store in your application using the keyboard shortcuts. Experiment with ways to use your still store or reference images to improve your corrections. It may seem like pulling these stills and referring to them will slow you down, but they can also keep you from straying too far down an unproductive path.

Also, as you see by the example of the colorists throughout the book, you need to decide in which cases you want to cut back and forth between the still store and in which cases you want to wipe between it and your working image. Some prefer one method and some prefer the other, but most of them use both methods at one time or another.

"So," I ask Leffel, "Making a perfect match won't be possible in this case, because one or more of the color channels has either become clipped or compressed in one area and not another?"

"Yes," he responds. "So you have to say, 'I want to get as much as I can get right.' Like this is already better, just to take that blue out of the black."

I ask him what he sees as the difference in the images. "It's mostly red gamma. But if you start worrying about that particular detail, you're going to lose the rest of it. It's more an overall perception thing. If you just try and watch the whole image, not trying to see too many details, what your eyeball is going to catch is the overall hue shift. Your eyeball is not going to catch necessarily that change in the doorway." See Figures 9-6 through 9-8.

I ask Leffel to describe what he did as he cuts back and forth between the corrected and uncorrected cool image? "I looked at that blue and said, 'Most of that is happening in the brightest parts of the picture or gain,' and I immediately tried to take out that blue tone and lean more toward the target image overall—throwing warmth in. Once I had that even remotely close, I started dialing contrast in. So then it was time to hit blacks and gamma and dial in some contrast, then working black and gamma against each other to try to get full tonal separation again in the shadows and the midtones so that I wasn't crushing or hitting anything too hard."

I press him further, asking, "By saying 'full tonal separation' and 'working black and gamma against each other,' do you mean how far you pull down the blacks and how high you pull up the midtones, or how high you bring up the blacks and how low you pull down the mid-

Fig. 9-6 The split between the two corrected shots; the "cool" image is on the top. Yes. There is a split there! Notice that the bottom corner of the dark blue banner is cut off.

a

Fig. 9-7 **(a)** The primary correction for the "cool" image and **(b)** the data from the Primary room.

b

Fig. 9-8 **(a)** The secondary correction, pulling added warmth out of the sky and **(b)** the data from the Secondary room.

a

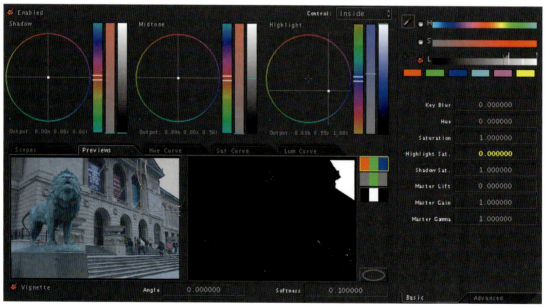

b

tones? And you're doing that with both hands. Then you do that on the other side with the highlights?"

"Exactly," he responds. "You open the midtones and darken the whites. It's a lot easier to match an image if you have some full tones to work with, so I added black. I added gamma. I added color saturation. I mostly manipulated midtones. I brought the black down, but I also brought the whole midtone down. You can see that the white values don't change a whole lot, but the midtones and the blacks do."

The tonal separation really makes the detail pop. "It looks like you can see individual bricks in the façade," I comment.

"Absolutely, and that midtone kind of really stretches out. One of the things I tell colorists is that you have to discern rather quickly, where's the white? What's a white point? What is white, what is black, and everything else is midtone. Then if you manipulate that midtone and think of midtone as a curve that you're kind of sliding down, you can sort of round this image out to have some richness," he explains.

"So you've added a bunch of black and stretched out the image, not to the point where it's harsh or that you're clipping anything unnecessarily — in an image like this you kind of have to clip — but you've stretched it out to have dynamic range: a black, a little-bit-higher than black, a middle gray, a slightly-higher than middle gray, something approaching white, and then white. If you can get 16 steps of gray into an image, you're doing a great job . . . or at least my buddy Ansel Adams said so," Leffel jokes. "I still use The Zone System every day. I'm really surprised that I do, but I come from printing photographs and the mark of a good printer of photographs is tonal separation. If the creative direction is to eliminate it, then of course that's what you do, but as a base way to color correct or as a base way to approach an image, I always approach it as a full-tone image," Leffel concludes.

Craig Leffel

Craig Leffel is a senior colorist and partner at Chicago's Optimus. He works on national TV spots for virtually every major ad agency in the United States.

Leffel got a B.F.A. in photography from Indiana University in the late 1980s before being hired at Skyview, where he apprenticed under one of this book's other featured colorists, Pete Jannotta, at the now-shuttered Skyview. From there, Leffel moved on to Editel until it closed and then to Optimus where he's been for over 12 years.

In addition to his TV spot work, he worked on *Hoop Dreams* and indie features *Yes Men* and *The Pool* with director Chris Smith.

Bob Sliga of Apple Inc. also took on the challenge of the Art Institute lions. His approach was that, even though the "base" image wasn't ideal, he would treat that as the "hero" grade and would match directly to the uncorrected, slightly warm shot. This is almost the reverse of Kassner's approach later in the chapter.

Sliga explains, "I look at the waveform monitor, vectorscope. I like to look at the vectorscope blown up a lot. I blow it up as far as I can go, because it helps me find a neutral black and a neutral white. I also look at the RGB parade display, then I look at the picture. What I have up right now is in the still store, I've saved a picture that I want to match to. The white balance is extremely different. The exposure level is different on the scope. I can see where I have to put the signals in order to help match the image. I'll utilize the wipe to the reference image, then I'll rotate the split so I have a little bit more of the picture," he says as he rotates the wipe so that it goes from the bottom left corner to the top right corner.

Sliga continues, "So if I go to Primary In [room] and I'm just going to brighten this up really high. So one of the things I'm looking for is a match in the waveform. Then it'll be by eye after that. So you kind of get it in the ballpark of the overall video level. I'm also looking at the black level; how we're higher over here, so it's not balanced out. So as I come back over here to my parade display, what I'm trying to do is balance these off as close as possible. To do this, I'm going to start by making my blacks black."

Sliga uses the shadow trackball to balance blacks. "You can see as I move around what happens on the vectorscope. You want to have things coming out of the center. We still have a big-time white balance difference and I'm not even looking at the monitor. I can do this in the joyball area and move all three tonal ranges, or I can come over here to the advanced side (the Advanced tab in the Primary room) and grab the channels one at a time. I'm going to bring my red lift down just a little bit more in the blacks. Now that we're in the Advanced tab, it's easier than moving three joyballs at once. This is just another way of doing this."

Sliga switches from adjusting the red, green, and blue shadow levels to working on highlights. "So we're just going to try to get the highlights in the ballpark," Sliga states as he checks the waveform monitor. "Now we need to take some of the blueness out of this, which I can look to do in one of a couple ways. First I'm going to start with the blue gamma and bring it down into this area here. Then I'm going to bring the red gamma up a tad and then go back and forth."

Sliga changes gears again and jumps from the Advanced tab corrections back to the trackball for midtones. "Now this is one of those places where it's easier to do with the trackballs, so I'm going to do the rest of the correction over here. We're getting warmer overall. We're probably not going to match it totally 100% exactly, but the idea is to get it pretty darn close, and we should be able to. If we had to use windows and that, we could. Remember I'm just in the Primary In room for this right now. So I'm just going to add a bit of color to it. Looks like we have a little bit of a green balance," he says as he adjusts the highlight trackball. "I'm doing this by eye at this point. Then I'll come back to the gamma with a little bit more green. Now I'm using shadow sat (saturation) and pulling down some of the saturation that was building up in the shadows." See Figures 9-9 and 9-10.

With most of the work done in the Primary room, Sliga moves to secondaries, explaining, "I'm going to use the Saturation curve. What I really want to do is deal with that yellow that's coming in to the warmth of the bricks." He pulls the saturation down on the yellow vector of the curve. "When you're actually doing matching like this, you end up trying a lot of

a

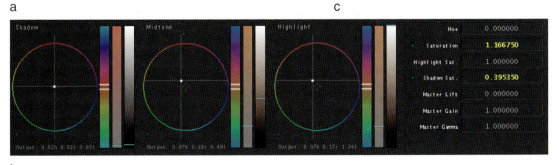

b

Fig. 9-9 The "hero" shot Sliga used for his match.

Red Lift	−0.027550
Green Lift	0.000000
Blue Lift	0.000000
Red Gain	1.095700
Green Gain	1.000000
Blue Gain	0.949250
Red Gamma	1.072500
Green Gamma	1.000000
Blue Gamma	0.770900

c

Hue	0.000000
Saturation	1.166750
Highlight Sat.	1.000000
Shadow Sat.	0.395350
Master Lift	0.000000
Master Gain	1.000000
Master Gamma	1.000000

Fig. 9-10 **(a)** The primary correction of the "cool" shot, **(b)** the main Primary room data, **(c)** the data from the Advanced tab of the Primary room.

things to make it happen, because you're forcing one into the other. And so this one here, by pulling the yellow out, it got our stone (the foundation of the lion) a lot closer, except we've got a little bit of color up in there that's different," he explains, pointing to the building's façade between the lion and the first doorway. "So I came back up here figuring I could get away with a gain change, that gets it in the ballpark. And if we wipe between the two just to see where we're at, the building itself is pretty darn close."

Using another secondary, Sliga tries to bring the color of the lions closer. He positions the split screen diagonally across the lion, then goes to the Saturation curve and moves the cyan point, moving it up and down radically. "That's the wrong point. That ain't going to work, so I'll try the green point." Sliga lifts and lowers the green saturation point radically, seeing that it is affecting the right portion of the image. He settles into a lowered saturation on green. "Maybe somewhere in that area," he determines. "And if we go to the still store and wipe across . . . I pulled too much out, but we can go back to that and raise it a little." A few minor tweaks to the Saturation curve later and his match of the lion is complete. See Figure 9-12.

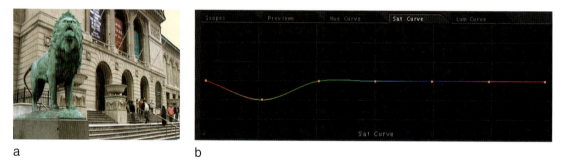

a   b

Fig. 9-11 **(a)** The first secondary correction, pulling yellow out of the façade and **(b)** the data from the first Sat Curve of the secondary correction.

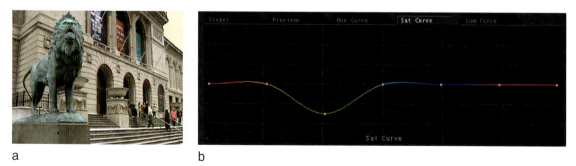

a   b

Fig. 9-12 **(a)** The second secondary correction, pulling saturation out of the "cool" image and **(b)** the data for the Sat Curve of the second secondary correction.

Sliga then added another correction to match the sky, pulling a luminance HSL (hue, saturation, and luminance) qualification and a circular garbage matte (see Figs. 9-13 and 9-14).

Neal Kassner takes the next crack at matching the lions. His initial corrections are to the "cool" lions. "Alright the first thing I'm going to do is try to balance the blacks a little bit. And I'm looking at a combination of the waveform and the vectorscope. I'm going to warm up the gammas a little. Now, I don't know what kind of stone that is (referring to the façade of the building), but I know it's not as yellow as one or as blue as the other, so I'm just going to try to make it neutral. I'm also going to wind down the overall gain and see what that does to the sky."

Then he switches over to the warmer lion shot. "So now what I have to do is go the other way with it. And I'm going to take some of the warmth out of the lowlights and also out of the midrange. Okay, so this is where it's getting

a   b

Fig. 9-13 **(a)** The third secondary correction, pulling warmth out of the sky and **(b)** the data from the third secondary correction, pulling the Highlight Sat. numerical entry to 0.

Fig. 9-14 The split between the "base" shot and the corrected "cool" shot.

there, but it's not close, so I'll cut back and forth between this and the still. What I'm going to do is match the luminance using the waveform."

In order to get the contrast ratios right between the two images, Kassner plays the gammas and highlights off each other, bringing the gammas down and the highlights up, then bringing shadows up, then playing shadows up and highlights down at the same time, before his correction is in a comfortable range for him. "Okay, the luminance is closer than it was. Now I'm going to concentrate on color. Now I'm running into a situation where I like *this* better than *that*," he says, preferring his semi-adjusted shot two over his completed correction on shot one.

Kassner starts his grade over using grade three in the timeline. I ask him if he's trying to get the shapes in the waveform to line up. "Exactly. So now there's a color cast . . . a little cyan. It appears to be mostly in the gammas. Now I'm looking at the vectorscope, just trying to match the shapes a little better. It almost looks like there's a black stretch going on in this grade. This," he says, pointing at the shadow area on waveform monitor, "up to here is a fairly close match, color aside, just luminance. But then, this," he points at the high midtones, "is getting stretched out more. If I just go and bring up the highlights it's also dragging up the lowlights with it. So if I work the two against each other . . . now we're getting some place. That's actually a little bit closer." Kassner has been moving the gammas down and the highlights up at the same time. "Then there's just a question of trimming the colors. A little overall hue correction would be a good cheat." See Figures 9-15 through 9-17.

Janet Falcon of Shooters Post in Philadelphia, PA, is next up. She starts in on the correction with her eyes almost completely on the video monitor. "I'm just trying to get it somewhere close to a starting point before I bother going back and forth." Falcon wipes between the "correct" and "cool" lion, deciding, "There's way too much red in the blacks. I need to brighten this up. So basically I need more yellow in the highlights because there's too much blue in the highlights. Then put a little blue back in the lowlights." Falcon points at the middle of the doorway arch closest to the lion, commenting, "I'm going back and forth between looking here for blacks, here for gammas," as she points to the top edge of same archway, "and up here for whites," she says, pointing to the far right square of the building's façade above the far right archway. "It's a little pinker." See Figures 9-18 and 9-19.

Falcon points out that as you get closer to getting a match, it's easy to forget which side of the correction you're adjusting. "With FinalTouch (Color) you don't know if you are looking at the reference frame or live picture because there is no indication in the GUI. On the DaVinci there is a green bar on the Graphical interface that shows whether you are on the reference frame or live picture," Falcon explains.

With the buildings matching fairly close, Falcon pulls a secondary HSL key for the lion and matches it as well. She also adds a simple HSL qualification to both the images to correct for the clipped sky

15a

16a

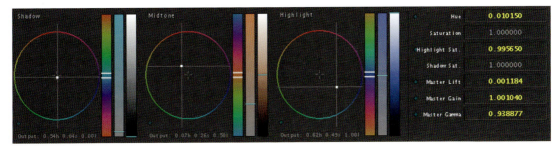

15b

Fig. 9-15 **(a)** Kassner chose to balance to the Art Institute shot entirely in the Primary room. This is the primary grade for the warm or "base" shot. The sky would be fixed with a secondary. **(b)** The data from the "base" image in the Primary room.

16b

Fig. 9-16 **(a)** The "cool" image graded in the Primary room and **(b)** the data from the "cool" image in the Primary room.

Fig. 9-17 The split between shots; the "base" image is on the bottom.

Fig. 9-18 (a) The primary correction on the warm, "base" image and (b) the data from the primary correction to the "base" image.

a

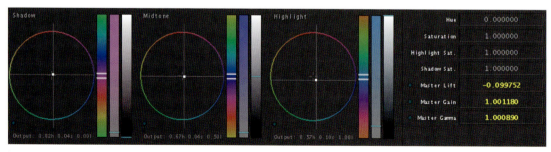

b

a

Fig. 9-19 (a) The primary correction on the "cool" image and (b) the data from the primary correction to the "cool" image.

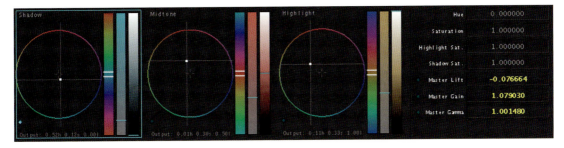

b

(see Figs. 9-20 and 9-21). The corrections are nearly identical to those done by the previous colorists in this chapter.

Falcon offers a final tip at the end of her matching session. "Unless the final product will be a split screen or some other type of special effect, where matching details can be very important, matching one shot to another is mostly about overall perception. As long as the basic balance and contrast ratio are the same you can get away with smaller details that may not be exact. Often a shot like the one I worked on here would never be cut to itself, there would be a close up or some other shot next, so by the time the 'matched' shot appears again the smaller differences would never be noticed."

Fig. 9-20 **(a)** The secondary correction to the hue and saturation of the lion and **(b)** the data from the secondary correction.

a

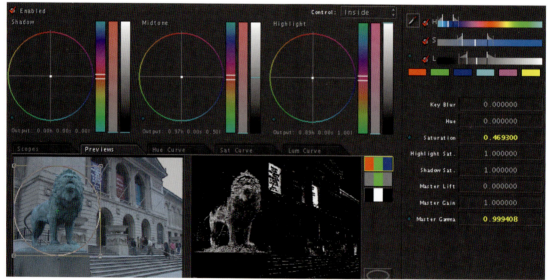

b

Fig. 9-21 The split between shots; the "cool" image is on the top.

Matching Scene to Scene

Figs. 9-22 though 9-25 are images from footage from a project I produced for Exclaim Entertainment's "BOZ the Bear." In the project, these two shots—the "b-roll" shot of the woman with her son (see Fig. 9-22) and the interview scene of the woman (see Fig. 9-24)—were not cutting together well. I tried trimming the shots one way and then the other with no success. Finally, I decided to color correct the shots so that they'd match better. That was the solution.

Figuring that our panel of experts could match them better than I could, I included the scenes in the sessions for the book. Here Bob Sliga takes a crack at matching the scenes. Follow along using the images in the tutorial folder of the DVD: "Jackie_and_Nick_b-roll.mov" and "Jackie_interview.mov"

Fig. 9-22 Source footage of the "b-roll" shot. Image courtesy of Exclaim Entertainment.

Fig. 9-24 An image from the source footage of the interview. Image courtesy of Exclaim Entertainment.

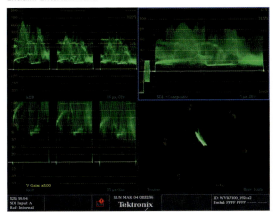

Fig. 9-23 Scopes showing the source image: the RGB parade (top left quadrant), the RGB parade zoomed in to show the black balance (bottom left quadrant), the composite waveform (top right quadrant), and the vectorscope (bottom right quadrant). From Tektronix WVR7100.

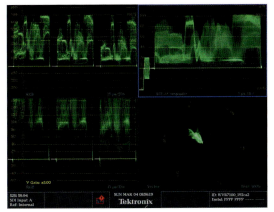

Fig. 9-25 Scopes showing the source image: the RGB parade (top left quadrant), the RGB parade zoomed in to show the black balance (bottom left quadrant), the composite waveform (top right quadrant), and the vectorscope (bottom right quadrant). From Tektronix WVR7100.

Bob Sliga

Bob Sliga graduated from Illinois State University and has been a colorist since 1979. He has been senior colorist for three different facilities.

In 1983, he moved to Post Pro Video in Chicago, IL, with the first Rank Cintel Mark III C with full zoom and repositioning capability. Sliga was then recruited by Henninger Video to open the first film transfer suite in Baltimore, MD. He returned to Chicago in August 1997 to oversee the opening of The Film & Tape Works Datacine Suite. Bob has served as a demo colorist for da Vinci and the Spirit Datacine.

Specializing in commercials for 20 years, his clients have included Leo Burnett USA; DDB Needham; Foote, Cone, & Belding; J. Walter Thompson; Ogilvie & Mather; ESPN; NBC; CBS; ABC; Major League Baseball; and The Discovery Channel.

In the fall of 2001, he began teaching a telecine and color correction course at Columbia College in Chicago. In September 2005, he became a freelancer to pursue digital intermediate (DI) color correction with Silicon Color's FinalTouch HD. In June 2006, he became the director of training for Silicon Color and served as demo artist for Silicon Color's FinalTouch HD. In December 2006, Sliga was hired by Apple Inc. for Color's new quality assurance team in Cupertino, CA.

Sliga starts by correcting the interview scene first. "I'm bringing the whites down out of clip. Then I balanced my blacks and brought them down a bit, which got me to here (See Fig. 9-26). I forgot I even did it. Sometimes it seems like my hands think for me."

With a basic correction to the interview scene, Sliga turns his attention to the shot of the mother and son. "Okay, so now we come over here. I'm going to balance him out too. I'm just going to pull the blacks down to zero. I'm going to bring the overall warmth of this down a little bit in the gain because we see how high that is," Sliga remarks, referring to the red channel in the RGB parade scope being much brighter than blue or green. "I'm going to choose to do it this time on the individual channel. It's a little easier." Sliga brings the gain of the red channel down, but not so that it is perfectly even with blue and green. "It is still slightly higher, which it should be because the image is mostly skin tone," he explains. See Figure 9-27. Then he plays the shot through. "A lot of times I'll advance the clip to the next scene and then back it up one frame to see how the shot ends."

Sliga returns to the interview shot. "So this shot is a lot warmer than the other shot. I could pull the warmth out. People generally look better warmer, so I try to use the warmth to its advantage. I'm going to try to richen her up at first, then I'll match the other to this."

Sliga continues, "I'm going to keep what I've got here and go to the Secondary room. The reason is that if I like where I'm at in primaries,

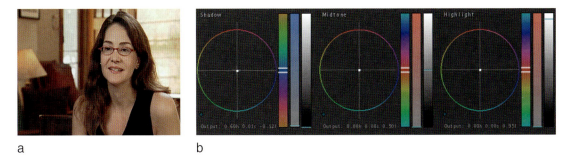

a   b

Fig. 9-26 **(a)** The primary correction to the interview scene and **(b)** the data for the Primary room.

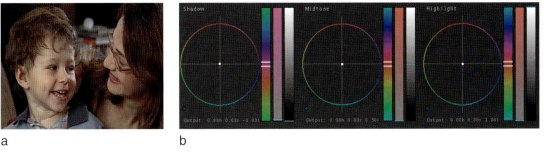

a   b

c

Fig. 9-27 **(a)** The primary correction to "b-roll" scene, **(b)** the data from the Primary room, **(c)** the data for the Advanced tab of the Primary room.

but I want to do some more, then I don't have to sacrifice what I've already done. There's more than one way to color correct with this software, and it all depends on the type of job and the type of work that you're doing. So I'm going to richen her up a bit by pulling the gammas down a bit. I'm going to warm it up a tad. The black is looking nice and black and we've got a nice clean white back here. I just richened it up a bit, okay? And by doing that, the saturation kind of came into play on its own. . . . I added more saturation by just darkening it down. So I'm going to keep this and hit control-I, which will make a still of this."

Sliga continues with his explanation of his workflow. "Then I'm going to call up the other scene and cut back and forth to the still. I'm more of a cut person instead of using a wipe. First thing I'm going to do is richen this up, warm it up a little here. I'm going to leave primaries where they're at and I'm going to come into secondaries." See Figure 9-28.

Sliga enables a secondary, but doesn't qualify anything at all, using it as another layer of primary. "I'll richen it up a bit," he continues, pulling down the gamma. Then he warms the image by dragging the midtone wheel toward red/yellow. "Now I'll kick up the whites a bit, bring my blacks back down. That's going to be a little too warm, I have a feeling," he speculates as he brings red back down in the midtones. "Let's just see where this is at," he says as he hits control-U, checking his match. "So I've made this a little bit too warm in comparison," he says, altering the shot slightly, before completing his grade. See Figure 9-29.

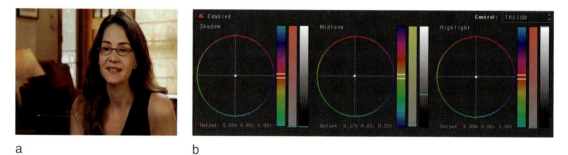

a   b

Fig. 9-28 **(a)** The secondary correction of the interview image used "unqualified" as essentially an additional layer of the primary correction and **(b)** the data from the Secondary room.

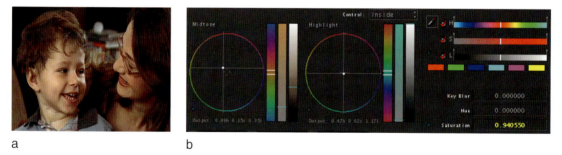

a   b

Fig. 9-29 **(a)** The secondary correction of the "b-roll" image used "unqualified" as essentially an additional layer of the primary correction and **(b)** the data from the Secondary room.

Matching When Lighting Changes in a Scene

The following shots (see Figs. 9-30 through 9-33) are from a documentary I produced about my family's bicycle trip across the United States. During the interview with my brother, which I shot on BetaSP without lights, the sun started to go down, so the beginning (see Fig. 9-30) and end (see Fig. 9-32) of the interview look somewhat different. Follow along with the "brian_overexposed.mov" and "brian_low_contrast.mov" files from the

Fig. 9-30 The image from source footage of the interview from early in the day called "brian_overexposed" on the DVD.

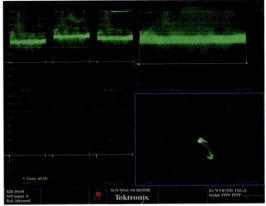

Fig. 9-31 Scopes showing the source image: the RGB parade (top left quadrant), the RGB parade waveform zoomed in to show the black balance (bottom left quadrant), the composite waveform (top right quadrant), and the vectorscope (bottom right quadrant). From Tektronix WVR7100.

Fig. 9-32 The image from source footage of the interview from later in the day, called "brian_interview_low_contrast" on the DVD.

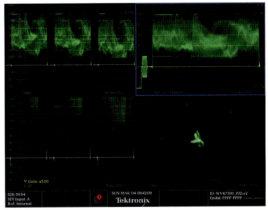

Fig. 9-33 Scopes showing the source image: the RGB parade (top left quadrant), the RGB parade waveform zoomed in to show the black balance (bottom left quadrant), the composite waveform (bottom left quadrant), and the vectorscope (bottom right quadrant). From Tektronix WVR7100.

Tutorial folder on the DVD. The color temperature didn't actually change much, but the contrast as it got closer to dusk definitely changed.

Nolo Digital's Mike Matusek starts by correcting the first shot from the interview, then he corrects the second shot to match the first. "This would be a combination of midtones and blacks that I'd bring down. Midtone may not have enough range," he says as his eyes go back and forth between the scopes and the monitor as he adjusts.

I ask him what the challenge is in getting these shots to match. "I think you said that the sun was out in this first image and then it started to go down in this second image," he replies. "The first shot has more contrast and the highlight of his right side is up, so I'll probably put a window on it, then, probably increase the contrast on [the second shot] to try to get them closer, then just match the flesh tone." See Figs. 9-34 and 9-35.

34a   35a

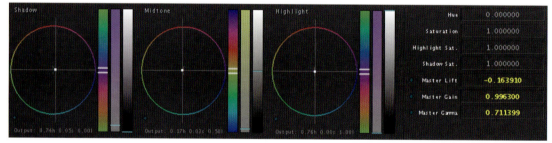

b

Fig. 9-34 (a) Early "overexposed" interview footage with the primary correction, and **(b)** the data from the Primary room.

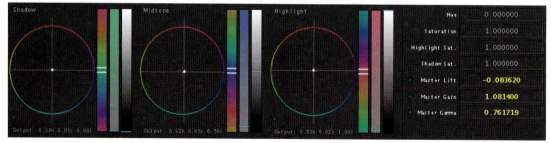

b

Fig. 9-35 (a) Later interview footage with the primary correction and **(b)** the data from the Primary room.

a   b

Fig. 9-36 (a) Early "overexposed" interview footage with the secondary correction and (b) the data from the Secondary room.

Fig. 9-37 The split between the two shots shows how close the skin tones and background tonality match (and this Picasso-like image is sure to make my brother laugh).

Matusek puts a window on left side and lowers the brightness of the background and the face highlight. "See? That's all it really needed." See Figures 9-36 and 9-37.

Conclusion

The colorists I did sessions with for this book have such a depth of experience that most of them did these matches very much by eye. For the less-experienced colorist, you will find that one of the greatest ways to match shots is by using the split screens and the RGB parade waveform monitors, matching the various "shapes" in the trace between each color channel or cell.

Another good way to assist your eye in matching is rapidly cutting back and forth. At first, you can look at the overall image and try to ascertain the differences, but as you get closer, your eye will have to isolate various tonal ranges as the shots cut back and forth. Therefore, you can determine if the thing making one shot look redder than the other shot is red coming from the shadows, midtones, or highlights.

CHAPTER 10

Creating Looks

Creating "looks." This is probably why some colorists make as much as CEOs of Fortune 500 companies and drive around in Lamborghinis. This is the sexy stuff. It's also the stuff that is virtually unquantifiable. It's part of what takes color correction from craft to art.

Craig Leffel of Chicago's Optimus explains some of his process for coming up with looks. "Well I think it's always a process of working wider and then narrowing."

I ask if some of the time when he's spinning the trackballs, he's not really color correcting as much as getting a sense of where the image can go. He explains: "Yeah. Sometimes when you make an extreme change you see that you've either grabbed the wrong thing or you've grabbed too much. It's certainly the subtle stuff that begins to appear to you when you've made a huge change. Then you can narrow down and narrow down and narrow down from there. Also, sometimes when you're starting to play with a new image, you work in extremes unless you're being told a very specific thing. But if it's up to you to kind of come up with a look, then making extreme, radical changes is sometimes helpful. It may not be helpful to the people sitting behind you, but it helps you kind of see where an image can go. How much it can handle. If you really do make those extreme changes up front, I quite often see things that I didn't think of. Like maybe this image looks really good pink and I never considered that. Or maybe hicon or way more crushed than you would have ever thought would look good."

"You say, "Holy Moley that looks great. I didn't really mean to do that. I was just kind of rolling through my ranges but that looks really good. I think I'll work toward that." Because quite often that first impression of an image—no matter who you are, no matter how experienced you are, no matter how much background you have—the first time somebody says, "Do something really cool with that," that first impression that you have may not be the one you really want to go with. And you kind of have to be willing to let yourself find where you might want to go. And obviously it's a collaborative effort with the people behind you, but quite often, if I'm by myself, I don't like to trust my first instinct. I like to kind of challenge myself and see if there's something I didn't think of. I call it 'going through my ranges.' You know, really pushing it around—light and dark—pushing it all the way around the vectorscope. If I have a huge time crunch I don't do it, and if I've got someone behind me saying something very specific I won't typically do it, but I will push for a little bit of time with the film by myself where I do run through those ranges. Especially if it's kind of open ended, like 'Do something cool with this.' So that's my trick. Push it around hard at the very beginning and then narrow down and narrow down and narrow down."

Enough Is Enough

I ask Leffel when he knows to stop, since they say that great art is all about knowing when to stop. "Certainly in my line of work, knowing when to stop . . . there's a point of diminishing returns. I think I'm usually done when I don't see anything objectionable in the picture anymore. If everything has lived up to what I was trying to do and I don't see any objections, then I'm usually feeling pretty good about being done. The truth is, you could keep working forever and you'd never be done. You'd just keep going and going and going."

I ask him to be specific about how he knows where his boundaries are. He explains, "Those are the hard things to even verbalize. I think if the lighting I've set feels like it's actually motivated by something outside and I feel like that's not going to be able to go anywhere past that. If I like their flesh tones; if I like the details in the image. I'm always scanning the image all over the place to see if something is standing out to me or bothering me or drawing my attention. And I'm usually trying to consider all things at once, so in a shot, if I'm really trying to be critical, I'm saying to myself, 'Is anything distracting me? Is anything bothering me? Is anything pulling my eye away from what I should be looking at?' When I can answer all of those questions and say, 'I'm not being distracted. I feel I'm looking at what I'm supposed to be looking at. I've achieved the goal that I've set out to do,' if I can answer all those questions then I'm usually feeling like I'm pretty done."

Preset Looks

Bob Festa of R!OT Santa Monica was one of the few people who I spoke with who described some of the looks that he starts to show clients. Festa is clearly talented enough to develop these looks from scratch on every shot, but he's also a big proponent of reusing selected elements of these looks as easy-to-apply presets.

"I've been doing this for a long time and I've been the architect of a couple of features in the da Vinci, and one of those is something called PowerGrade. PowerGrade is a browser that lets me keep 20–25 of my top techniques in there, and once I get an image balanced and into a place that I like, then I can ripple those PowerGrade effects back on top of it. Those might be everything from a four-corner pin to a bleach bypass to a **cross-process look**. These are things that might take five or ten minutes to build up from scratch; I can quickly double-click it and dial it in on top of my base, well-balanced image. So that PowerGrade library is very influential. And I had a lot of arguments about that with people about, 'should we be able to dial things on top, with just a single keystroke, of images, or should they be rebuilt from scratch?' My feeling is, if you want to give your clients a choice, I'd rather show them 25 things that I can do with a single key-stroke than 4 things that I've had to build from scratch."

Festa's PowerGrade Library Revealed

Bob Festa generously shared a glimpse at some of his trade secrets. "Some of the things that are in there are prebuilt Power Tiers. So basically I always start with a nice balanced image. Then I've got a bunch of Power Tiers that I can ripple on top of that. They'd be one or two channels of window or a channel of defocus combined with a key.

Festa is sitting at his da Vinci and walks through the presets with me. "Just to give you an idea off the top of my head what I have in there. In the top row I have a complete line of bleach bypass, ranging from 20% to 70% in 10% increments. In a single keystroke I can ripple that on top without having to go through a whole building process. So I can show somebody 20%, 30%, 40%, boom, boom, boom, just like that."

Festa opines, "The da Vinci is really clumsy when it comes to setting up soft effects like ProMists, defocus, pearlized whites. So I have all of those set up on single keystrokes. Of course, what that does is build a defocus channel and a key channel and a channel of Power Window just to support it all."

Continuing through the presets, Festa explains, "I have the Pearlizer, which is just soft whites. I have the swing and tilt, which is just the corner's softened. I have the ProMist. The ProMist is divided up into ProMist 1 through 6. And I also have a mist with what I call 'de-min' added to it, which is like a richer ProMist also. The ProMist settings don't have much correlation to the on-camera ProMist filters."

Festa explains, "Textures, which are really hard to create, like bleach bypass and soft effects, I have all those on single-keystroke things. In addition to those I have the usual kinds of stuff like Blue Wash #2, duo-tones, day-for-night 1 and 2, film noir black and white. Then I have my cross process looks."

Festa describes what his cross-processed looks actually do. "So I have those two things built as layers and those use multiple layers because a C41 to E6 look really gives a super golden white with a lot of blue-cyan in the blacks. So I use a separate channel for each one of those effects.

Cross-process Look: The look of film when it is processed chemically in a "bath" or "soup" that is *supposed* to be used to process a *different kind* of film. For example, using a C41 development bath on a piece of film that should be developed in an E6 bath, or vice versa. This cross-processing alters the characteristics of the film. (See the subhead "Cross Process Looks" and Figs. 10-1 through 10-4) later in this chapter for more information.

One channel to warm up the whites gives it a golden, dirty look. And also a channel to get that 'cyan-ey' blue stuff in the blacks."

Festa summarizes, "To build any of these effects from the ground up is really a five-minute job. So I found, if I had all of this stuff at the top, I could open up this PowerGrade and just quickly show somebody not only my warm, cool, and balanced looks, but here's some really wacky stuff if you want to stretch out."

I respond, "Everybody's got a deadline, so why spend it recreating something you know you've done over and over again."

"Exactly," Festa agrees, "that was my thought."

Preset Looks in Apple's Color

Apple's Color, and many other applications, have the same ability as Power-Grade to create preset looks and apply them at the touch of a button. Most of the preset looks that were delivered with the initial release of Color were created by Bob Sliga, who is featured in this book. There are also fantastic preset looks available from third-party vendors, like Graeme Nattress, who sells a collection of effects nodes that work in Color. Many of the colorists who are experienced Color/FinalTouch users highly recommend the Nattress plug-ins, which not only come with the effects nodes themselves, but with entire prebuilt process trees. A demo of the Nattress effects is on the DVD.

Film Processing Looks

Many of the highly desired looks that colorists are asked to do actually mimic chemical film processes. We briefly touched on cross-processing and we'll take a deeper look into the electronic reproduction of the skip bleach and bleach bypass looks later in the chapter, but the following looks give you a quick overview of some of the ways that various film processes can affect the look of an image. The images below are not color corrections but motion picture film processed chemically in various ways. Understanding how these processes affect the look of an image will help you build your "visual vocabulary." Since directors of photography are frequent collaborators with colorists, understanding what these processes do to an image will help you communicate better with them.

Often, directors of photography (DPs) will choose to attempt to reproduce these looks electronically in color correction sessions instead of applying them chemically because these chemical processes are somewhat risky to apply since they can't be "undone." Although Kodak educates filmmakers in how to execute and utilize these processes, they do not recommend them due to the inherent dangers of developing film in ways that were not intended. Cross-processing creates higher contrast and saturation and distorts colors in sometimes unexpected ways. See Figures 10-1 and 10-2 for examples.

a

b

Fig. 10-1 **(a)** This image is a print from Kodak 5245 negative film processed normally with the ECN-2 process. **(b)** This image is a print from one of Kodak's reversal films, Ektachrome 5285, which has been processed using ECN-2. Images courtesy of Eastman Kodak Company.

a

b

c

Fig. 10-2 **(a)** This image shows a print from Kodak reversal film Ektachrome 100D, processed normally. **(b)** This image shows a print from Kodak negative film 5279, processed normally. **(c)** This image shows a print from Kodak Ektrachrome 100D cross-processed. Images courtesy of Eastman Kodak Company.

Pushing film, which overdevelops the negative, is used in combination with underexposing the negative to increase contrast and add grain (see Fig. 10-3). In color films it also creates lifted, blue shadows and a color imbalance. It is also possible to "pull" process film, which is essentially the exact opposite of push processing.

Fig. 10-3 **(a)** This image is printed from a black-and-white negative with normal processing. **(b)** This image is printed from a black-and-white negative pushed two stops. Images courtesy of Eastman Kodak Company.

a

b

Skip bleach and bleach bypass are processes where the film is either not bleached at all to remove silver or is partially bleached, leaving various amounts of silver. The remaining silver increases the contrast of the film. Wherever there is more developed dye, there is more silver, so you get higher contrast, blacker blacks, and less saturation. See Figure 10-4.

Now that you've seen how these looks are created photo-chemically, the following section will describe how to electronically attain one of the most common of these looks: skip bleach or bleach bypass.

a   b   c

Fig. 10-4 **(a)** This is a print from normally developed Kodak 5274 film. **(b)** This is 5274 film with bleach bypass processing of the camera negative. **(c)** This is 5274 film with skip bleach processing of the print. Images courtesy of Eastman Kodak Company.

Skip Bleach or Bleach Bypass

Bob Sliga did his first pass at the image in Figure 10-5 by simply dropping Graeme Nattress' bleach bypass effect on it in Color Effects (see Fig. 10-6).

I ask Sliga if he could reproduce the look just using the Primary and Secondary rooms. "This shot is pretty nicely balanced, and the blacks all match, but in the gammas, there's a bit of an 'angle,' with red higher than green higher than blue," Sliga explains. "That's because this

Fig. 10-5 The original source image. Image courtesy of Artbeats' "Lifestyles—Mixed Cuts 1" collection..

Bleach Effect Amount	0.425800
Over Exposure	0.072000
Desaturation	0.500000

a   b

Fig. 10-6 (a) The image with the Nattress bleach bypass effect dropped on it in Color Effects and (b) the data from the Nattress bleach bypass node in Color Effects.

shot is balanced a little warm. And there are purists who might say that this shot needs to be balanced perfectly and that those levels should match."

I explain to Sliga that I've been looking at this shot with the basic grade of the original Artbeats' image, so I'm used to seeing it a little warm. Sliga agrees, "It should be warm. This shot wants to be warm. When I think of balance, I think of making the blacks black." See Figure 10-7.

With the shot in a good starting position, Sliga turns his attention to giving it a classic bleach bypass look. "We'll favor the bleach bypass on the cool side," he says as he takes the gamma and highlights toward blue a little with the hue offset wheels. "Then we'll go to secondaries." In a secondary, Sliga doesn't bother qualifying anything before he pulls the blacks down in the entire image, using the secondary like a second level of primary correction. See Figure 10-8.

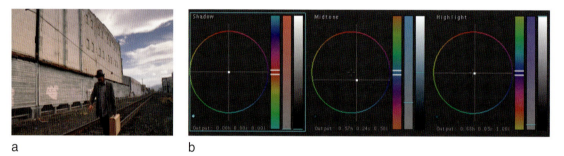

a   b

Fig. 10-7 **(a)** Sliga's primary correction and **(b)** the data from the Primary room.

Fig. 10-8 **(a)** The first secondary correction and **(b)** the data from the Secondary room.

a   b

"I'm going to be clipping the blacks and blowing the whites out," Sliga explains as he stretches the gamma back up a bit to compensate for his big black drop. He drops saturation in each of the tonal ranges, adds another secondary, and qualifies the brightest portions of the sky and building. Then Sliga corrects outside of this qualification pulling down the midtones, making the shadows darker. See Figure 10-9.

a

Fig. 10-9 **(a)** The second secondary correction and **(b)** the data from the second secondary correction.

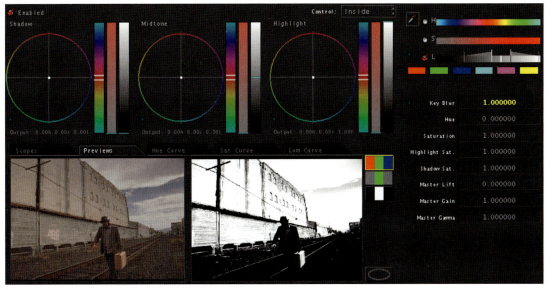

b

"It hurts the eyes after a while when you look back and you see how far it went," Sliga comments. "That's one way we could go. Bleach bypass is a matter of crushing gammas, crushing blacks, blowing out whites. How far that you want the blacks to be is really the key. You have to have a broadcast safe filter on it, because you're blowing it all out. If you don't have a broadcast safe filter on it, you're going to get hosed."

Greg Creaser expounds on the look of bleach bypass as he drops a bleach bypass effect on the Artbeats' Marines scene (see Fig. 10-10). This is in the Artbeats Tutorial files as "Marines_MAR115H1.mov" "Typically bleach bypass has more saturation than that (See Fig 10-11a) depending on how it was done or how long it was let out of the bleach." To correct it to a more classic bleach bypass look, he goes back to primary, adds saturation, pulls down blacks, and pumps up highlights. "It would be a little edgier, like that," he says. See Figure 10-11(b).

Fig. 10-10 The source image. Image courtesy of Artbeats.

a   b

Fig. 10-11 **(a)** The image with no correction except the bleach bypass node in Color Effects. **(b)** The "edgier" version after Creaser adds saturation, lowers blacks, and raises highlights.

> ### Greg Creaser
>
> Greg Creaser is a freelance digital intermediate (DI) colorist in Los Angeles, CA, with an impressive list of over 60 feature films to his credit as either digital color timing supervisor or DI colorist: *The Ring Two*, *Seabiscuit*, *Terminator 3*, *Pirates of the Caribbean: The Curse of the Black Pearl*, *xXx*, *Spider-Man*, *The Fast and the Furious*, *The Mummy Returns*, *Hannibal*, *Mission Impossible II*, and *Gladiator*.
>
> Greg has been working in the industry since 1977, starting in the laboratory as a technician/color timer and moving into upper management by 1985. Greg also studied photography at Art Center in Pasadena, CA, and his father was a cinematographer.

I ask Creaser to define the look of bleach bypass. "That's an interesting question," he says. "There's multiple ways to do bleach skip. You can skip the whole bleach or half of the bleach. What usually happens with skip bleach is you end up with a saturated/grainy/gritty image. It changes the contrast of the film. It really depends on what kind of film stock it is and how it was bypassed and whether it was overdeveloped or underdeveloped on top of that."

Match the Look

One of the common requests to colorists is to give an image a look from a popular movie, TV show, or music video. Obviously for the colorist, this requires a fairly decent command of popular culture and a decent color memory.

I ask Mike Matusek of Nolo Digital Film if it's a big help when someone provides visual references to other media? "Do you feel like you have to be up on the latest movies or watch a lot of media or TV so that if somebody says, 'Hey I want it to look like *Crash*,' you can say 'I know what that means.'"

Matusek responds, "Totally. I get Netflix. Newer films are a good place to look for looks. With older films, it was color timing and they were not as extreme. Commercials are great resources to look for really pushed looks. I did the "GoDaddy" spots the last few years, and the look we were going for in those spots was "CSI: Miami." Hypersaturated . . . well, not hypersaturated, but make the sky yellow and the water cyan and push the contrast. Generalizing, that campaign had that look. Or the "Diamonds Are Forever" spots were kind of contrasty and cyan, duotone with a flesh tone that's desaturated. It's tough to have seen the same movie as your client, or see the same spots as your client. It's mostly about saying "Is this what you mean?" and doing a look and then trying something else. Usually you can find something you've both seen."

Matusek picks out the Marines shot from Artbeats (see Fig. 10-12) and decides to give it a look of another popular movie. "For this image, I'm just trying to give it a more high contrast, maybe go for a skip bleach kind of a look. Kind of a *Blackhawk Down*—I hate to be cliché, but it is kind of a cool look."

Matusek begins his grade. "So this shot I'm just playing on the contrasty image, because there's already nice highlights here. I'm just kind of pushing that. Letting the sky blow. There's some nice blue there. Sometimes a client will have you spend 20 minutes on making the sky blue—[but] the subject is the soldiers." See Figure 10-13.

Matusek points to the highlights on the bright sides of the helmets, and continues with a great tip. "I'd probably grab a highlight defocus on some of that stuff, because if you defocus the highlights, you can push the contrast

Fig. 10-12 The source image. Image courtesy of Artbeats.

Fig. 10-13 (a) Matusek's primary correction and (b) the data from the Primary room.

a

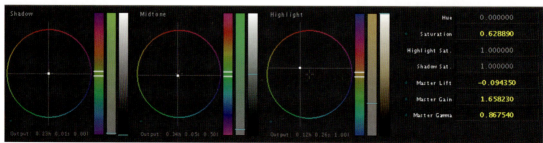

b

even more. Because when you go too much, some of these pushed high-lights start to look a little clipped, which doesn't look that good. So if you throw a nice, soft defocused highlight, that kind of smoothes out that transition and allows you to go a little more heavy-handed with the contrast."

Matusek takes some time working on getting a saturated sky before explaining, "I'm doing what I said I disliked when the clients asked for it, but I'm putting a little blue in the sky. Usually it works out to look pretty good." He creates a big oval window along the top. "I would prefer it without the blue sky, but a lot of clients would prefer that," he says, showing off his newly tweaked sky. See Figure 10-14.

a

Fig. 10-14 **(a)** the data from the outside of the qualification in the Secondary room and **(b)** The secondary correction to tweak the sky.

b

Continuing with the "soldier look" theme, Matusek comments on a recent project of his. "I worked on a documentary called *War Tapes*. They gave a bunch of cameras to soldiers and they documented their year's stay in Iraq. So what we did was, all the footage in Iraq, we gave it a higher contrast, warmer look. We gave it a little grittier look. And then they would cut from the soldiers to their families. On the home front, it was a little softer, it was more saturated and truer colors. Just trying to create a separation. And it's all subtle. It was a documentary, so the Iraq footage wasn't like *Blackhawk Down*."

Looks for Promos and Opens

One of the popular images that the colorists in this book chose to give a look to was Artbeats' image of a football being readied by the center (see Fig. 10-15). This is available as "Football_SP123H1.mov" in the Artbeats Tutorial folder on the DVD.

To give some context, I ask Shooters Post colorist Janet Falcon to grade the image as if it will be used in an open for the SuperBowl.

She considers the request, then dives in to the grade. "Then you'd go for something a lot more contrasty and a lot more pushed and forced. Depending on what other things are in there, you may stick with normal color. I just want to save it along the way so I can play with a few different things. Everytime I get something, I save it. I use my da Vinci Notepads a lot. Maybe go with a blue-black if you want not 'off' colors, but not normal colors."

She continues, "Opens are usually high color. Like if you've seen the open for 'Survivor.' Really bold, wild colors. You could go something more like that." See Figure 10-16.

Fig. 10-15 The original source image. Image courtesy of Artbeats' Sports 1 HD Vol 1 collection.

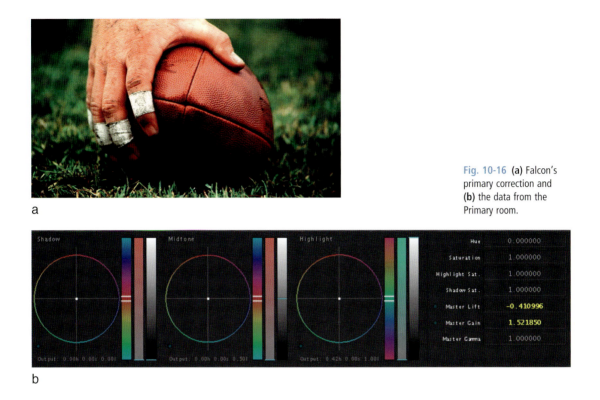

a

b

Fig. 10-16 **(a)** Falcon's primary correction and **(b)** the data from the Primary room.

I ask for a different look, since the year we did this, Chicago was in the SuperBowl: cold and tough. (GO BEARS!) "We could go here for cooler. You can shift colors when you're doing Master Gain and Master Lift. As you track up and down, you shift color. I usually like to do luminance only in my vignettes and then go in separately and adjust more or less saturation." See Figures 10-18, 10-19, and 10-20. Falcon's last sentence describes a fairly unique ability of the da Vinci to affect luminance without affecting RGB. Many other color correctors, including Apple's Color, don't have this capability, so the workaround is to go back and change saturation after gain and setup adjustments that raise or lower saturation.

Pete Jannotta also gives the football image a look of his own. He works for awhile before I prompt him to tell me what he's doing. "I desaturated it," he explains. "I'm just experimenting. I want this one to feel strong. Not too clean. Feel gutsier, because of his tape, the dirty tape, and go with that suggestion of it being tough." It's a telling point that he derives the direction of his correction from an element of the picture, like the tape on the player's fingers.

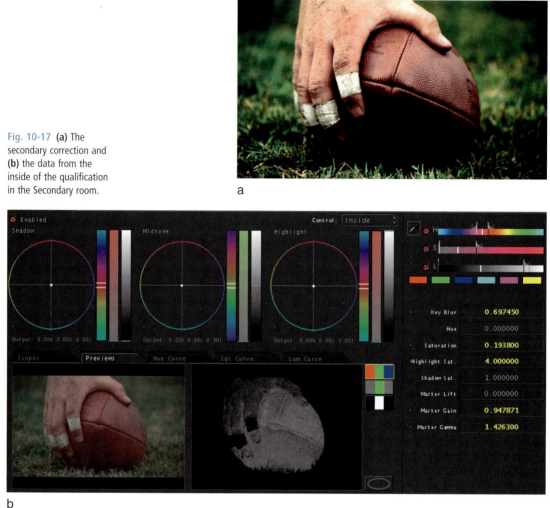

Fig. 10-17 (a) The secondary correction and **(b)** the data from the inside of the qualification in the Secondary room.

Jannotta continues, "Then the other thing I was thinking of with this picture is softening the outside. But then I looked at it and it's kind of already done. It does it naturally. I don't know if I really need to get on top of that and mess it up. But I do think I can do more with the fingers." Jannotta cranks up the highlights and pulls down setup. "Maybe just make it burn a little. White's go up, blacks go down, gamma goes down. It always makes it more theatrical . . . printlike. It looks more like it's on a movie screen this way." See Figure 10-21.

Fig. 10-18 **(a)** Falcon's new "Chicago cool" primary correction and **(b)** the data from the Primary room.

Jannotta continues, "I don't like that his hand is so flat. The ball looks good, the grass looks pretty good. His hand's kind of not happening. Boring. So I'm going to go into secondaries and put a vignette on, and enable this, and enable the vignette, and draw something. I'm going to make a sloppy shape around here like this," he says, drawing a mitten shape around the hand. "I'm not sure how it's going to work when he moves, but I'll figure that out later."

He saves his shape and goes back to secondaries to adjust inside the mitten shape. Jannotta spins the midtones down a lot and the blacks down some, exclaiming "Now I've got dirt! Make that dirt pop." He cranks up the highlights. "Now on the outside of the hand vignette I might desaturate that a bit. I like what's happening there. Maybe not the *areas* it's happening in, but I like that blend of the warm with the more neutral. Let's watch it as it moves. Yeah, not too bad," he says approvingly before he pulls down the mitten shape to include more of the football. See Figure 10-22.

Fig. 10-19 (a) The vignette correction in the first secondary and (b) the data from the outside of the first secondary correction from Secondary room.

a

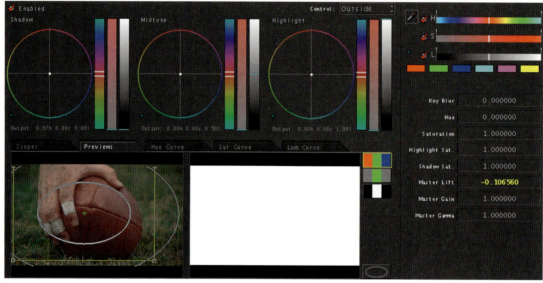

b

a

Fig. 10-20 (a) An HSL (hue, saturation, and luminance) qualification for the second secondary correction and **(b)** the data from the second secondary.

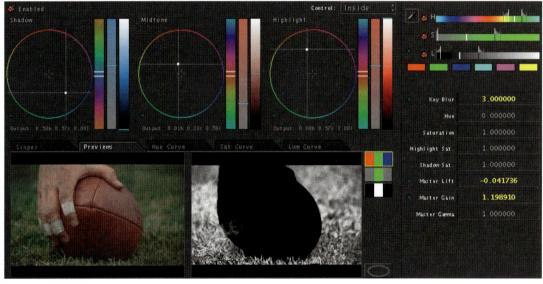

b

Fig. 10-21 (a) Jannotta's primary correction and (b) the data from the Primary room.

a

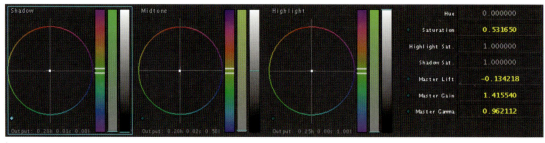

b

Pete Jannotta

Pete Jannotta has worked in the television industry since 1975 and has been a colorist for almost 30 years. Pete has worked with a myriad of color correction systems, including every permutation of da Vinci since its inception.

Pete was a colorist at Editel Chicago for 13 years, working on national and international advertising accounts until becoming a partner in Skyview Film and Video. While there, he continued to hone his craft for 10 years, working with A-list clients from Chicago, IL, as well as all over the midwest and the world. Currently, Pete is a senior colorist at Filmworker's Club in Chicago, IL, where he continues to work on advertising accounts as well as feature films, documentaries, and music videos.

a

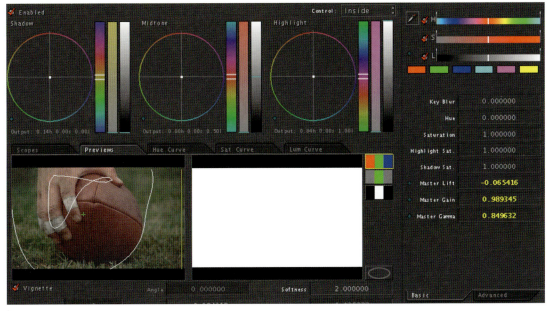

b

Fig. 10-22 **(a)** This image is the final look in secondaries, though the correction to the outside of the vignette is made later. **(b)** The data from the inside of the vignette in the Secondary room.

"I'm thinking the blacks are too compressed on the inside, but boy I like the hand that way," Jannotta explains, as he goes to the Color Effects room and adds sharpness, bringing it down a little from the default sharpness setting. See Figure 10-23.

As a final touch, Jannotta proposes one last change, "I feel like adding blue to the outside. It's going to pop the ball more and his hand. It doesn't necessarily make sense that it's that desaturated on the right side but it's interesting." See Figure 10-24 for the data on this last correction.

Fig. 10-23 Jannotta's color effect is just a sharpen set to 0.621550.

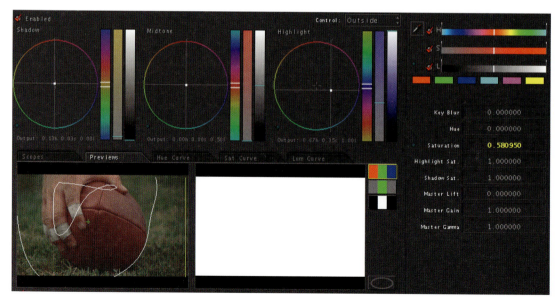

Fig. 10-24 The data from the outside of the vignette in the Secondary room.

Of course, the natural colorist to take on this image is NFL Films' Chris Pepperman. Pepperman starts with primaries. "I wanna make everything black and white." (So the primary correction is simply pulling all of the saturation out.) He pulls an HSL key in secondaries, qualifying warm tones. Then he cranks the contrast, crushing the blacks. See Figure 10-25.

When Pep realizes that some posterizing was starting to happen in his correction, he stops to refine the qualification of the HSL key, saying, "I always want to push the limit and then come back, because I want

a

Fig. 10-25 **(a)** The first secondary correction to the warmer tones and **(b)** the data from the first secondary correction.

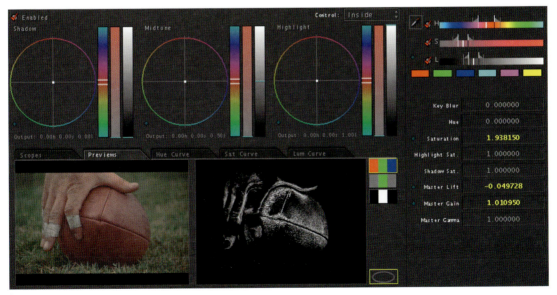

b

to know what my range is. I reference it to a golf club. You swing a
nine iron. You swing it as hard as you can. You know how far you're
going to hit it. And then, when the target is closer, you soften it
up a bit. You don't swing as hard until you get the right distance." See
Figure 10-26.

Pepperman explains, "So what I've done here is just create a contrasty
image, and I just desaturated the red a little bit and I'm really pushing
the blacks and I'm giving it a very contrasty look, because this is for an
open and they tend to be glossy. I might add some blur to it. I might add

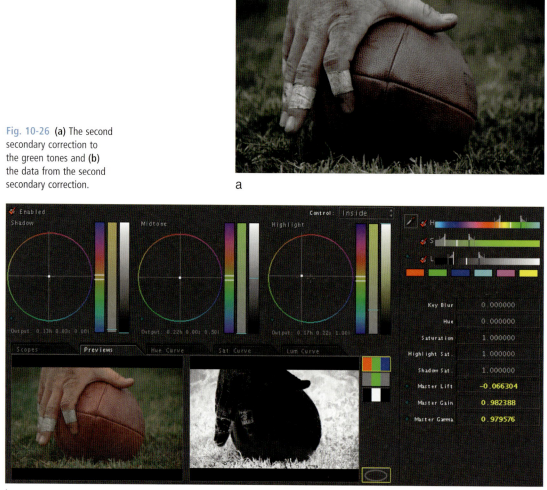

Fig. 10-26 **(a)** The second
secondary correction to
the green tones and **(b)**
the data from the second
secondary correction.

a

b

some grain. I might add sharpness to it. Make it sizzle a little bit. So it gives it a very gritty 8-mm type look. I see grain structure. I see maybe film scratches. I also like to do desaturated looks where you desaturate everything and then just feather back in a little bit of color. That might work very well here too. Keep everything black and white, then just add a little of the red and black back in."

Chris Pepperman

Before joining NFL Films, Chris Pepperman worked as a colorist for Manhattan Transfer in New York, NY. Pepperman then joined NFL Films in 1993. In addition to working on NFL Films' television series and specials, Pepperman's list of credits include national TV spots, "Survivor: Africa" for CBS, and numerous other documentary and film projects.

Pepperman's partial client list includes, NASCAR, HBO, Harley-Davidson, Sprint, Wal-Mart, Comcast, Pepsi, and the U.S. Army.

True Grit

One of the images that definitely called out for a tough, gritty look was the scene from *Chasing Ghosts* of the SWAT team storming out of the truck (see Fig. 10-27). Several colorists were inspired to give that scene a shot.

Fig. 10-27 The ungraded source image from *Chasing Ghosts* (the green tint came from a bad film scan). Image courtesy of Wingman Productions, Inc.

Pete Jannotta starts off. "Well, what's coming to mind for me on this one is gritty, desaturated, crispy, which I don't know how to make it on this machine."

I ask Jannotta to define "crispy" for me, since it's a term that I've heard lots of colorists use. He responds, "Crispy is sharpening and highlight accentuation, which I would do with a curve in da Vinci. Really peak the top end only. Stretch it. That makes all the highlights pop up. And sharpening makes the grain pop; it makes all the edges pop. I'm looking at this thinking it needs to be meaner. It has to have a mean feel. It's too sweet. So again we'll look at our contrast on this stuff over here and balance," Jannotta says, checking out his RGB scopes.

Then he points to his vectorscope, explaining, "I see a lot of green down here and I see a lot of green up here." He points to the monitor. I point out that the green is not only coming from the grass behind the truck. Jannotta agrees, "No. It's not just the grass. He looks over at his RGB parade. "Whoa. That's not good. Blue is way out of line in the blacks," he says before he balances it out with the shadow trackball.

"Now I'm looking at that gray courthouse wall and trying to get a better balance overall than what we had before." He cuts back and forth between the source and the correction. I just wanted to get it more balanced to begin with, then I can start doing the weird stuff. As long as I know what kind of picture I really have here."

Jannotta's ready to move on, saying, "Now I want to desaturate it. Then really stretch the heck out of the top." He rolls the highlights *way* up as he says, "Burn it and compress the bottom end of the grayscale so that everything gets pulled out." Jannotta makes a hand gesture like he's pulling taffy. "There's more tension that way I think." See Figure 10-28.

With the primary color correction out of the way, Jannotta wants to sharpen the image, so we go to FinalTouch/Color Effects room and add sharpening. The process tree was simply a sharpen node set to 0.671350, a fairly similar setting to the sharpening he did in the last correction. "There you go. Now it's a SWAT team. That sharpening effect is pretty cool. It makes it really dangerous looking."

Jannotta is pleased with his correction and decides to take it one step further. "I'm going to try, just for fun, a more simple vignette on this one." I notice that his "simple" vignette is, as usual for him, a hand-drawn shape instead of a simple geometric shape.

I tease, "And once again you refuse to use a square or a circle." He responds, "Yeah, I do. I don't like them, because I want to have the handle . . . the control and the ability to move."

He finishes drawing a big D shape and darkens the edges, then starts adjusting the shape with the correction in place. "I had the shape too

a

Fig. 10-28 **(a)** Jannotta's primary correction and **(b)** the data from the Primary room.

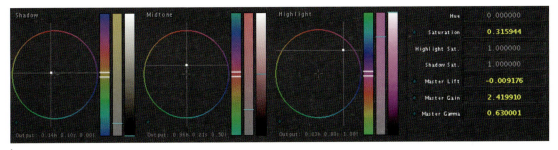

b

tight. But you don't know until you do it. That's why I like these custom shapes and adding the softness up front to the shape."

Jannotta starts pulling out even more saturation. I ask him what the saturation move is accomplishing. He replies, "I want it to feel colder and more scary. More tension. So pulling the color out and adding a little blue to it, making it real crispy like that. Closing it in," he says, pointing to his vignette with darkened edges. I note that he's got deep shadows and punched highlights. "Yeah," he says, "I think of pulling the picture like this." He makes a motion like pulling a scroll open from top to bottom. See Figure 10-29.

Feeling in his element with the action of the scene, the colorist for "24," Larry Field, also gives the image a try. Field explains his approach. "It's yellow-green. It could be changed to a few different things. I'll just quickly balance it. We can neutralize it somewhere in there. Those white-balanced gammas weren't too bad. You may want contrast in a

Fig. 10-29 **(a)** Janotta's image after the secondary was added, **(b)** the data from the inside of the qualification,

a

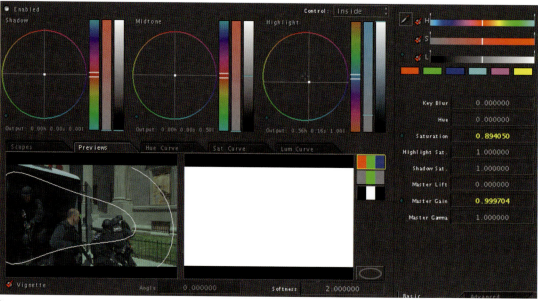

b

c

Fig. 10-29 (*Continued*) (c) the data from the outside of the qualification.

shot like this because crazy things are happening. It would add to the excitement . . . the intensity of the shot. If this was '24,' we'd have this nice and warm, desaturated, and as grainy as we could get it. Then do a lift of luma only, which grits it out and gives it a bleachy feel. Then since its film, we can really push the grain, desaturate it. Very high contrast, low saturation to bring up a grit of it and the intensity."

(Unfortunately the settings for Field's corrections were lost, so I can't show the final or the settings he used to get there. From memory, it was similar to Jannotta's correction.)

This shot also appeals to Chris Pepperman, who works on a look for it. Pep starts, "Okay, this is a good shot. I want to make sure I'm out of the clip." He pulls the gain down a bit before continuing, "and I want to balance everything. I know it has a green texture to it. I see that. But what I'm trying to do is eliminate that and balance it to what it would look normally by eye."

"You're assuming that the green is not something the DP wants," I interject.

He responds, "That's right. Assuming that that's not what he wants. Now I'm going to take this image and do it like we're doing a very high-contrast almost reenactment kind of scene, and what I would do is, in this particular case, I'm going to take the primaries and I'm really going to go to town and crank the video levels up and bring the black levels down and create this very, very high contrasty look. Now as I'm doing that, it's affecting the greens in the highs and the midrange, so I'm going to clean that up a little bit as we go along. I can see it in the wall. The background is almost blue and the pillars themselves almost have a green texture to them, which doesn't bother me. I like it. Everybody tries to stay away from that green, green, green. I kind of like it where you can really stylize. Everybody always used to stay away from that yellowish green because it always looked like it was bad video. Looks come and go. Everybody does windows. Everybody does the cross-processed look. It's the guys who innovate and try to melt those looks together and come up with different images." "So right now I'm adding just a little warmth into it. There's still a little contamination in the blacks, so I'm really trying to clean that up a little bit. I'm seeing a little bit of purplish in the blue. I just want to add some cyan. I'm liking what I see, though it's cyanish here (pointing to the shadows in the truck). Now once I got that look, I would isolate the reds and bring the reds down a little bit. (See Fig. 10-30.)"

Fig. 10-30 **(a)** Pepperman's primary correction and **(b)** the data from the Primary room.

a

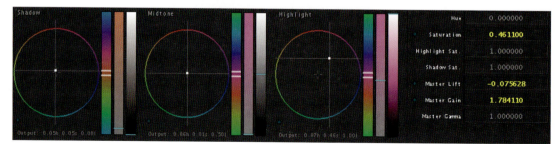

b

Pepperman qualifies the skin tones with an HSL key and starts to add a vignette to garbage mask them when I warn him that the shot is a Steadicam shot that follows the team. Pep continues, "I use vignettes all the time on motion, and I just track it and keep it very soft." See Figure 10-31.

Pep adds another secondary, creating an oval, and rotates it to changes its position and aspect. I notice that Pepperman falls into the "grade with vignettes sharp" camp. He agrees, "Right, because I want to see the differ-

a

Fig. 10-31 (a) The image after the first secondary and (b) the data from the first secondary correction.

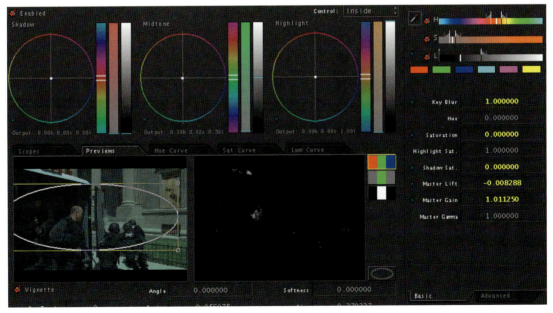

b

ence between the two. I always do softness last. I want to see the difference."
He cranks down the gain outside and cranks up the gain inside before softening the oval. "See now I went too far, so I'm just backing off the vignette
a little bit. See how I like to go deep, and now I've come off of it a bit. So
now you can't see the vignette. It's transparent." See Figure 10-32.

a

Fig. 10-32 (a) The image
after the second secondary
correction and (b) the data
from the second secondary
correction.

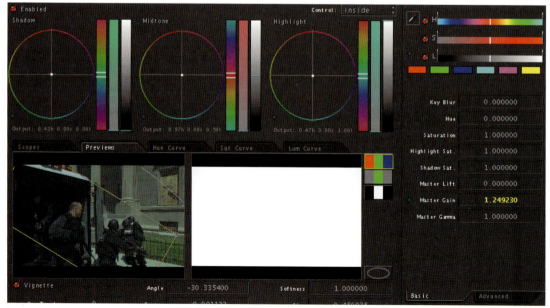

b

In an interesting sidenote, Pep's vignette was transparent on the eCinema display, but on the Dell computer monitors attached to the Mac, it was still pretty obvious. This is one place where the gamma display differences between the computer monitors and the real grading monitor were obvious.

Pep continues tweaking the look of the shot by adding another secondary and qualifies the green grass using an HSL key, being careful to select the grass but not the green of the pillars. "So once again I'm trying to give it this chromatic look. A high-intensity Ektachrome look. So what I'm doing is I'm almost wanting that green of the grass to glow and look ultragreen." Obviously feeling liberated by the ability to add up to eight secondaries in Color, Pepperman adds yet another secondary, qualifying and tweaking the blue of the SWAT team uniforms. See Figure 10-33.

a

Fig. 10-33 (a) The image after the final secondary correction and (b) the data from the final secondary correction.

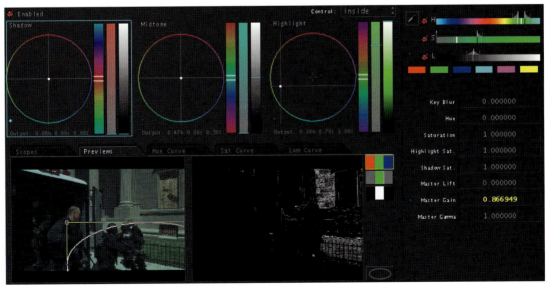

b

Graphic Looks

From the frantic energy and grittiness of the SWAT scene, we'll transition to the Zen-like simplicity of Artbeats' image of a man sitting at the end of a pier (see Fig. 10-34). It was an image that spoke to Mike Matusek. This file is called "Pier_LM110" and is available in the Artbeats Tutorial folder on the DVD.

"I look at this one and I think of it as more of a graphic image," Matusek explains, "So I'll try doing a few looks. First a silhouette, maybe crush it a little bit and see where that goes. Maybe that'll be too muddy. Then sometimes what I do is bring the blacks to zero and don't crush, but I want to get it darker that that, so then I'll go to the midtones and bring the midtones down, so I'm not necessarily crushing the blacks."

Matusek continues, "Sometimes when you go blue, you get kind of hypersensitive to the hue and you see a little pink in there. You almost see a little bit of magenta in the water. So, do you want to go more cyan-blue? Do you want to go a little more true blue? If you go to more true blue on the scope, it looks more magenta all the time, at least to me, so I tend to go a little bit more toward cyan. There's a lens flare there, so that clues me in that the sun is maybe still a little bit out. Maybe get more contrast. Throw a vignette on their real quick to see what that does to the mood of it." See Figure 10-35.

Matusek adds an oval vignette with softness and rotates it, then darkens the upper left corner. I comment that as I watch a lot of people use vignettes, it is a way to focus attention, but it also seems to be a way to take a flat expanse of color and give it some depth or texture. Matusek

Fig. 10-34 The source image. Image courtesy of Artbeats' Lifestyles— Mixed Cuts 1 Collection.

a

b

Fig. 10-35 (a) Matusek's primary correction and **(b)** the data from the Primary room.

says, "Exactly. Once you get a vignette on there, it's a little more shaped. Because it seems just flat and uninteresting, so if you add a vignette to it, there's much more depth to it. So now there's more depth *and* it brings your focus to him." See Figure 10-36.

"He looks like an old guy reminiscing. That's why I went cooler with it. I think if I'd gone golden, that evokes a different emotion." I ask if it would be hard to get this image to be golden, and Matusek seems ready for the challenge.

Matusek starts off by mentioning that his blacks are close to being clipped and I ask how he knows how to stretch a specific tonal range. "If I wanted to get detail out of the blanket over his legs, bringing the black up would just make it milky, so riding the lift down and the gamma up until I'd stretched that little area and get more detail out of it. If this was shot on video, it'd just be noise."

Matusek continues, "If I'm going to go golden, I'd probably go a little more contrasty with it. This is more of a graphic image, so you don't have to be realistic. You can definitely have some more fun with it. It's really the color of the water, and then the guy and the pier is pretty much grayscale. There's not much color information. So you can really be more graphic with it." See Figure 10-37.

Fig. 10-36 (a) The secondary correction was applied to the inside and outside of the vignette. (b) The data from the inside of the vignette,

a

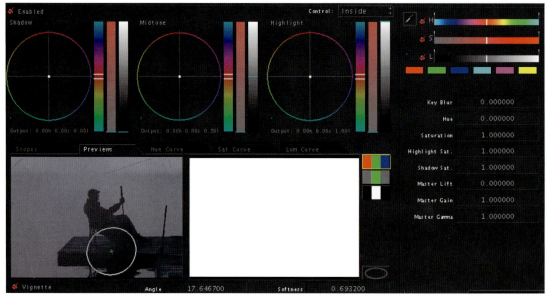

b

c

Fig. 10-36 (*Continued*) (c) the data from the outside of the vignette.

a

Fig. 10-37 (a) Matusek's primary correction for the "gold" look and (b) the data from the Primary room.

b

Matusek goes to the secondaries and adds a soft oval in the top left corner. "You can do a few things here. Maybe add some more color in there. You can even do this, which is interesting sometimes," he says as he makes the vignetted area cyan. See Figure 10-38.

"So you're playing one color off another?" I ask.

"Right," he responds. "That's not creating contrast with luminance, that's doing it with color."

Fig. 10-38 **(a)** The secondary correction done both inside and outside of the vignette. **(b)** The data from the inside of the secondary vignette,

a

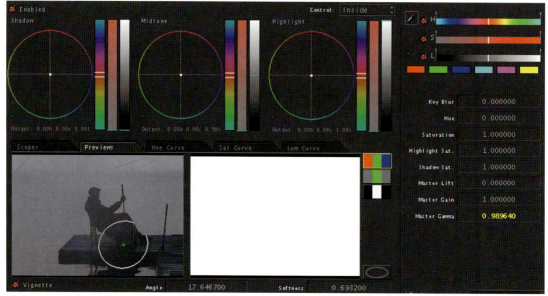

b

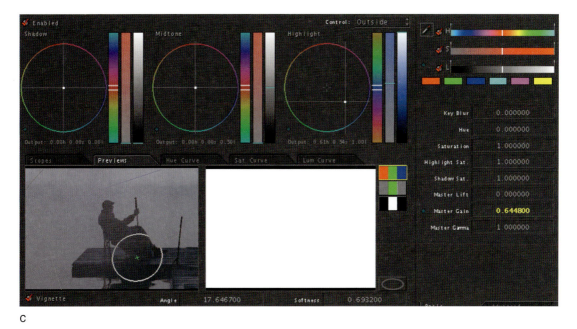

c

Fig. 10-38 (*Continued*) **(c)** the data from the outside of the secondary vignette.

Matusek continues with his experimentation. "I can do one more thing with this, because, as you said, the planks are kind of cool on the pier," he says, increasing the contrast in the planks of the pier, creating a nice texture to the shot (see Fig. 10-39).

a

Fig. 10-39 **(a)** The second secondary correction to increase contrast in the planks and

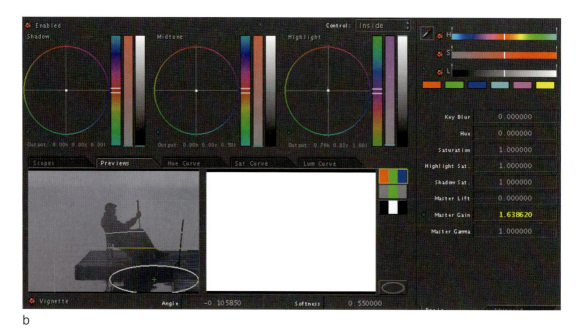

b

Fig. 10-39 (*Continued*) **(b)** the data from the second secondary correction.

Day-for-Night

Day-for-night shots are one of the requests that colorists have to pull off on occasion. We tasked several colorists to walk us through day-for-night shots on several scenes.

Bob Sliga starts on an indoor scene that was shot as a camera test image by my good friend and respected documentary and feature cinematographer, Rich Lerner (see Fig. 10-40).

"One of the things to remember in day-for-night is that saturation isn't plentiful. A lot of people really overdo blue," states Sliga. "You should feel it, but you shouldn't be hit in the face with blue."

Fig. 10-40 The original source image. Image courtesy of Rich Lerner.

I ask, "So you use the science of how the eye sees at nighttime?"

Sliga responds, "Exactly. And that's how I come across a lot of my looks. I'll walk around and look at things and almost reference them like I have a video scope. I mean, I've done it for so long. I'll look into shadows. I'll look into other areas. Overall color textures. Highlights off of building reflections downtown. Then thinking, how would I emulate that in here? Then at night, you go outside, after awhile, obviously your eyes will adjust and you can see more and more into the night, but you never see more and more color. It's not there."

"I remember reading that your eye has a harder time seeing red saturation in low light," I say.

"Exactly," Sliga agrees. "So you feel the cooler tones. I'm doing this all in my Primary In Room, and what I'm doing is throwing away the detail that I don't want to keep. But I'm not clamping it off. I'm not plugging it in the basement," he says as he points to the fact that the blacks aren't incredibly crushed. Then, as Sliga lowers gammas and shadows, the saturation increases and he compensates by lowering saturation in those areas as well as using the wheels to push a little bit of coolness into all of the tonal ranges. See Figure 10-41.

a

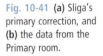

Fig. 10-41 **(a)** Sliga's primary correction, and **(b)** the data from the Primary room.

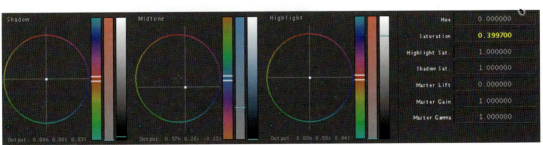

b

"Let's go into a Secondary room now," Sliga continues. "The first thing I'd like to use on this is a luminance key." He qualifies mostly the lamp and spill on the wall with a little of the highlight on her forehead and arm. "Now I'm going to go outside the qualification and throw more stuff away. Now I'm sliding some of that blueness in. Not a lot, just a little bit." See Figure 10-42.

Sliga notices the strong red tones of the blanket. "This is still coming through pretty strong," he complains as he goes to the Saturation curve in secondaries. "So I'm just going to go in and try to grab reds in the Saturation curve and pull them down." Attempting to fix the redness of the blankets with the Saturation curve did not create the look he was after, so he resets the curve and tries another tack.

Fig. 10-42 (a) The first secondary correction and **(b)** the data from the first secondary correction.

a

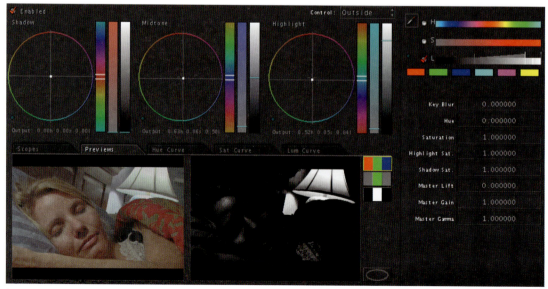

b

Rich Lerner

Rich Lerner was the DP for the Academy Award–winning short documentary, *A Story of Healing*. He also developed and coproduced *Instinct* with Anthony Hopkins and Cuba Gooding, Jr. He worked on the national Emmy-winning episode of *Nature* titled "Urban Elephant," and has shot over 1,000 fashion retail spots. He has also worked extensively as a cinematographer for *National Geographic*. He has shot several feature films and feature documentaries. His background was primarily in shooting 35-mm and Super 16-mm film, but currently does a lot of his work in HD.

"I'm going to go into another secondary and pick that red. That's a very strong selection, because it's looking back at the *original* color of the source. So I'm going to use the color picker to isolate that down just a little bit more. Then I'll throw a little blur on it. So on the inside of that qualification I'm just going to pull saturation down. We can even come down on the outside of the qualification and bring the red gain down as well," Sliga adds as he goes into the Advanced tab to affect the red gain. See Figure 10-43.

Sliga adds a third secondary to qualify the lamp and the spill on the wall using luminance (see Fig. 10-44). Then he softens the qualification, picking up some of the highlights on the woman's skin. With that done, he pushes a good deal of warmth into the highlights, making her face quite warm.

I ask about the change to the woman's face. "You're not worrying about what happens to her face, just the lamp, right?"

"Right," he says, explaining, "I'm trying to find something symbolizing a little bit of warmth coming out of that lamp." To fix the face, he creates a soft vignette and positions it over the lamp, eliminating the corrections on the woman's skin. So we came from here to there," he concludes as he checks back and forth between the starting source image and where he ended up.

Mike Most also works this same image into a day-for-night. "What I would do is bring this way down," Most begins by pulling down midtones and shadows. And I've also got to bring down saturation first, because one of the things about night is that saturation is much lower and, point of fact, red saturation is much, *much* lower. It's not so much that things go blue. They don't really, but what they do go is minus red, because the red disappears. You don't want it too greenish but cyanish is probably okay. What I'd really try to do is put a little bit of a window around

Fig. 10-43 **(a)** The second secondary correction bringing down the red saturation in the blanket mainly. **(b)** The data from the inside of the second secondary, plus, to the correction of 0.908650 down on the red gain in the Advanced tab.

a

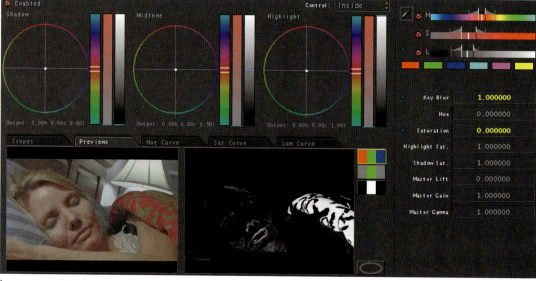

b

a

Fig. 10-44 **(a)** The third secondary correction bringing warmth to the lamp and **(b)** the data from the third secondary.

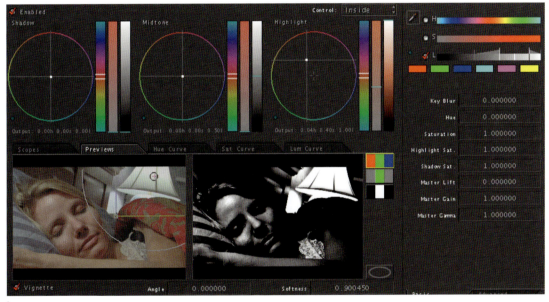

b

her. It doesn't make physical sense, but I'm going to play this as if there's another key down here. It doesn't make sense, but sometimes it just works." See Figure 10-45.

Most draws an oval around her face, raises the gain inside the vignette, then softens the edge. "I'd have to do something very different with the outside area," he comments. "What I'd actually like to do with the outside area is make it a little warmer. That whole green thing is driving me nuts. Once again, take some of the saturation out. I'm desaturating the outside." Most cuts back and forth between the original image and his correction. "Considering that you started from that . . . it's not great but it's not horrible."

"Looks like night to me," I say. See Fig. 10-46.

Fig. 10-45 **(a)** Most's primary correction. (This data was created in FinalTouch 2K and reimported into a Color Project. I feel like the correction is not quite the same as the way Mike was seeing it.) **(b)** The data from the Primary room.

a

b

Pete Jannotta takes on the Artbeats' scene of the Marines to attempt another day-for-night shot (see Fig. 10-11).

Jannotta goes straight to secondaries to try to select the sky. He picks a spot that selects the left side of the sky then widens the qualification with the HSL selection sliders, grabbing almost the entire sky. Switching the HSL selection so it *only* used luminance improved the qualification.

Jannotta thinks this selection will be good enough, but it isn't, because as he brings down the luminance in the qualification, it brings down the

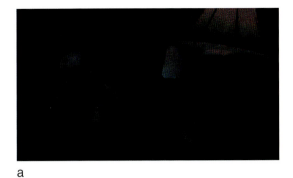

a

Fig. 10-46 **(a)** The secondary correction inside and outside of vignette. **(b)** The data from the inside of the vignette, **(c)** the data from the outside of the vignette.

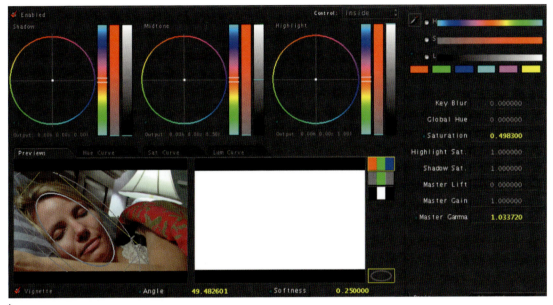

b

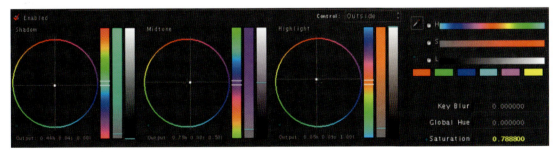

c

right side of the sky before it brings down the left side. "A little blue always helps for the suggestion of night. But this," he says as he points to the sky and the way the matte transitions to the helmets, "is not good."

Instead of being impatient with the mistake, the challenge of the shot energizes Jannotta. "This is fun. This is a real shot that someone would come in and say, 'I want this to be nighttime.' And whether or not it's easy, doesn't matter. So it's actually a good exercise."

I ask Jannotta what things he has to do to create the day-for-night effect. "Desaturation, all the levels come down, a little blue added. Pretty much that's it," Jannotta responds. He starts with desaturation. "I'm just compressing the bottom and bringing the highlights up a bit. We could cool those off a bit too. I'm pushing it into the flesh tones. It can get pretty trite to get really blue, because it just looks hokey. But most everyone sees blue and dark and they think 'night.' If you go overboard, then it's sad and sick looking. It could almost be okay to do a little bit of cyan. A little bit of green-blue is okay too." See Figure 10-47.

Greg Creaser completes our final day-for-night scene. Actually it's more of a night-for-night scene as he works on the "Nightgown" scene from *Kiss Me in the Dark* (see Figs. 10-48). This shot is available in the Tutorials folder of the DVD as file "Kiss_nightgown." "If this was typically

Fig. 10-47 (a) Jannotta's primary correction for day-for-night and (b) the data from the Primary room.

a

b

moonlight, it's not going to be warm. We started out a little warm and a little bright, so around in there . . . would be a good starting point. I think this would be a creative decision on the part of the client. I'd stick it there and say, 'Where do you want to go with it?' It'd be maybe more to the cyan side or the bluer side. My own opinion on night stuff is that I don't like to see it always blue. I like to see it clean. Maybe cool, yet not blue-blue. A lot of time you see night shots and they're just extremely blue. I kind of try to stay away from that, but that's my personal choice, and that's not what a client may want, so maybe I'd put it here and they'd say, 'We want it cooler,' or this or that." See Figure 10-49.

Fig. 10-48 The ungraded source image from *Kiss Me in the Dark*. Image courtesy of Seduced and Exploited Entertainment.

a

Fig. 10-49 **(a)** Creaser's final day-for-night correction, and **(b)** the data from the correction in FinalTouch UI.

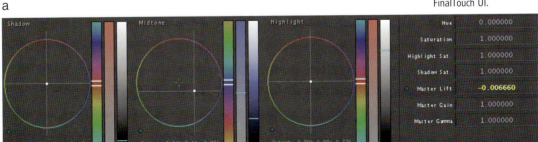

b

The Look of the Feature Film

David Mullen, A.S.C., describes the modern look of feature films.

Most movies nowadays are on the contrasty side, compared to movies in the past. They tend to be a single-source look with a lot of falloff into the shadows, which is nice because it gives the film a certain three-dimensional quality to it. There's always a technical reason for wanting more contrast and that is that it makes things look sharper and more three dimensional. But it's mainly a mood issue. It's like asking a cook, "How much salt should I put in it?" One of the comments I always get from film students is, "I'm working with a director and we're trying to make these scenes look dark and we're not agreeing on what that means." And that's partly because it's completely a taste issue. I mean, one thing I tell people is that you have to define what dark means. Does it mean dim, which can be low contrast and nothing is at key exposure and everything is fairly murky and low key and soft? Or it can mean that there's a lot of contrast, where there are small areas of the screen within the frame at full exposure but there's lots of big areas of the exposure that are black or near black. A lot of them don't realize that the terms are all vague. I remember once telling a director that we should shoot the scene in silhouette and he said, "Oh that's great." So I lit the scene in silhouette and he goes, "I can't see the actor's face." I go, "That's because he's in silhouette." And he said, "Well, can't we have some fill light on him?" Well, then it wouldn't be a silhouette! A silhouette means a dark shape against a bright background. But some people think a silhouette means a backlit person with very dim lighting on them. So that's "silhouettey" but it's not in silhouette.

CHAPTER 11

Miscellaneous Wisdom

Consider this chapter to be like the bonus track on a CD from your favorite band. It wasn't in the plans for the book, but I had so many great little nuggets of information left over that didn't make it into the rest of the book that I really wanted to share. There's not a great way to tie them all together, so I'll just share them in a stream-of-conscious sort of way and hopefully you'll find them influencing your corrections in important ways.

Starting Off

Bob Festa describes how he approaches a shot: "When I throw up a shot, the first thing I do, before I talk to anybody, is kind of peer into the corners of the negative and look for my visual signposts; my references in the shot that I look for. I'm actually looking for handles in the film like: What would I bring forward? What would I drop back? Is there a white light reference in the shot? Would I sniff around and try to find that and try to find a reference to create a quick dynamic image that we can start to talk with? Basically I look for signposts that point to balance and white, then I also look for traditional photographic techniques—stuff I can either bring up or bring back. Getting the blacks to a malleable area and getting the whites to a malleable area. When I first put up a shot and get it balanced, I use the blacks and whites almost like a throttle on a motorcycle. Kind of revving the engine to see what you've got. I use the Master Gains and master blacks to get a feel for how it behaves."

I give Festa my camera focusing analogy. He agrees, "I think that's true. You're looking for the sweet spot. And the only way to find that is to go too far. That's probably true for color correction in general. You really have to push it around to somewhere you *don't* want to go to find out where you *do* want to go. I think that's a good statement." "Then I can look into the neg (negative) and look for things that I can bring to life. So I look at the ratio of foreground and background. But in addition to balancing, I'm also looking at adding value. I like to show my commercial clients a whole range of opportunities based on that. The most classic thing I like to do is show three or four different opportunities based on either warmer, cooler exposures, more or less dynamic range, more or less contrast. And then we start getting very, very specific using the classic photographic techniques of the day, dodging and burning and actually creating the look that's based on that." "What I like to do is show people some choices. If you give them one, two, or three different choices, they can actually point their finger up at the screen and say, "I like A, B, or C," instead of being very general about "Where do you think you guys want to go from here?" I also like to look at the work picture, just to see what these people are used to looking at. Whether it's right or wrong in *my* mind, they may have fallen in love with it and not even know it to some extent. So I'll give them an option that might have some relationship to the work picture. That makes the dialog a little easier I think. I think initially I tell them that this is going to be very general, for starters. And it's very broad-stroke based. And once you get dialed in through a series of "1, 2, 3," after a while you get into a very close place. Then the brushstrokes become much more fine and more dynamic, I think."

Communicating with Clients

Festa continues with a discussion on communicating with clients: "It wasn't so much techniques or tools that helped me communicate more with my clients, but I actually started listening. I would actually not say a darn word, but I would tell people, "Before we get started, tell me in 20 words or less what today's theme is going to be." I'd rather let them spill their guts for 20 words or 20 minutes and then turn around and deliver the goods, because then I have a good idea about what their perception is and what their ambitions are for the session. So if anything, I've become a good listener in my old age."

Chris Pepperman extends this conversation: "Typically the way I work when I color correct is, I'm one of those guys who verbally expresses or talks out loud what I'm doing. A lot of my clients actually like that because as I'm doing it, I'm talking my way through it and explaining to them what I'm doing, and that's a habit that I picked up very early in the business when I was working with guys like Nick D'antona and Howie Burch who were the principal owners of Manhattan Transfer, and I spent years assisting those guys. I always found it to be a very good tool. I consider myself not to be a technical colorist. There are guys out there who are really technically inclined. Chris Ryan is one of them. He knows these systems inside and out. "There are two aspects to color correction. One is being able to emulate the aesthetic look or direction that the DP or director is expressing to you and that's essentially your primary objective, right? That's what you want to do. Somebody comes in and they have a visual idea of what they want and you try to give them that. The other one is being able to have the "room savvy," and what I mean by that is being able to communicate effectively with the client. It's a personality thing. I try to be personable."

Having hung out in a session with one of Pep's clients, I agree, "People like to hang with you."

He responds, "Exactly. And I feel that's one of my strong points why people like to come here. You definitely have to have talent, technical-wise, to be able to interpret what they want visually. But you also have to have the personality to sit in a room with an A-type personality or a B-type personality, understand what they want, give it to them, and all along keep them comfortable.

Taking It to Extremes

David Mullen, A.S.C., explains how he likes to communicate with colorists. "When I see them trying to get a certain color I say 'just go overboard.' Show me *beyond* what we're talking about, because when you're fiddling with something subtle it's sometimes a problem that you're not quite seeing the effect you want. It's better if you just overcrank it for a moment and then pull it back down."

The Importance of Color Contrast

Pete Jannotta explains that the *traditional* way to think of contrast is certainly not the *only* way. "Luminance contrast is important, but *color* contrast is just as important."

Jannotta is examining the "Banker's Light" shot from *Chasing Ghosts* that he's trying to tweak. (See the file on the DVD "Ghosts_Bankerslight.mov") "Before, when I was looking at it, I wasn't feeling the color contrast was right. It was too much in one part of the palette. It looked kind of brown, so it needs a little blue and green back into it. I've taken too much green out of it. This is a real common thing that I do all the time," explains Jannotta. "What did I have to start with? So: Am I ruining anything? Am I taking away something that I want to retain? I'm always looking for that."

Maintaining a Look

Neal Kassner talks about one of his biggest challenges: "My show, "48 Hours," has to match itself from one segment to the next and the characters reappear all the way through. Even though the same source reels are used by as many as six different editors working on different Avids. The first time I correct a character, I grab a reference of it, and each time that character appears, even in the same segment, I'll reference back. Because I've found that when they're shooting, it's not unusual for the camera guy to adjust the iris. So the same character, even in the same setting may be a little darker or a little brighter than the first time I saw him. So I want to keep it consistent all the way through."

Looking at Real Life for Inspiration

Neal Kassner tries to look at real life for inspiration in the color suite: "One of the things I find helpful to do is you have to look at life as objectively as you can. Grass isn't really green in television. There's a *lot* of yellow in grass. So if you try to make it look green, it's going to look phoney. It's going to look like Astroturf. You need to look around. You have a white barn in the middle of a field. At noon it's going to be white. Late afternoon, it's still going to be a white barn, but it's not going to look white to your eye. Your brain is going to filter what your eye sees. In news, that's a kind of fine line that I walk. Do I make it a white barn in the afternoon and destroy the overall look and feel? Or do I maintain that? And what I often end up doing is sort of splitting the difference. There's a way in the da Vinci to put in two color corrections and mix between them."

This advice jibes with similar advice given earlier in the book by Bob Sliga, who claims that he consciously walks around examining real life as though he has a video scope with him. It's a very interesting exercise. Look up at the sky and the clouds and imagine that you can color correct them. Are the clouds pure white? How pale is the sky? Is it cyan or blue? How yellow is the grass? How dark are the blacks in a car's tire? What about up under the wheel well? In a room indoors, can you detect the various colors of mixed light? Does that make the room more visually interesting?

Multitasking

Larry Field explains how and why he prefers using the trackballs on something like the Tangent Devices control panel. "While I'm grabbing the blacks, I'll be balancing them while I'm bringing them down. It's all interactive and it's all simultaneous. While that's going on, I may be using my other hand and working on the highlights. The idea is to get home at the end of the day."

Smoke

As Craig Leffel prepares to work on the Artbeats' image of the boxer, he discusses what he considers to be the bane of the colorist: "This shot's got all the bad things colorists hate, like smoke. God knows I hate smoke. Photographers love it, but I hate it. Light doesn't travel predictably through it, so when you filter a light source, especially if you mix incandescent or mix practicals in a lighting scenario, like right here, you've got this green light coming from maybe a practical, maybe a lighting source, and you've got this cleaner source over here. If you were to walk through there, his skin and his face and his body would change color, because smoke dissipates the light quite a bit, so it quite often corrupts whatever it is that you're trying to do. And most of these color correctors are set up with hue, saturation, and luminance and the smoke affects HSL in a way that's really unpredictable and color correctors have a really hard time with it, which makes *you* have a really hard time with it."

Keeping Butts in the Seats

In the end, the colorists who make the most money are the ones who keep the butts in the seats. In other words, having new clients coming in the door and old clients coming back. Chris Pepperman describes what he thinks delivers that desired result: "Clients respond to colorists who work quickly. Colorists who get them what they want and stay within their budget and deadline. I assess what I have. I look at the rough cut. I look at the film. I look how it's shot and I say, this isn't going to take as long, or this might take more time. But I typically always run quicker than slower, because I'm the kind of guy who, once I get an image the way I like it, I'm gone. I'm not messing with it. If you like it and you're happy with it, I'm moving on. I'm not going to teeter around with it any more. I go to the next scene. I want to get it done, because if something goes wrong, now we're ten hours into a project. My eyes are tired. I'm compromising the look of my project the longer I'm in the room, the more frustrating it becomes for the client. I'd rather always have the extra time in the backend of the session to say, "You know what, I wasn't happy with this shot, let's go back and tweak it," rather than get to the clock and have five shots still to go and then you've got to rush through them. And that's something I learned in New York, working under the gun with agencies just kind of lined up at your door, waiting to come in, four or five a day, because you can really get yourself in a tizzy if you're slowing down and it's five o'clock and there's still clients out there waiting."

The Future of Color Correction

I ask Festa about the trend away from telecine color correction, where the image that is being manipulated is coming directly from the film, toward corrections done from flat data transfers on central servers or from flat transfers to D5 or some other tape. The episodic world of color correction has already turned toward this workflow, as have digital intermediate workflows. The TV spot world seems to be the sole holdout, and I wonder if spots will join the rest of the industry in this regard. Since Festa is definitely a veteran of the industry, I expect some resistance from him on this point, but he surprises me. Festa exclaims: "God, I sure hope so. I really don't know what it's going to take. I really think it's going to be an application like the Color app, where people are exposed to it on a fundamental, early level. The youngsters who are familiar with Final Cut—today's runners or assistant editors, they're all familiar with Final Cut—maybe it'll seed the industry at an early age and these people will all be influenced early on that there's no reason to pay big money and spend an inordinate amount of time slinging film. Quite frankly I'd rather have the flexibility and the speed to make contributions that are possibly not quite the same quality but are equally satisfying on a more artistic level."

Trying to understand his point, I ask, "Because you'd do more color correcting than waiting for the film to get set up on the telecine?"

Festa responds: "Yes. The way I see it, I've only got so much patience left, and I'd rather spend it color correcting something in context than threading film up. I think we're really witnessing the Avidization of telecine, where hopefully color decisions and color correction as we know it can be a lot more interactive and face to face and project based as opposed to service bureau based. Quite frankly, I'd be much happier if I was working on a per-project basis, face to face, much more interlocked with my client, as opposed to just acting as a service bureau. I'm excited about the future, because I think that's what it's going to be."

Books of Note

Here's a short list of books about color and color correction in my library. Of course, my previous book with Jaime Fowler, *Color Correction for Digital Video*, would be at the top of the list!

Patti Bellantoni, *If It's Purple, Someone's Gonna Die*: *The Power of Color in visual storytelling*. Focal Press, 2005.

Bruce Block, *The Visual Story*: *Seeing the Structure of Film, TV, and New Media*. Focal Press, 2001.

Leatrice Eiseman, *Pantone Guide to Communicating with Color*, Grafix Press, 2000.

Tom Fraser and Adam Banks, *Designer's Color Manual*: *The Complete Guide to Color Theory and Application*. Chronicle Books, 2004.

Edward J. Giorgianni and Thomas E. Madden, *Digital Color Management*: *Encoding Solutions. Addison Wesley*, 1998. (authors are color scientists at Kodak).

Johannes Itten, *The Art of Color*: *The Subjective Experience and Objective Rationale of Color*. John Wiley and Sons, 1961.

Michael Kieran, *Photoshop Color Correction*: *The Essential Guide to Color Quality for Digital Images*. Peachpit Press, 2003.

Alexis Van Hurkman, *Advanced Color Correction and Effects in Final Cut Pro 5*: *An Apple Pro Training Series*. Peachpit Press, 2006.

Moritz Zwimpfer, *Color, Light, Sight Sense*: *An Elementary Theory of Color in Pictures*. Schiffer Publishing, 1985.

Conclusion

I hope having a glimpse into the worlds of some of these great colorists inspires you to dig deeper and delve into the world of color correction with renewed confidence.

Getting to meet and watch these talented men and women was really a treat, and I've been excited throughout the two-year journey of writing and researching this book to bring their experience and wisdom to you.

Happy Coloring!

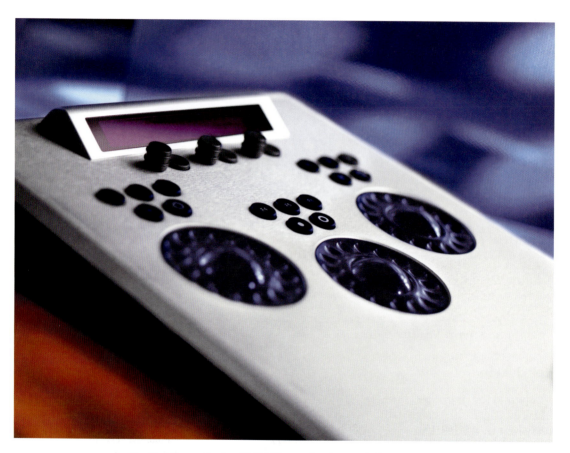

Fig. 11-1 Tangent Devices CP-200-BK controller photographed by Greg Gills.

Index

A

Adams, Ansel, 78
Adobe Photoshop, *see* Photoshop
After Effects
    Channel Mixer, 125
    channels, 123
    RGB color balance user interface,
       114
Alleyway scene, manipulation
    approaches, 221–228
Alpha Dogs, 46, 94
Angle of Attack, 94
Apple Color
    color balance controls, 91
    Curves, 106, 247–252
    da Vinci secondaries comparison,
       169
    eyedropper, 82
    preset looks, 314
    Primary In room, 35–37, 67, 106,
       116
    printer lights, 126
    Secondary room, 130, 136,
       159–160
    secondary curves, 160–162
Arrowhead display, 8
Artbeats
    color vector with garbage matte,
       157
    Food 1 collection, 2
    Marines HD Vol. 1 collection,
       258, 320
    Sports 1 HD collection, 12–13
Attention focusing, secondary color
    correction, 191–194
Automatic corrections, limitations,
    2–3

Avid
    automatic corrections, 2–3
    eyedropper, 82
    Symphony
       Channels, 103
       channels, 123
       color vector isolation, 138–143
       Curves tool, 44
       hue, saturation, and luminance
          tab, 38
       Luma Range, 59
       secondary color correction tab,
          131
       warning systems, 11
       XpressCurves tool, 44

B

Balance
    color cast analysis, 63–89
    definition, 63
    eyedropper, 82–86
    flat-pass waveform monitor,
       86–89
    histograms, 78–82
    RGB parade, 65–74
    vectorscope, 73–77
Banding, definition, 32
Banker's Light scene, manipulation
    approaches, 185, 205–216
Base mem, definition, 91
BetaSP, 239
Bezier curves, 56
Big Shoulders Digital Video
    Productions, 229
Bit depth, definition, 34
Black level, setting, 11–12, 15–21
Blackhawk Down, 322, 324

Bleach bypass
    definition, 126
    film processing looks, 316–321
Blow out, definition, 23
Bottom, language of music and
    color, 17
Brightness control, avoidance in
    tonal correction, 33–35
Budget, Luma Range considerations,
    61–62
Burch, Howie, 362

C

Cathode ray tube (CRT), monitors, 5
CCIR601, 16
Cell, definition, 10
Channel Mixer, After Effects, 125
Channels, Avid Symphony, 103
Chasing Ghosts, 185, 205–216,
    221–228, 268, 270–275, 335,
    363
Chip chart, definition, 32–33
ChromaduMonde, chip chart, 84, 123
Clients
    communication, 362–363
    responsiveness, 365
Clipping, definition, 16
Color, *see* Apple Color
Color cast
    analysis
       eyedropper, 82–86
       flat-pass waveform monitor,
          86–89
       histograms, 78–82
       RGB parade, 65–74
       vectorscope, 73–77
    definition, 63

Color contrast
    color balancing, 89
    importance, 363
Color Finesse
    Curves tutorial, 47
    eyedropper, 82–86
    Luma Range, 59
    Secondary tab, 131
    sliders, 112
ColorFiX, sliders, 112
Colorista, sliders, 112
Color vector isolation
    Avid symphony, 138–143
    Final Cut Pro, 143–145
    garbage matte, 157–160
    practice, 146–147
    qualification, 133–138
Color wheels, *see* Hue offset
    wheels
Contrast
    defining, 25–29
    luminance key for contrast
        building, 201–204
    saturation effects, 281
    visual clues, 78
Contrast control, avoidance in tonal
    correction, 33–35
Crash, 321
Creaser, Greg, 227–228, 266–268,
    320–321, 358–360
Cross-process look, definition, 313
Crowley, Teague, 210
CRT, *see* Cathode ray tube
Crush, definition, 12
"CSI: Miami", 321
Curren, Terry, 94, 247–253
Curves
    Color Primary In room, 32
    grading with in Color's Primary
        In room, 247–252
    S curve, 45–47
    tabs in software, 44–45
    tonal correction, 31–32
    tonal range isolation, 53–56
    tutorials, 47–53, 105–112
Custom shapes, 156

D

Da Vinci
    historical perspective, 105
    Power Curves, 105
    PowerGrade, 312–314

Power Windows, 148, 164, 215,
    220
secondaries comparison with
    Apple Color, 169
Daylight balanced, viewing
    environment, 5
Day-for-night
    look creation, 350–360
    vignette creation, 177–184
Delores Clayburn, 256
Deluxe Labs, 126
Density, definitions, 267
DI, *see* Digital intermediate
Digital intermediate (DI), 266–267
Director of Photography (DP)
    colorist collaboration, 255–256,
        264–266
    definition, 156
    film processing looks, 314
Discreet, 16
DP, *see* Director of Photography
DR Group, 210
DSC Labs, chip charts, 32–33,
    84
Duotone, definition, 126

E

eCinema, 5
Eclipse-CX, 36
8 bit image, 32
Excursion, definition, 87
Eye Display, 8
Eyedropper
    color cast analysis and balancing,
        82–86
    tips, 83
Eye One Display 2, 5

F

Faking Spot Corrections, 149
Falcon, Janet, 186–188, 191, 205,
    258–261, 264–265, 298, 301,
    324
Feature film, look, 360
Festa, Bob, 164–165, 257, 312–314,
    361–362
Field, Larry, 176, 191, 214–216,
    337, 339, 364
Film processing look, creation, 314,
    316
Filmworker's Club, 205, 268
Filters, types, 126, 128

Final Cut Pro
    color vector isolation, 143–145
    eyedropper, 82
    Limit Effect, 130, 152
    warning systems, 11
FinalTouch, 178, 186, 227
"48 Hours", 62, 176, 216, 363
Fuji film, versus Kodak, 256

G

Gain, sliders, 116–118
Gamma
    definition, 36
    playing against highlights and
        shadows, 29–30
    setting, 24–25
    sliders, 120–121
Gamut, definition, 2–3
Garbage matte
    color vector isolation, 157–160
    definition, 157
Gilbert, Barry, 172, 268
Gradated filter, definition, 126
Grade, definition, 12, 14
Graphic looks, creation, 344–349
Graphical user interface (GUI),
    definition, 7
Grass, coloring, 154, 364
Graticule, definition, 10
Gretagmacbeth, 5
Gritty look, creation, 335–343
GUI, *see* Graphical user interface

H

Hapkido, training and coloring
    analogy, 19
Highlights
    balancing, 68–69
    Gamma playing against highlights
        and shadows, 29–30
    setting, 21–23
Histogram
    color balancing tools, 102–104
    color cast analysis and balancing,
        78–82
    forms and functions, 43–44
    Levels controls, 39–43
HSL, *see* Hue, saturation, and
    luminance
Hue offset wheels
    color cast analysis, 74
    definition, 36

hue offset with RGB parade, 95–101
Hue, saturation, and luminance (HSL)
  Avid Symphony, 38
  definition, 38
  secondary curves in Apple Color, 160

I

I line, 94, 115
IRE, definition, 2–3
IRIDAS SpeedGrade, *see* SpeedGrade
Isolation, *see* Color vector isolation

J

Jackson, Kyle, 210, 270
Jannotta, Pete, 156, 205–208, 268, 270–275, 325–332, 336–337, 356–358, 363
JLCooper, MCS Spectrum, 36

K

Kassner, Neal, 62, 64, 176, 209–214, 216–219, 258, 297–298, 363
Kassner's Balancing Tricks, 220
Key Blur, 137
Kiss Me in the Dark, 170–176, 266–268
Kodak film, versus Fuji, 256

L

LCD, *see* Liquid crystal display
Leffel, Craig, 62, 166–169, 287–293, 311–312, 365
Legal, definition, 1–2
Lerner, Rich, 353
Letters from Iwo Jima, 256
Level 3 Post, 191
Levels controls, 39–43
Lift
  color cast analysis, 66–67
  definition, 66
Lighting changes, matching within scene, 306–309
Lightning Display, 9
Limit Effect, Final Cut Pro, 130, 152
Liquid crystal display (LCD), limitations, 4–5
Little Buddha, 256

Looks creation
  boundaries, 312
  day-for-night, 350–360
  feature film, 360
  film processing looks, 314, 316
  graphic looks, 344–349
  gritty look, 335–343
  maintaining look between scenes, 363–364
  matching looks, 321–324
  overview, 311–312
  preset looks, 312–314
  promos and opens, 324–327, 332–335
Look-up table (LUT), monitors, 5
Lovejoy, Robert, 195–200, 261–262
Low Pass, definition, 12
Luma Range
  alternative, 61
  budgeting considerations, 61–62
  definitions, 58
  display, 57–58
  editing, 58–60
Luminance, relationship to reds, 74
Luminance key
  contrast building, 201–204
  creation, 203–204
Lustre, 16
LUT, *see* Look-up table

M

Manhattan Transfer, 362
Master Colorist Awards, 165
Matching looks, creation, 321–324
Matching shots
  examples
    lighting changes in scene, 306–309
    lions of the Art Institute, 287–302
    scene to scene, 303–306, 363–364
  secondaries, 195, 195–199
  visual matching tips, 309–310
Matte, Apple Color controls, 135–136
Matusek, Mike, 170–176, 229–230, 276–277, 307–309, 321–324, 344–349
MCS Spectrum, 36
Midtones, setting, 24–25
Miller, Robin, 172

Monitor
  types, 4–5
  viewing environment, 5–7
Monitoring
  surround environment interview with Randy Starnes, 7
  vectorscopes, 9
  video monitor, 4–5
  viewing environment, 5–7
  waveform monitors, 7–9
Most, Mike, 11–12, 24, 227, 230–234, 353, 355
Mullen, David, 255, 257–258, 266, 285, 360, 363
Multitasking, 364
Music, language of music and color, 17

N

Nattress, Graeme, 314, 317
Nattress effects, 314, 317
Netflix, looks resource, 321
NFL Films, 166, 177, 221, 276, 335
NLE, *see* Nonlinear editor
Nolo Digital Film, 170, 176, 229, 276, 307
Nonlinear editor (NLE), definition, 34
Nucoda, 170

O

OCN, *see* Original camera negative
Opens, look creation, 324–327, 332–335
Optimus, 166, 287, 293
Original camera negative (OCN), racking on telecine, 62

P

Paint, *see* Shade
Painting cameras, 209
Pandora, 165
Pedestal, *see* Peds
Peds, definition, 222
Pepperman, Chris, 166, 177–184, 221–226, 239–241, 277, 280–284, 333–335, 339–343, 362–363, 365
Photoshop
  color correction, 125
  Curves, 106
Plug-ins, filters, 126, 128
Posterization, definition, 32

Power Curves, da Vinci, 105
Power Windows
  da Vinci, 148, 164, 215, 220
  sunrise creation, 176
PowerGrade, preset looks, 312–314
Practical lights, definition, 23
Premiere, 16
Primary color correction, definition, 63
Printer lights, 126
Promos, look creation, 324–327, 332–335

Q
Q line, 115
Qualify
  color vector isolation
    Avid symphony, 138–143
    Final Cut Pro, 143–145
    practice, 146–147
    qualification, 133–138
  definition, 132
  qualifications in secondaries, 133

R
Racked, original camera negative on telecine, 62
Raster, definition, 129
Regional color differences, 64
Resetting, eyes, 74
RGB parade
  color cast analysis, 65–73
  definition, 9
  highlight setting, 22
  hue offsets, 95–101
  image balancing, 94
RGB sliders, 112–113
Riesen, Randy, 177, 228–229, 242
R!OT, 164–165, 312
Ryan, Chris, 362

S
Sat, definition, 222
Saturation
  contrast effects, 281
  controls, 101–102
Scene matching, 303–306
S Curve, tip, 45–47
Secondaries, see also Spot color correction
  attention focusing, 191–194
  changing uses, 200

color vector isolation
  Avid symphony, 138–143
  Final Cut Pro, 143–145
  practice, 146–147
  qualification, 133–138
  da Vinci comparison with Apple Color, 169
  definition, 131
  importance, 162, 185
  matching problems, 195–199
  purpose, 129, 131
  qualifications, 132, 133
Secondary color correction, see Secondaries
SED, see Surface-conduction electron-emitter display
Sepia tone, definition, 126
Shade
  color balancing with flat-pass waveform monitor, 86–89
  definition, 86
Shake, 16
Shaw, Kevin, 188
Shooters Post, 261, 298
Shot matching, see Matching shots
Silicon Color, 46, 210
Skin tone, the-I line as skin tone reference, 94, 115
Skip bleach, see Bleach bypass
Sky, coloring, 154, 364
Sliga, Bob, 169, 200–204, 234, 236, 242–246, 293–297, 303–306, 317–320, 350–353, 364
Smoke, challenges, 365
SpeedGrade
  color balance controls, 91
  primary color correction controls, 114
  printer lights, 126
  secondary correction mode, 131
Spill
  definition, 156
  removal, 156–157
Spot color correction, see also Vignette
  examples, 176–184
  faking, 149
  geographic color fix, 152–155
  Power Windows, 148, 164
  rationale, 148
  user-defined shapes, 156
  vignettes, 148–151

Starnes, Randy, 7
Still store, applications, 290
Storytelling, colorist role, 255–285
Surface-conduction electron-emitter display (SED), 16
Surround environment, Randy Starnes interview, 7
"Survivor", 324
Symphony, see Avid
Symphony Nitris, 46
Synthetic Aperture, Color Finesse HDF, 47
Syringe, sampling large areas, 134

T
Tangent Devices
  CP-100, 29
  CP-200, 26, 29
  CP200-BK trackball knob panel, 36, 75, 91–92
Tektronix
  WFM700, 8
  WVR7100, 8, 10, 12, 14, 115, 201
Telecine
  definition, 62
  original camera negative racking, 62
  prospects, 366
10 bit image, 32
Time, definition, 234
Tobacco, definition, 259
Tonal Range
  color correction considerations, 110
  definition, 4
Tonal Ranges, definition, 4–5
Trace, definition, 10
Tungsten, lighting, 5
Tunnel Post, 270
"24", 176, 192, 257, 337

U
UI, see User interface
Under your fingers, definition, 44
User interface (UI), 87–88, 93, 117

V
Valid levels, definition, 2–3
Vanderpool, Charles, 192
Vector
  definition, 1
  isolation, see Color vector isolation

Vectorscope
    advantages and limitations, 7–8
    color cast analysis, 73–77
    definition, 9–10
    the-I line as skin tone reference,
        94, 115
Viewing environment, monitors,
    5–7
Vignette
    definition, 132, 164
    examples
        day-for-night shot creation,
            177–184
        Kiss Me in the Dark, 170–176
    ultralight flyover scene,
        166–169
    spot color correction, 148–151

W
War Tapes, 324
Waveform monitor
    advantages and limitations, 7–8
    color balancing with flat-pass
        waveform monitor, 86–89
    color cast analysis, 65–73
    definition, 7
    reading, 12
Wood, Roland, 227

X
Xpress Pro, *see* Avid

Y
YRGB parade
    black level setting, 17–18
    color cast analysis, 65
    waveform monitor reading, 12,
        14

Z
Zebra pattern, superimposition,
    11
Zone System, 78, 289, 293

DATE DUE
